ALSO BY BRUNO BETTELHEIM

Love Is Not Enough:
The Treatment of Emotionally Disturbed Children (1950)

Symbolic Wounds: Puberty Rites and the Envious Male (1954)

Truants from Life:
The Rehabilitation of Emotionally Disturbed Children (1955)

The Informed Heart: Autonomy in a Mass Age (1960)

Paul and Mary: Two Cases from Truants from Life *(1961)*

Dialogues with Mothers (1962)

Social Change and Prejudice (co-author with M. B. Janowitz)
(1964)

The Empty Fortress (1967)

Children of the Dream (1969)

A Home for the Heart (1974)

The Uses of Enchantment:
The Meaning and Importance of Fairy Tales (1977)

Surviving and Other Essays (1979)

On Learning to Read

On Learning to Read

THE CHILD'S FASCINATION WITH MEANING

Bruno Bettelheim &

Karen Zelan

THAMES AND HUDSON

First published in Great Britain in 1982 by
Thames and Hudson Ltd, London
© 1981 by Bruno Bettelheim and Karen Zelan

*Printed and bound in the United States of America by
American Book–Stratford Press, Saddle Brook, New Jersey*

Contents

Preface

Since my student days I have been interested in the role un-conscious processes play in determining human behavior, my own as well as that of others. During the nearly thirty years I directed the work of the University of Chicago's Orthogenic School, I set this interest to practical use in the treatment and education of most severely disturbed children. Many of them originally had been totally unable to learn; others had such severe reading disabilities that they had been diagnosed as suffering from incurable alexia.

Despite such ominous diagnoses, however, careful atten-tion to the unconscious processes at work in these children and application of therapeutic and educational methods based on psychoanalytic thinking permitted practically all of them to overcome the severe handicaps from which they had suf-fered. This suggested that the methods applied at the Ortho-genic School might also benefit the education of normal chil-dren. But fully occupied with meeting the exacting demands of the work of the Orthogenic School, I did not have time to investigate this idea further.

After my retirement from the university, a generous grant from the Spencer Foundation enabled me to direct a study, the purpose of which was to investigate the contributions psycho-analytic thinking could make to teaching children beginning to read in school. Much that follows is based on observations that were largely made possible by the Spencer Foundation. I am grateful for its support, and particularly also for the in-valuable personal encouragement of its president, Tom James.

After the plan for the research was formulated, a small

staff was assembled to help with its execution. Karen Zelan, who for eight years had been associated with me at the Orthogenic School, joined this staff as its most important member. In making and evaluating the observations here reported, Karen Zelan and I were helped considerably by Margot Griffin. In addition to her contributions, those of Kristin Field, Gail Donovan Levinson, Judy Schulman, Carol Slobodin, Margaret Thé, and of the many teachers in whose classrooms we made our observations ought to be gratefully acknowledged.

Chapters 2, 4 through 9, and Chapter 11 are based on the work of the entire staff and were written by both authors. I assumed sole responsibility for Chapters 1, 3, 10, and the last two chapters.

The original manuscript was most sensitively edited by Joyce Jack. We are greatly indebted to her for her many splendid suggestions; her skill and subtle understanding made this book ever so much more readable. Theron Raines made many and most valuable suggestions for improving the book; we are very grateful for his help and interest. Last but certainly not least, we wish to thank Robert Gottlieb for his guidance and continuing interest and encouragement, as well as his editing. It was our very good fortune that he devoted himself to this task. We are deeply grateful for his support and enthusiasm.

B.B.

My interest in children's reading came about as part of a general endeavor to treat and teach seriously disturbed children at the Orthogenic School. The power of the unconscious was impressed upon me as I worked with these children, including the meaning involved in misreadings, or other academic "errors." Understanding unconscious meaning was, I felt, my central task, and paying attention to misreadings was one among many ways in which I tried to facilitate therapeutic growth.

Gradually I became interested in educational issues in themselves. If the children in my care could be taught academic subjects, their rehabilitation would be that much more complete. And if severely disturbed youngsters could profit from insights as they tried to learn, normal youngsters, being so much more ready to understand, ought to benefit even more from self-understanding while learning.

A child who suffered from the most serious of childhood disturbances, infantile autism, was my special concern. When finally willing to talk she also began to read, albeit in a negative fashion. She dictated words she wished to read, which I printed on separate pieces of paper, so they could be arranged in a variety of sentences. Like most younger children who are learning to read, she chose to learn the names of important people, such as her parents. When angry at the birth of a sibling, she gleefully threw out the pieces of paper on which were printed "Daddy" and "Mommy." My impulse was to retrieve the words from the wastebasket. What stopped me was the realization that she must have silently read the words correctly, or else she wouldn't have singled these out to throw away, out of some twenty words. Musing about the power of the printed word, I did nothing. The girl who for years had not spoken to anyone was so delighted at throwing the offending words away that she then systematically read all the remaining words in her pile correctly.

After some eight years spent as staff member of the Orthogenic School, I left to complete my work for a Ph.D. in Educational Psychology. Since then I have been engaged for some fifteen years in searching for the psychological reasons why children are unable to learn in school, or are unable to read, although they have been assessed as normal in most or all other respects. These children are brought to me for psychotherapy by parents who are concerned about the many serious psychological spinoffs of not learning in school: anxiety, low self-esteem, hyperactivity, or a variety of other symptoms, all attributed to the child's failure to learn, or to read. Positive attention to what the child makes of reading or other academic assignments, and to his or her motives for not wanting to do what is expected, have led in every single case to improved academic performance.

It was these and similar experiences that induced me to participate in the study on which this book is based.

K.Z.

PART ONE

Literacy

CHAPTER 1

Achieving Literacy

The first day of school for the child is not just another new experience along the lines of many, often startling ones he has met in his past. Instead, it adds a new dimension to his life, which will never again be the same. In school, the child has to cope entirely on his own—usually for the first time—with a world quite different from that of his family, home, and friends, all he has known until now. Even more important, in school he is exposed to one of the most important institutions of society, whose avowed purpose is to develop him as a person by educating his mind and sensitivities.

Education has become the largest single enterprise of our society. More persons are employed in education than in any other undertaking short of government itself, of which education is a part. In consequence, a large and well-entrenched bureaucracy serves not only the interests of children but also its own interests, which are not always in accord with what will best serve the education of children. (An obvious example of the legitimate interests of children being short-changed by the understandable self-interest of teachers is a teachers' strike.)

Many of the daily procedures of schools are permeated by the needs of the educational establishment, and these needs often take precedence over those of the children. The excuse given is that unless the school system is enabled to function well, the education of the children will suffer. So the child is exposed in school not just to experiences that are designed to benefit him but to others that mainly serve to benefit the bureaucracy. This creates tension within the educational enterprise, from which the child and his education suffer. Children feel these tensions, even if in the early grades they are too young to become aware of them consciously.

Despite these conflicts between what is done in the best interest of the child, and what is done to satisfy the requirements of the bureaucracy, the child responds to the fact that schools are created and maintained by society to serve him by fostering his intellectual and personal growth. In fact, since schools are especially designed for him and his age group, the child tends to form his views of society on the basis of his school experiences, which is why early experiences with school not only create the foundations on which all his later educational experiences rest, but to a considerable degree influence how he comes to think of himself in relation to the wider world. These first experiences with learning in school are often decisive in forming the child's view of himself as part of society; depending on them, either he may feel welcomed and well served by it, and conclude that he will be successful within it, or he may feel that since this institution supposedly created for him is at best indifferent to his needs and at worst outright inimical, then the same is probably true for the rest of society and its institutions. If this happens, the child feels defeated by society from an early age.

In nursery school and kindergarten, particularly if academic studies are not pushed too soon or too hard, the child learns more or less how to play with other children and becomes acquainted with materials that prepare him for formal learning. Possibly the most influential of these early experiences for the child's future academic career is his encounter with his teacher. Through her, he encounters the educational system. If things go well, the child learns to cope adequately with academic demands and derives satisfaction from being able to do so. If things go badly, he becomes suspicious of the teacher's and the system's purposes. He then closes his mind to the teacher's efforts and either learns to beat the system, withdraws into himself, or becomes a little rebel.

The ability to read is of such singular importance to a child's life in school that his experience in learning it more often than not seals the fate, once and for all, of his academic career. What he has experienced in school up to the time he is taught reading is only preparation for learning in earnest; it has made it easier or harder for him to succeed in this crucial learning task. If his past experiences in home and school have equipped him poorly, what happens when reading is taught to him can undo the damage, although it won't be easy. If he finds reading rewarding, all will be well. But when he fails to learn reading properly, the consequences are usually irremediable.

If the child did not know it before, it will soon be impressed on him that of all school learning, nothing compares in importance with reading; it is of unparalleled significance. This is why how it is taught is so important: the way in which learning to read is experienced by the child will determine how he will view learning in general, how he will conceive of himself as a learner and even as a person.

Whether, how soon, how easily, and how well the child will be able to learn to read will depend to some measure on his native endowment and to a considerable degree on his home background. This includes how well his ability to understand, to use, and to enjoy language has been developed; whether reading has been impressed upon him as something desirable; and how much confidence in his intelligence and academic abilities has been instilled in him. Where the impact of the home has been negative, the child's school experiences may under optimal conditions exert a corrective influence, though only over time.

Irrespective of what the child brings from home to school, once he is in class, the most important factor in his learning to read is how reading and literature—its value and meaning —are presented to him by his teacher. If reading seems an interesting, valuable, and enjoyable experience, then the exertions that learning to read require will seem a small price to pay, considering the vast advantage one gains from being literate. To give the child this impression is quite easy if his home background supports it; if his background has not prepared him to see reading in a positive way, then it will be considerably more difficult for the teacher to convince the child that being able to read is both important in general and of highly personal interest to him right now.

There is great pleasure and satisfaction in becoming able to read some words. The child is proud that he is able to do it. But the excitement of being able to read some words soon fades when the texts the child must read force him to reread the same word endlessly. Word recognition deteriorates quickly into empty rote learning when it does not lead directly to the reading of meaningful content.

To be able to read with ease unquestionably presupposes the acquisition of pertinent skills, such as being able to decode and sound out words one does not know, and of this the child is well aware. But he also knows that these skills in and by themselves have little or no merit, aside from their training value. And he will not be interested in learning these skills if the impression he receives is that he is expected to master them for their own sake. That is why so much depends on where the teacher's, the school's, and the textbook's emphases lie. From the very beginning, the child must be convinced that mastering such skills is but a means to achieve a goal, and that the only thing of importance is that he should become literate—that is, come to enjoy literature and benefit from what it has to offer.

A child who is made to read: "Nan had a pad. Nan had a tan pad. Dan ran. Dan ran to the pad . . ." and worse nonsense, does not receive the impression that he is being guided toward becoming literate, because what he is being made to read is obviously not literature. It is not that children do not enjoy playing with words; they love making up words, including nonsense words and rhymes, and revel in their newly gained abilities in doing so. But for such word play to remain enjoyable, it must not be made into a chore, for then all the pleasure goes out of it, and with it out of reading. The child plays with words because he finds it amusing and clever. Unlike the child's spontaneous creations, however, the word play in pre-primers and primers is far from clever, it is in fact utterly boring; worse, these books are an insult to the child's intelligence.

Children recognize that repeated exercise may be needed to acquire some skills, such as those necessary for becoming literate, and if a child is drilled in the recognition of letters or phonemes, or in the decoding of words, without any pretense that he is reading a story worth his attention, then such practice, while it does not help his becoming literate, at least does not seriously interfere with it. Indeed, children may enjoy the exercise of reading drills when they first learn reading, just as they enjoy practicing other new skills. A brief period of "practice games" usually occurs after a child has become able to run, jump, or skip, and something akin to this may happen when the child first becomes able to decode.[1] For example, children will read signs along the road, much to their own and their parents' delight, as they are driving somewhere in a car. These and similar events show that during such periods of practicing a newly acquired function—in our example, decoding—it matters little what is decoded; it is the fact that he can decode that delights the child.

Children mature at different ages, and some learn to read

[1] Piaget discusses what he calls "practice games" in *Play, Dreams and Imagination.* New York: W. W. Norton, 1962. These consist of exercises engaged in "for no other purpose than the pleasure of functioning." Such practice games usually appear during the earlier sensorimotor period of development, but also later in instances of higher functions.

much sooner than others. Thus the age at which the child enjoys decoding "for the fun of it" varies a great deal, but most children will have gone beyond that stage by the middle or end of first grade. By then, having read words just for the fun of reading them, children now expect something even more interesting to follow. It is at this crucial point that their primers are found wanting, because the pretense is made that repetitive exercises make up a story that can be enjoyed. When the story to which the drill leads is stupid, boring, and offensive to the child's intelligence, self-respect, and budding literacy, then the skill that results in the reading of such a story becomes meaningless. That is why the emphasis on the technical aspects of learning to read, which characterizes the teaching methods used at present in this country, is detrimental and often actually destructive to the child's ability to enjoy reading and literature.

However, when newly acquired abilities can be separately applied directly to content which, because of its merit, makes reading definitely a worthwhile experience, this turns the rather empty achievement, "Now I can decode some words," into the eminently satisfying feeling, "I am reading something that adds to my life." This is why the technical aspects of learning to read ought to be clearly separated from the child's introduction to literature, although it is preferable by far that this two-step process of acquiring literacy be avoided, and that reading be learned from the start as a result of the child's spontaneous desire to become literate—that is, to become able to read books by himself.

Indeed, quite a few children learn to read before or after they enter school without receiving any training in decoding or other skills. They learn it at home, more or less independently from what they are taught in class, being children who have acquired a love of reading as they were being read to. The child who enjoys being read to learns to love books. Impressed by his parents' interest in reading and their enjoyment of reading to him, the child studies with keen interest the stories that fascinate him. All on his own, then, he begins to pick out words and learns to recognize them with his parents' help or that of an older sibling. In this way the child teaches himself to read.

I have known many preschool children who taught themselves to read thus; but I also knew some who first learned to read words upside down. They did this as they watched an older sibling read from the opposite side of the table, or from across a desk. The younger child would point out words, asking what they meant, and be answered without the book being turned around for him, so that he first learned to recognize words upside down. When these children entered school, it was difficult initially for them to read words right side up; but, given their interest in reading, they were soon able to do so.

Children who acquire a great interest in reading in their homes have an easy time reading in school, and they form the overwhelming majority of those who later become the good readers. The educational establishment points to them as demonstrating that the methods used to teach reading in school are successful. But it is not these methods that turned them into good readers and eventually literate persons; one is tempted to say that these are attitudes which these children acquired and maintained *despite* the experiences to which they have been exposed in school. Were it not so, why should the children of more highly educated parents have such an advantage in educational achievement over the children of less well educated parents who are of equal intelligence? Why would so many children who come from culturally disadvantaged homes not become literate persons, although they have acquired the necessary skills for reading in school? One major difference between the children who teach themselves to read at home and those who learn it only in school is that the first group learn to read from texts that fascinate them, while the second learn to read by being drilled in skills of

decoding and word recognition from texts devoid of meaningful content that are demeaning to the child's intelligence.

What is meant by being literate? *Webster's New World
Dictionary* gives as its first definition of literate: "able to read
and write," and as its second: "well educated; having or showing extensive knowledge, learning, or culture." The first definition seems too narrow, because in common parlance we would
hardly call literate a person who is barely able to read and
write. The second definition, by contrast, seems too demanding, because it allows only for the final accomplishment and
not for the many intermediate steps needed to reach it. These
two definitions reflect the lack of clarity in methods (if not
also in purpose) of our teaching for literacy. Our schools manage
to teach Johnny sometimes more and sometimes less well to
read and write; but the result of their methods is that all too
many children neither then nor later are able to find reading
truly meaningful.

In December 1969, the United States Commissioner of
Education, deeply concerned about the ineffectiveness of our
methods of teaching reading, requested help from the
National Academy of Education. Trying to meet this challenge,
the Academy, composed of the most prominent scholars of education and related fields, studied the problem, and its Committee on Reading prepared an authoritative report.[2] It states:
" 'Illiteracy' does not necessarily mean the complete absence of
ability to read, and 'literacy' covers a wide spectrum of capabilities—all the way from, say, being able to decipher a want
ad in a newspaper to being able to enjoy a novel by Thomas
Mann or read a scientific treatise with understanding." While
a number of literate people may not enjoy the novels of
Thomas Mann or read many scientific treatises, one would ex-

---

[2] John B. Carroll and Jeanne S. Chall, eds., *Toward a Literate Society.
Report of the Committee on Reading of the National Academy of
Education.* New York: McGraw-Hill, 1975. The following quotations
are from this report.

pect that reading has an important place in their lives, that they read regularly for both enjoyment and meaning, and most of all that they feel that reading enriches their experience.

Since literacy has so many facets, it is readily understandable that the report asks: "What does 'literacy' mean? What does it mean to say a person is 'able to read?' " and answers its questions with some examples used to illustrate the problem that "there are some millions of our citizens who cannot read, or who as schoolchildren are not learning to read to a level sufficient to satisfy their personal needs, and who are thereby precluded from full participation in our society."

Case histories present typical examples of a black child, a foreign-born child, and one suffering from minimal brain damage. Although fictitious, all these cases "reflect real, true-to-life conditions that are repeated over and over across the land." One case study is that of Sandy, an intelligent eleventh grader. Sandy's is the only case history of a native-born white, lower-middle-class boy about whose inherent capabilities there was never any doubt. Through Sandy's story, the authors highlight the elements crucial in cases of functional illiteracy when the child comes from an average home, is of good intelligence, and has attended a typical middle-class public school for the entire course of primary and secondary education:

> Sandy can "read," if you define the word generously enough. He could manage to read aloud an item in the newspaper, but he would do so haltingly and with little semblance of normal expression. He would understand very little of what it said. The process of reading is so arduous for Sandy that he avoids reading whenever possible. The star of his school basketball team, Sandy has pushed through to the eleventh grade merely by time-serving. He hadn't learned to read by third grade, but somehow, because of the long dreary exposure to printed material through the rest of the grades, he has

learned at least to "decode" print to the point of being able to express some of it audibly. Sandy talks and understands ordinary conversation as well as his peers. He is outwardly well adjusted and popular with his classmates. . . . When asked to explain his poor grades and test scores, Sandy says that somehow none of his teachers ever got him interested in reading.

Sandy—technically literate but functionally illiterate despite his native intelligence and age-appropriate ability to express himself verbally—blames his teachers. He is not knowledgeable enough to recognize where else the blame also belongs; on his home background, which failed to instill in him a love of reading, a desire to become educated; and on the methods by which he was taught reading and the content of the books from which he was taught. But he is right to blame the educational system, which his teachers symbolize to him. So many children have home backgrounds which do not motivate them sufficiently to want to learn to read that it should be the task of the educational system to counteract and compensate for what is missing in the child's home, so far as the wish to become literate is concerned. Since such children do not come to school eager to learn to read, it is particularly important that a boy like Sandy should not be exposed to books and teaching methods that fail to arouse his interest in and love of reading, and so prevent him from recognizing the great merit of becoming literate.

As far as schools are concerned, Sandy's story emphasizes two major points. The first is that learning to decode—which Sandy did accomplish—often does not lead to reading that is experienced as meaningful at the moment, or felt to be potentially valuable. Mastering a technical skill such as decoding might be likened to the ability to open a door: whether one will actually open the door depends on what one believes to lie behind it. When one has received the impression that behind the door are more or less the same disagreeable things one experienced while gaining the skill to open it, there is no motivation to go on.

The second point is that what happens to his reading during the first two or three grades is crucial for the future of a child's literacy. The third grade is a kind of watershed in this respect. Unfortunately, the texts predominantly used during kindergarten, and the first two and sometimes three grades are uninteresting and without merit, if not outright offensive. (Since this type of reading material continues to be used with poor readers well past third grade, things can only get worse for them, because as they grow in age, understanding, and maturity, the beginners' texts become still more repugnant.) This is why if by third grade a child is well started on becoming literate, in all likelihood he will continue in the same direction, since from then on his text materials become more interesting and worth his attention.

In contrast, by third grade children like Sandy have become completely uninterested in reading because of their earlier experiences with it. To protect themselves from what they have come to loathe on the basis of their previous encounters, they refuse to become acquainted with more advanced reading matter, as would happen in and after third grade had they reached the appropriate reading levels. But since they have not, nothing changes their views about what reading can offer them.

Approaching the problem differently, other scholars, too, came to the conclusion that what has happened by third grade is decisive for a child's future academic achievement. Benjamin Bloom, for example, points out that "approximately 50% of general achievement at grade 12 (age 18) has been reached by the end of grade 3 (age 9). This suggests the great importance of the first few years of school as well as the preschool period in the development of learning patterns and general achievement. These are the years in which general learning patterns develop most rapidly, and failure to develop appropriate achievement and learning in these years is likely to lead to continued failure or near failure throughout the remainder of the individual's school career."[3]

Sandy never became literate enough to develop the critical faculties required for evaluating a text. To be able to do so, one must have been exposed to meaningful reading; without it, one is unable to judge what is literature and what is only pretending to be. Having not read any texts that could have touched him and made a difference in his life, Sandy could not know that it was less his teachers' fault than that of his primers that he was not literate. Fourth and fifth graders who are able to read well and who have left behind their boring beginners' books are very clear that it is the books that ought to be blamed for such failures. Some spontaneous evaluations of these books from good readers may illustrate this.

In connection with our research on reading—some details of which are discussed in Chapter 4—I visited children in their classrooms in public schools. Only after many months, when the children had gotten to know me well from my repeated visits during which we had talked about a wide variety of topics, did I think the time was ripe to talk with them about their primers and readers. Initially, they were hesitant to express their opinions. Being good students, they wished to protect their teachers and their schools, which they liked. But when they began to realize that I was interested in their honest opinions about the way they had been taught reading, it was as if a sluice gate had suddenly opened and a flood of angry criticisms poured forth concerning not their teachers or their schools, but the books they had been required to read. Without exception, the children complained about how stupid the stories in their basic readers had been, and said how much they had hated having to read them. With venom they spoke

[3] Benjamin S. Bloom, *Stability and Change in Human Characteristics.* New York: John Wiley & Sons, 1964.

of "all these sweet little kids in the stories," furious that the stories assumed they were so simple-minded as to believe that children were like that. Only after they all, more or less in unison, had vented their accumulated annoyance at these texts could they individually be more specific about what had been most obnoxious to them.

A rather quiet boy who preferred to read or work by himself, who participated only rarely in class discussions and then only when specifically asked to do so, now spoke up all on his own, and with deep feeling. This was obviously an issue of great importance to him. Although he now liked reading a lot, he said, he still had a hard time reading aloud. His reason was that when in first grade he had been asked to read aloud, he had felt so ashamed at saying the stupid things written in the primer, he had blocked; he simply could not do it. Henceforth he had resented reading until the middle of third grade, when he began to read stories that were "really good."

Another boy hated the stories because they were neither realistic nor fantastic. He would have had a much easier time learning to read—and would have enjoyed it—he said, had the stories been either true to life, describing how people really are, or truly fantastic, like fairy tales. He had finally overcome his resentment of reading when he became acquainted with fairy tales, because then after he had read a story, he would contemplate its content "for a long while." These were meaningful experiences for him; those he had from reading in class were not.

When asked in what sense the stories were not "true to life," every child had some different objection. One was that in these stories only two age groups existed: children of their own age and adults, mostly parents; furthermore, children and parents alike were depicted as insipid. These children wanted to encounter stories about teenagers and old people as well.

Another universal objection was that nobody in these

stories showed their true feelings, such as being angry. Other complaints of these ten-year-olds were that there was no new information for them in these stories, that everything they read about they knew much better and in greater detail than was set out in the books from which they were supposed to learn great things.

When asked why they had not expressed their opinions about these readers before, the answer was that nobody was interested in their true thoughts on this matter; everybody wanted only to hear that they liked the stories. One mature fourth-grade girl remarked: "In none of the stories does anybody ever say his true opinion, so how could we?" To which all heartily agreed.

Their negative views were in stark contrast to those they had expressed to their teachers, who had frequently asked them their opinion of what they had to read, particularly when they had read some story by themselves. The teachers had asked mainly two questions: whether they had liked the story, and whether they would recommend reading it to some other child; in essence, whether it was a good story. The children nearly always had blandly said, "Yes." In most cases their lack of enthusiasm in doing so had been more impressive than their affirmative statements.

In further conversations they told me that they pretended to like the stories in their readers because they thought—not without reason—that had their teacher not been convinced they would like these books, she would not have suggested that they read them. Since their teacher expected them to like this type of story, they felt obliged to say that they did.

The unanimity and eagerness with which the children, when given half a chance, severely criticized the basic texts from which they had been taught to read ought to be evaluated in light of the readiness and candor with which they spoke of liking and disliking other stories they had read in and outside of class, and of the wide variety of opinions they held about them. For example, while a vast majority very much liked reading the *Pooh* books, or *Black Beauty*, there were some who found these wanting. While some loved baseball stories, others had no use for them. Some were full of praise for science fiction, others for fairy tales, and so it went. About all these stories they felt free to state their opinions and readily disagree with each other.

While the primers and their so-called stories are by no means the only cause of the frequent dishonesty that mars the dealings of many children with their teachers and the educational system, they add to the children's assumption that they had better tell the teacher what the teacher wants to hear. This, after all, is a well-known defense of the weak when dealing with the strong, and children are weak in relation to their teachers, not to mention the educational system in general, and they feel particularly weak, inexperienced, and doubting of their judgment when they cannot yet read well.

Encouraged by the direct and forceful way in which the fourth and fifth graders had expressed themselves, we also asked first and second graders about the widely used readers from which they were being taught in class at the moment. The children were unanimous in not liking any of the stories, said that they read them only because they had to, and that on their own they would never read such "junk." Their reasons were that "It's all impossible!" Asked why, they answered: "Because none of them are real!", referring to the people in the stories. "They aren't shy!", "They aren't afraid!", "They aren't angry!", "They aren't upset!" When one explained: "They aren't anything!", they all agreed that this summed it up perfectly and that there was nothing more to be said.

Any adult reading these texts feels the same way. When I asked graduate students in education to read the primers presently used in teaching reading and recollect their reactions when they had been taught reading from them, every one of them was shocked (see Chapter 12). The teachers themselves had nothing good to say about the stories in the readers they used, although they expressed their opinions circumspectly. Since it was they who asked the children to read the books, they were hesitant to be openly critical of them; but they, too, could not understand why the authors of these books thought such stories would make an appeal to children.

Actually, these series of primers have no "authors." Producing them is such an extensive enterprise that no one author could possibly do it. Many people are involved in creating them, and the financial investment required is enormous. In 1966, the cost of producing an entire series from preprimer to sixth grade was estimated to range from $10 million to $25 million. For example, the sizable staff of one large publishing house involved in creating its series' first-grade program devoted five years to this task alone. Yet despite the efforts and expenditures that go into developing a new series, all basic series are alike. As one publisher put it: "My basal series is pretty much the same as three or four leading basals. They are alike in that they have a controlled vocabulary through the sixth grade. . . . Similar to other basals, we created a family and maintained it through the first grade."[4]

Given the large investment involved in producing such a series, the publisher must be able to sell it to as many schools as possible, all over the country. He cannot risk objections to the individual reader's content; hence anything possibly objectionable has to be eliminated. The result is that by trying to please everybody, these readers end up pleasing nobody. Yet since they are utterly vacuous, their contents also offend nobody but the children who have to read them.

Two personal experiences may illustrate why the stories are so totally lacking in interest, why they are so completely empty. The first happened many years ago. I was randomly

[4] Jeanne S. Chall, *Learning to Read: The Great Debate*. New York: McGraw-Hill, 1967.

involved in an experimental effort to produce a more attractive reader for the first grade. One of its stories tried to arouse some interest by narrating a small tragedy of childhood. Children had gotten a balloon at a fair. They took the balloon home, where a cat jumped on it and it burst. This seemed harmless enough, but when a school system in Illinois tested out this book before it went into large-scale production, the cat lovers of Illinois raised outraged objections: the story maligned cats, set children against animals, and so on. They threatened a campaign against the local school superintendent, who was soon up for reelection. He thought it best to withdraw the book. Fearing similar setbacks for his new series, the publisher decided to include only content against which nobody could possibly object.

The second experience is more recent. The publisher of one widely used series was in the process of preparing a new one. The president of the company asked me to study the plans for the series and give him my opinion. After I had completed my review, he asked me to confer with the company's vice-president in charge of textbooks. I told him in some detail why I thought that the stories he planned to use were excruciatingly boring, and listed many other objections. He listened to me patiently, without reacting.

Finally I asked him what he thought of what I was telling him. He politely remarked that it made good sense, that he had thought in many respects along the same lines. But, he added, unfortunately what was most important was not what he thought, but whether the series would sell widely. He reminded me that neither children nor teachers buy such series, but only superintendents and boards of education. Their concern is that they should not be criticized for anything possibly objectionable in the stories, and practically every type of story I suggested might be objectionable to some voters. Having just suggested the use of fairy tales as possible materials, I knew he was right, because some people would be upset that these stories showed stepmothers in a bad light, others would find the punishment of the evil-doers too cruel, and so on.

What results from these conditions are readers containing an agglomeration of endlessly repeated words that pretend to be stories, although they are not. These books are given to the teachers for teaching reading. The teachers don't like them, but feel they have to use them. Many teachers with whom we talked firmly asserted that the content of the stories did not matter. All that the books were good for—and the reason the teachers were using them—was to develop reading skills, such as familiarity with phonemes, ability to decode, and so on. Since these books had been put together by experts, and approved for use by other experts, these teachers did not question the teaching of reading skills by means of content which they themselves considered irrelevant, if not obnoxious—feelings which, though never expressed to the children, did not fail to make an impression on them. The children concluded either that their teacher faked an interest in the stories, or that she thought so little of the children's intelligence that she believed they liked them. It made the children angry that they were considered so stupid.

The basic trouble is that teachers, although they don't believe that being able to read is synonymous with being literate, do believe that the first will necessarily lead to the second. This raises again the question of how one ought to consider what is involved in being "literate." The *Shorter Oxford English Dictionary* explains the concept by means of the following quotation: "to beguile . . . with some literate diversion, the tedious length of those days."

Observing children who are learning to read in school convinces one that, far from reading being a beguiling diversion, it greatly adds to the tedious length of their day. Nothing is more boring than having to spend one's time and concentrate one's mental energy on such things as phonemes, sight recognition, decoding of words, and reading senseless combinations and tiresome repetitions of words. All this—when the child could spend the same time on the "beguiling diversion" of reading a truly engrossing story!

The reasons for teaching reading by means of these tedious texts are based on two assumptions: never mind how the child acquires the skills necessary for reading, they will automatically make him literate in due course; and only through many repetitions can a child become able to recognize a word. Both assumptions are erroneous. If a child is truly interested in a word, he learns it easily and fast, as the graffiti written and readily read by children should have demonstrated long ago. And having laboriously met the boring preconditions for doing something does not guarantee that one will wish to do it.

If, rather than concentrating on developing reading skills, educational efforts from the very beginning were concentrated on developing the desire to become literate—essentially, an inner attitude to reading—then the final result might be that a much larger segment of the adult population would be literate. In our present situation, most adults are able to read but see little purpose in reading, beyond gaining some specific information in which they are interested or as a means for killing time through some trite diversion.

Learning to read "now" in order to be able to enjoy literature at some much later time—which for the kindergarten child or first grader often means some three or more years later, at that age experienced as infinity—is a sterile experience in the present. And even if by chance a rare child should be able to look forward with confidence to the distant future and believe that he will then find reading meaningful, the way he is taught reading at the moment still makes it an odious task. To be motivated by distant rewards requires a commitment to the reality principle in preference to the pleasure principle. Yet the vast majority of children have not made this commitment in respect to academic studies as they enter school or in the early grades, not to mention the many who fail to make it even later on. Such a commitment to academic education comes about only as an accumulated result of many rewarding learning experiences. It cannot be expected to exist as they begin school.

The worst aspect of the way reading is presently taught is the impression the child receives during his earliest years in school that skills such as decoding are what reading is all about. There is nothing wrong with teaching a skill, as long as it is not done in ways that do damage to the purposes for which the particular skill is needed or desirable. But the teacher's emphasis on decoding and word recognition—and these are all she can emphasize, since the utter emptiness of the texts does not permit her to stress meaning—gives the child the idea that these are all-important.

That this is the wrong way to teach reading was recognized over seventy years ago, in the first important treatise on the teaching of reading written in this country. Edmund Huey strongly stressed that the teaching, or drill, in the technique of reading must be entirely separated from reading as such.[5] "The school," he wrote, "should cease to make primary reading the fetish that it long has been," and added: "the technique of reading should not appear in the early years, and the very little work that should be tolerated in phonics should be entirely distinct from reading." He emphasized that "The child should never be permitted to read for the sake of reading, as a formal process or end in itself. The reading should always be for the intrinsic interest or value of what is read, reading never being done or thought of as 'an exercise.' Word-pronouncing will therefore always be secondary to getting whole sentence-meanings, and this from the very first. . . . The learning of real literature should begin in the home and in the very first days of school, and should continue uninter-

[5] Edmund Burke Huey, *The Psychology and Pedagogy of Reading*. New York: Macmillan, 1908.

ruptedly." Such convictions led Huey quite naturally to conclude that "School readers, especially primers, should largely disappear, except as they may be competent editings of the real literature of the mother-tongue, presented in literary wholes, or as they may be records of the children's own experiences and thoughts."

Huey anticipated what is now called organic reading, based on the child's own stories. But he recognized that this alone would never make for literacy, because the stories the child invents all by himself, while of interest to him and revealing of his personality and preoccupations, are nearly always of mediocre literary quality unless his writings are refined by his knowledge and understanding of great literature. This is why the child's limited experience must become enlightened and enriched by what Huey called real literature.

Things have become much worse since the days when Huey spoke out so forcefully against the content of the primers in use in his time, and in favor of teaching children to read from "real literature" that should neither be simplified nor expurgated but used only in "literary wholes." Harris and Sipay report that first readers published in the 1920s contained on the average 645 different words. By the 1930s, this number had dropped to about 460 words. In the 1940s and 1950s, the vocabulary had become further reduced to about 350 words. Analyzing seven basic readers series published between 1960 and 1963, they found that "the total preprimer vocabulary ranged from a low of 54 to a high of 83 words; primer vocabularies from 113 to 173 words."[6]

Chall compared the first-grade readers of five different editions of the Scott, Foresman series, which is widely used. From 1920 to 1962, there was a continuous decline from edition to edition in the number of words used in these readers. Whereas in 1920 the number of running words per average

[6] Albert J. Harris and Edward R. Sipay, *Effective Teaching of Reading.* New York: David McKay, 1971.

story was 333, by 1962 it had shrunk to 230. In 1920, eight new words were introduced in the average story; in 1940, there were five, and in 1962, only four new words per story. The number of different words used in the entire book was 425 in 1920, 282 in 1930, 178 in 1940, and 153 in 1962. And as the number of words in the stories and the entire book declined from edition to edition, their contents became more boring and repetitious. During the same period, the number of pictures per 100 running words nearly doubled from less than one in 1920 to nearly two in 1962.[7] The more illustrations there are to reveal the story's simple content, the less reason there is to read the story for meaning.

Harper & Row's *Janet and Mark* series (formerly *Dick and Jane*) is probably among the most widely used today. It contains in its four preprimers only seventy-eight different words. The first primer increases this vocabulary to a meager 182 words, although by then the children have studied reading for nearly two years, and have read five books of the basic series as well as many other books and workbooks, all of which feature an equally limited vocabulary. But at this age most children already know and use a vocabulary of 4,000 words or more. Nobody had to make any deliberate efforts to teach them these words, with the exception of the first few, which their parents taught them in infancy. All the rest they learned because they wanted to—because they found talking and using these words useful, enjoyable, and necessary for doing what they wanted to do, such as communicating with others. The least verbal group of first graders masters on the average well over 2,000 words, thus rendering useless and irrelevant the claim that these first primers must employ very few words so that they will not make things difficult for children coming from culturally deprived homes. This kind of cultural condescension ignores the reality of life in even the most disadvan-

---

[7] Chall, *op. cit.*

taged home environment. Although in the 1920s few children went to kindergarten and little preschool reading instruction took place, today, when many children attend kindergarten and reading is quite consistently taught there, our primers contain only 28 percent of the vocabulary presented to children fifty years ago.

It would be difficult to establish a direct connection between the reduction in the vocabulary taught to beginning readers and the drop in verbal abilities as reflected in the performance of college-bound high school juniors and seniors. Still, a decline in the verbal scores they earn when taking the Scholastic Aptitude Test suggests a lowered interest in serious reading. The average scores these high school students earned declined from a mean score of 473 in 1956–57 (on a scale of 200 to 800) to 434 in 1974–75.[8] This drop in verbal achievement—which actually measures reading achievement, since these are tests of reading and writing and not of speaking— was not restricted to the average students but extended to the top students as well. These are the students whose scores are above the 600- or 700-point level. The drop in their scores paralleled that of the average student.[9]

Research in reading, far from justifying the continuous reduction in the number of words used in primers, fails to find any reason for it. For example, Chall, "analyzing the research basis for basals' vocabulary control," found that "by the late 1940's this control was much stricter than any research justified."[10] Since then the vocabulary used in the primers has shrunk on the average by half, as just mentioned. Chall continued: "More recent research by Gates indicates that children in the middle of grade two and at the end of grade three [the

[8] Evelyn Stern Silver, Lawrence Johnson, and Associates, *Declining Test Scores: A Conference Report.* The National Institute of Education, February 1976.
[9] Annegret Harnischfeger and David E. Wiley, *Achievement Test Score Decline: Do We Need to Worry?* St. Louis: Cemrel, Inc., 1976.
[10] Chall, *op. cit.*

two groups studied by Gates] know most of the words in the readers of the grades beyond their own. Yet . . . each succeeding edition of a series had a lower vocabulary load."

Like Huey before her and others since, Chall is critical of the stories from which children are taught to read. "My own personal content preference for first and second graders is folktales and fairy tales. They have universal appeal. . . . These tales contain struggle and triumph, right and wrong, laughter and tears—themes that have disappeared from modern stories based on familiar experiences. Most authors who select and adapt stories for first and second grade readers seem to have forgotten that children, like adults, enjoy a good cry once in a while. To make all stories come out happily at the end is not only unrealistic but also dulling."

Sara Zimet also regrets that "reading texts emphasize skill, and reading is taught for the sake of the skill itself," and stresses that "we need to shift our emphasis from 'reading to learn to read' to 'reading about something meaningful while learning to read.' By emphasizing the process to the exclusion of meaningful ideas, we sacrifice the *raison d'être* for learning to read." She goes on to say that "both the fantasy and reality of children's lives are full and rich compared to the pallid scenes and words of the beginning reading texts."[11] This is exactly what the children themselves complained about.

Considering the views of the experts just quoted, it is hard to understand why textbook publishers during the last half century have successively restricted the vocabulary of their basic readers ever more, thus making them even less interesting to children; and why educators have used these ever more boring readers in preference to more challenging ones. One possible explanation (which tallies with the progressive decline in reading ability among American students) is that as the readers became more boring, children learned to read less well.

[11] Sara Goodman Zimet, *What Children Read in School*. New York: Grune & Stratton, 1972.

The conclusion drawn from this fact was not the obvious one that as the textbooks became more boring to children and teachers alike, children would have a harder time working up any interest in learning to read. Instead, it was concluded that the books were too *difficult* for the children and that things should be made easier for them, by asking them to learn fewer words! So each new edition of a primer contains fewer words in ever more frequent repetition, and in consequence is more boring than that which preceded it. With this, children are progressively less interested in what they are made to read and find learning ever less rewarding; their reading scores go down, and more of them develop serious reading difficulties. As this cycle continues up to the present day, things have gone from bad to worse.

Textbook writers and publishers have not remained unaware that their new books are of less interest to children, so they have tried to make them more attractive by adding more good and colorful illustrations. The trouble is that these pretty pictures make the printed text appear even less appealing by comparison, because it is less vivid and contains much less information than the illustrations. Being able to guess from the pictures what the accompanying text is all about, a child who initially is uninterested in reading sees no reason to struggle with learning the words when he can get ample information from the illustrations.

Classroom observations have demonstrated how children look at the pictures, decide what the text must be, and then pay little or no attention to it. Even adults cannot help looking first at the pictures, which are so much more appealing than the text with its endless repetitions, while each of the pictures is at least a bit different from the others. Teachers, knowing that the pictures are more attractive than the text, talk about them with the children before attending to the text. In fact, much more ground is covered in talking about the pictures than will ever be covered by the reading, which makes reading seem all the more pointless. It seems hardly necessary to note that the Bible stories from which children learned reading in times past either had no pictures, or if there were pictures, these did not permit guessing what the text would reveal; if one wanted to find out what the text said, one had to learn to read.

Some experts have remarked on how questionable the dominant use of pictures in basic texts is, and how apt to detract from interest in reading. To quote Chall once more: "No one has yet demonstrated that pictures help the child either to recognize words or comprehend the text. In fact, recent experimental evidence indicates that pictures may hinder the child's attempts at building comprehension. At any rate, if his attention is constantly directed to pictures, the beginner may be distracted from the words and get a completely erroneous idea of what reading is all about." And "first graders already know how to 'read' pictures . . . the task of beginning reading instruction is to teach them to read words. . . . Since the content of first grade readers is limited by the pupil's decoding skills, meaning and appreciation questions must naturally feed on the pictures." Typically, the elaborate teacher's guides accompanying each book of a series suggest that "the first question asked [in connection with] each page, from the preprimers through the second grade readers [should be one referring to] a picture. Only in the third grade reader [do the teacher's guides suggest calling] the child's attention first to the text." But "Even in the first of the third grade readers, about 30% of the questions [to be asked by the teacher] can be answered without reading the words."[12]

And this, even though experimental evidence suggests that pictures retard or interfere with learning to read:

Children in the second term of kindergarten were given practice with three-letter common words ("cat," "bed,"

[12] Chall, *op. cit.*

"dog," etc.) on flash cards. In one group, the word on the card was accompanied by the appropriate picture. In another, it appeared alone. Training trials, in which the experimenter pronounced the word as it was displayed to the child, alternated with test trials when the child was shown the word alone and asked to say what it was. The picture group made significantly more errors and took longer [to be able to read the word] than the group without pictures. The picture redundancy appeared to be distracting rather than useful.[13]

Similar results were obtained by S. J. Samuels.[14]

And yet, in the face of such evidence, primary reading texts remain full of pictures—presumably because (as is by now abundantly clear) the pictures are the only attractive aspect of these readers, their texts being so obviously stupid as to be unbearable alone. Even the publishers' guides to the readers concentrate on the messages contained in the pictures, recognizing that without them the teacher would have nothing to talk about with the children.

With the decline in vocabulary and the great emptiness of the text's content, teachers and children find reading instruction less and less to their liking. While teachers dutifully spend the time allocated to reading on it, only the very best can find ways to make learning to read attractive to children whose background has not conditioned them to want to do so. Since most teachers actually like children and try to make being in class attractive to them, their efforts become more and more concentrated on activities other than reading, and the modern classroom offers innumerable opportunities for this.

[13] Eleanor J. Gibson, "Theory-based Research on Reading and Its Implications for Instruction," in Carroll and Chall, eds., *op. cit.*
[14] S. J. Samuels, "Attention Process in Reading: The Effect of Pictures on the Acquisition of Reading Responses," *Journal of Educational Psychology*, 58 (1967).

In former times, when learning to read was much more exclusively the central issue in early education, the main way—often the only way—to gain the pleasure of receiving the teacher's attention and praise was to learn to read well. It was this reward that made learning to read a sensible reason—often the only one—to be in school as far as studies were concerned.

Today, as in times past, the child seeks the pleasure of receiving the teacher's approbation. But today this reward can be gained easily in ways which, in and by themselves, demand comparatively little application: by drawing, playing in kindergarten, even by napping. How much easier it is to receive the teacher's praise as reward for being a good nap-taker, block-builder, or participant in games played in class than through the arduous task of learning to read from an uninteresting text! Even if a child should on his own concentrate on reading, despite these other more enjoyable opportunities for gaining the teacher's praise, the text of the primer also diverts him by suggesting he seek pleasure in all sorts of ways such as running and jumping and through outdoor play, all completely unrelated to learning, reading, or literacy.

If we wish to induce children to become literate persons, our teaching methods should be in accordance with the richness of the child's spoken vocabulary, his intelligence, his natural curiosity, his eagerness to learn new things, his wish to develop his mind and his comprehension of the world, and his avid desire for the stimulation of his imagination—in short, by making reading an activity of intrinsic interest. This would "beguile" the child. When this is done, nonreaders of long standing, children who have rejected all learning, become fascinated with reading. At the Orthogenic School, some of them easily learned to recognize words that carried emotional significance for them after having seen them once or twice, and they learned to spell and write them after a few more repetitions. They did not find it difficult to learn to read ten or more such often complicated words in a day.[15] Sylvia Ashton-Warner reported similar experiences.[16]

Beginning readers who are "beguiled" can learn many words in a day, and not only words that are considered "easy." There are many historical examples demonstrating this—probably the most striking of them being found in the case of Helen Keller. Not yet seven, this blind deaf-mute, who had viciously fought all learning and socialized behavior, was taken in hand by Anne Sullivan. Within weeks Helen was able to "read," that is, to recognize some 400 words when spelled into her hand. She learned five or six new words a day. Anne Sullivan reports: "In one lesson I taught her these words: bedstead, mattress, sheet, blanket, comforter, spread, pillow. I found the next day that she remembered all but spread. The same day she learned at different times these words: house, weed, dust, raspberry, swing, molasses, fast, slow, maple sugar, counter. She had not forgotten one of these last."

True, in this case a most unusual though entirely inexperienced teacher met with a most brilliant child. But examples from our experience at the Orthogenic School involving children of quite ordinary intelligence and teachers who, though devoted and specially trained, were by no means miracle workers, suggest that such progress probably would be very frequent, if we used correct methods of teaching.

Characteristically, on the day that Helen Keller met Anne Sullivan, she spelled first the word "doll" and later "cake" into Helen's hand.[17] Both words have great emotional significance

[15] Bruno Bettelheim, "Violence: A Neglected Mode of Behavior," *Annals of the American Academy of Political and Social Science,* 364 (March 1966).
[16] Sylvia Ashton-Warner, *Teacher.* New York: Simon and Schuster, 1963.
[17] Nella Braddy, *Anne Sullivan Macy.* New York: Doubleday, Doran and Co., 1933.

for a little girl. Despite Helen's brilliance and Anne Sullivan's extraordinary talents, had she begun her efforts to teach reading by spelling into her hand: "Look," "and," and "see," which are the first words taught to children in our schools, or "Nan can tag Dan, Can Dan tag Sam?", little Helen might never have learned to read. There was, after all, a good reason why Anne Sullivan herself, on graduation from the Perkins Institution for the Blind, refused to become a teacher, as was strongly suggested to her, even though she did not know how else she might be able to make a living. She did not want to teach because "She had watched the teachers at Perkins toil day after day to teach an uninteresting subject matter with painfully meager results."[18] But there are no uninteresting subject matters, only uninteresting ways of teaching them. If taught in a boring way, any subject becomes uninteresting, and the results of teaching it painfully meager.

Teaching reading by introducing the child in the first year of instruction to some seventy uninterestingly simple words— that is, less than two a week—and this at a time when his functional vocabulary is some fifty times as large, consisting of quite complicated and, more important, emotionally very significant words, is in itself condescending. When in addition the stories built out of this pitifully small vocabulary abound with endless senseless repetitions of the same empty, boring, mostly monosyllabic words, then it becomes an insult to the child, who feels that he is being treated like a stupid person.

I know of no better way to characterize this method of instruction used to teach reading than by what Anne Sullivan wrote in 1887, at a time when readers contained at the least five times as many words as today, and when children were taught five to ten times as many words per week. She wrote: "They [the systems of teaching] seem to be built up on the

---

[18] Joseph P. Lash, *Helen and Teacher: The Story of Helen Keller and Anne Sullivan Macy*. New York: Delacorte Press, 1980.

supposition that every child is a kind of idiot who must be taught to think." Today, it seems that our system of teaching reading considers the child five times as much an idiot and five times as unable to think as it did some hundred years ago.

CHAPTER 2

Why Children
Resent Reading

Although there has been great concern about children who fail
to become literate, and much research into the causes of
children's inability to read and how to overcome it, by and
large there has been little sympathy for the valid psychological
reasons why a child may passively resist or actively refuse to
become literate, despite the obvious advantages that literacy
offers. The search has been predominantly for physical im-
pediments preventing the child's learning to read despite his
inclination to do so, such as visual disturbances that interfere
with correct recognition of letters, or central nervous impair-
ments that do not permit adequate reading. Almost completely
neglected are the valid reasons that may make a child wish
not to read and thus motivate him actively to resist efforts to
teach him.[1]

Something similar can be observed in relation to research
on the phenomenon called hyperkinesis, which also interferes
with the learning process. There the search is for central
nervous system causes and for pharmacological remedies, with
no consideration of the possibility that the child, far from
being unable to sit still, concentrate, and pay attention, may

[1] Years ago in Bruno Bettelheim, "The Decision to Fail," *The School
Review*, 69 (1961), it was emphasized that failures to learn are often
not the consequence of an inability to do so, but of the child's determined decision not to learn some subject matter.

do none of these because he does not wish to. Through his hyperkinetic behavior he may be attempting to assert himself against those who try to dominate him, wishing to defeat those he considers his enemies, or at least fighting back against what he experiences as insensitive persons or an inimical system.

Whereas in most other respects we have come to accept that even a very young child has a will of his own, which he tries to exert as well and as often as he possibly can, in respect to a child's nonreading, defective reading, or his so-called hyperactivity, we proceed as if these could not possibly be the consequences of his will. We assume that he would *like* to sit still and read, except that some defect he cannot help prevents him from doing so.[2] In order to begin to face this problem, we should ask: "What is the child feeling and what is its importance?" And we should then find an answer that is valid from *his* point of view, rather than an answer that simply reflects *our* point of view.

Most children do learn to read sooner or later, and learn it more or less well. Yet only a minority—albeit fortunately a sizable one—delight in reading, and later, all through their lives, derive great benefits from it. Our concern here is not with this happy minority but with the all too many for whom reading and what it has to offer is an experience they prefer to avoid. These are often children whose initial and pursuant experiences with reading were not ones in which they were able to involve themselves personally. On the contrary, reading was

---

[2] The reason we speak of a "so-called hyperactivity" is that in nearly all cases we observed, when the child felt welcome to express his honest opinion, he left no doubt that in his mind the amount of motor activity he displayed was entirely appropriate to his interests, his wishes, and the situation in which he found himself. His motility was excessive only in the eyes of those parents and teachers who did not want the child to be as active as his inner pressures forced him to be. They do not recognize that it may be demands which the child finds unacceptable in his environment that create the necessity for the child's responding to them with motor discharge.

The widely held erroneous opinions on these matters find support in

experienced as an essentially passive procedure of mere recognition of letters, words, and sentences that remained devoid of any deeper meaning.

Children may actively resist learning to read out of some anxiety connected with it, or because they experience it as utterly boring (which it is, when we fail to involve ourselves personally in what reading can offer us). Such children see reading as alien to their true interests; it is an imposed task that provides neither enjoyment nor other valuable rewards, an activity which, while potentially useful in the future, demands too much for what it can offer at the time.

Since most people will read only if they find it personally valuable, all efforts from the very beginning of teaching reading ought to be bent on making it that. Unfortunately, reading is most often taught as decoding instead, and decoding is essentially a meaningless activity—a process of mere recognition—in which we engage for some exterior reason, such as because a teacher requests it of us. Even if we do take in what the text tries to convey, as long as we do not respond to it and do not involve ourselves in it as the unique person we are, we permit ourselves to be passively impressed by what somebody else—the text writer, the teacher who asks us to read it—has chosen.

Only as we begin to respond personally to the text's content and open ourselves to its message (irrespective of whether the

---

the statements of children who, knowing that adults in authority will not accept as valid their desire not to learn to read or not to sit still, but *will* accept their excuse that they *cannot* do them, therefore claim that they cannot do these things. In some cases the child consciously believes that he would like to read and be able to concentrate, and not to be hyperactive. But unconscious processes prevent him from behaving in line with his conscious desires. In such cases the unconscious pressures and needs overpower the much weaker conscious wish to conform, and then it is true that the child cannot do what he wants to do because of this conflict.

consequence of this is an acceptance, modification, or rejection of it) do we go beyond a mere decoding or perception of the words and begin to perceive meanings. Then we are bringing our past experiences and present interests to bear on what we read; in short, we are actively involving ourselves in reading, at last able to comprehend what the text means to us, and what it can do to and for us. And this process of commitment to literacy is best and most easily established early in life.

The printed word is not a tangible object, but represents one. While the child may at some moments still equate words with tangible events or objects, he also struggles to get at a critical aspect of words—their intangibility. The word is what Piaget calls a "signifier," which refers to the object it signifies. In trying to make the distinction between the word (the signifier) and the object (the significate), the child vacillates between thinking that the word can exist apart from the object and that it is identical with it. When he tries to get at word meaning, he comes to understand that words are not objects, but nonetheless have a definite referent. As he is struggling with these complex thoughts, he is misled if the teacher conveys to him that he will solve the mystery by mastering the various letters that form the word. Concentration on studying the letters throws him back to the less mature view that it is the word—an object the elements of which must be mastered—that is all-important. But the word is not important because it is an object; it becomes important only as it signifies or imparts meaning. The child must learn this if reading is to become meaningful.

The teacher's concentration on developing basic language skills runs counter to the child's grasping the function of symbols, because too much attention is paid to decoding letters that in and by themselves have no intrinsic meaning. Even finding the little word within the bigger one makes it difficult to fathom the meaning of any given word, because it diverts attention to a little word, which has nothing to do with the one to be read, nor with the context of the story.

A visiting professorship at Kyoto University permitted one of us to visit classes in public schools where Japanese children were taught to read. It was amazing to observe the interesting stories, conveying complex thoughts, that were used to teach first graders, and it seemed that they all learned at least the basic skills involved. By the end of first grade, the Japanese school child is supposed to have mastered the two different syllabic alphabets—Hiragana and Katakana—each consisting of forty-six syllables, which themselves consist either of a single vowel, or of a consonant followed by a vowel. All Japanese words are built up out of these syllables. In addition, every Japanese child by the end of the first grade is supposed to have mastered seventy-six pictographs. Although the children are taught the strokes of the pen, or brush, out of which the syllables and particularly the pictographs are built up, the pictograph itself has to be learned as such, and its meaning must be comprehended if the child is to learn to read and write. Therefore, from the very beginning, the teaching of reading is concentrated only on the meaning of a pictograph, and not on the elements out of which it is built up.

There is no sounding out of elements forming a word in ideographic systems of writing and reading. The steps made in the teaching of an alphabetic language—from learning to recognize the letters of the alphabet to the sounding out of these letters, to hearing and pronouncing and recognizing the word, to comprehending the word as symbol for something it signifies—are all reduced in ideographic cultures to recognizing the symbol as something that symbolizes a specific referent. Thus from the very first, teaching to read concentrates on the meaning of the symbol and on nothing else. This seems to quickly make it possible to read sentences conveying complex thoughts.

It should, however, be mentioned that teaching the reading of pictographs is not like teaching whole word recognition as opposed to phonetic teaching. The emphasis is not on the recognition of the pictograph but on its meaning, which is necessary because the same pictographs reappear as elements in many different combinations, and only comprehension of the meaning of each pictograph permits comprehension of the meaning of these combinations. It would be practically impossible to learn each of these combinations all by itself; one must be able to build up an understanding of their meaning from the meaning of the single pictographs that are combined in them.

The relative speed with which Japanese first graders learn to read rather complex sentences, and to understand them, would suggest that we ought to give serious thought to basing our teaching of reading much more than is presently done on reading for meaning, and worrying less about the decoding of letters—at least so that the child from the very beginning, and all along, understands that the decoding of letters has no purpose or importance in itself, but has value only as leading to meaning.

Even an interesting text may have only idiosyncratic meanings, especially for the new reader. It takes time and experience for the child to understand that written material exists to impart messages to anyone who reads it, not just that it has specific messages for him. And so the transition from idiosyncratic to general can take place only through the meaning, not through the decoding of words. Significance, then, no longer resides in the word itself, but only in meaning, which in large measure is determined by common usage, but to some degree is also open to individual interpretation.

One significant element in making reading meaningful is the resonance the words evoke in our unconscious. We know that what goes on in an author's unconscious plays a significant role in his creation of a work of literature. Many of us feel that unless we succeed in comprehending not only the conscious phenomena that enter into the act of literary creation but also the contributions coming from the author's unconscious, we fail to understand important aspects of his work. A vast literature is devoted to the problem of how a writer's or an artist's unconscious influences his work.

Equally as important is the share the unconscious plays in shaping the *reader*'s appreciation of a work of literature. The unconscious of the reader significantly shapes his responses to the work he is reading, but so far this phenomenon has received little attention, although its investigation would help us to understand why some people derive great benefit from reading while others remain indifferent to it.

Any piece of writing contains overt and covert messages. The person who is reading it responds to both types of messages with both conscious and unconscious reactions. In consequence, the meanings intended by an author and those which the reader derives from what the author has written are by no means identical.

If the reader's personal concerns are somehow activated by what he is reading, and connected with it, he becomes emotionally involved in what he is reading. How far astray the reader's idiosyncratic reactions to a text will carry him depends on his ability to think abstractly, his propensity to control his extraneous thoughts from intruding, and on his experience in doing so. The less intellectually sophisticated the reader, the less he is accustomed to comprehend matters in accordance with abstract reasoning and the more he will be apt to be swayed by his dominant preoccupations or the mood of the moment. Thus the meaning of what he is reading is distorted both by the feelings he brings to it and by those feelings that the material he is reading arouses in him.

We do not yet know much about the unconscious forces within the reader that condition his responses to a piece of literature so that he wants to make it become part of his personal experience. We know even less about what is involved when there is a disparity between the messages intended by an author and those received by a reader. When this disparity occurs, we may read differently from the way the text is actually printed, or we may become resistant—and in extreme cases unable to read the text at all.

The younger and the less intellectually mature a reader is, the more powerfully his emotions affect all that he does. Consequently, he is not very able to experience things independently from his concerns and in objective ways, nor can he prevent his unconscious from obtruding and distorting what he consciously tries to comprehend. While these are well-known phenomena, when it comes to the teaching of reading to beginners, they are largely neglected. The unconscious is not even mentioned in the most highly regarded and widely used treatises on the teaching of reading.

The idea that when confronted with an external stimulus, such as a printed word, one tends to modify it to make it adjust better to one's expectations or preoccupations is not unique to Freud and psychoanalysis. Piaget has written extensively about how children in their thinking tend to assimilate—that is, make new material fit into their currently dominating system of meanings. In adults, there is normally a fairly harmonious balance between experiencing and interpreting external stimuli in terms of one's self-system (assimilation), and a readiness to do justice to them in more objective ways (accommodation). But the younger the child, the stronger is his tendency to assimilate outside stimuli, and the less developed is his ability to do justice to what is objectively inherent in the external stimulus.

Further, Piaget says that accommodation must always be preceded by a certain amount of assimilatory activity; that is, the individual must experiment with how the new information fits in with what he already knows, in order to adjust to the characteristics of the new material and reach a higher level of development. It is therefore entirely reasonable to assume that young children will treat the printed word, at least initially, in terms of what they already know, are thinking about, or how they feel.

A child who changes the text he is reading is thus behaving in accordance with the tendency of his age to actively manipulate things. Without being consciously aware of what he is doing, by modifying what he is reading, the child actively masters in personal ways that which otherwise he would only passively be taking in. This active manipulation endows the reading with a personal flavor, gives it a personal imprint, and makes reading more important. All this is common knowledge. It is the reason why the so-called stories in basic readers try to present topics thought to be personally attractive and meaningful to children of the age at which most are introduced to reading. But just because an activity is attractive to a child does not mean that reading about it in oversimplified form will also be attractive.

For example, a first grader may be familiar from his own experience with just how complex the personal interactions in a ball game are; therefore, when he reads a text about a ball game that uses only an extremely limited vocabulary, it seems completely devoid of interest. Such a text will convince the child that reading about ball games is trite indeed when compared with the vital events of a real game. Thus he has learned that reading is not worth the effort involved, because all it can offer is a very incomplete picture of its subject matter.

We teach children to read in the hope that what they read in the future will have meaning for them. But a skill that was not intrinsically meaningful when we first learned it is much less likely to become deeply meaningful later on, especially when compared with an activity that captivated the deepest layers of our being from the very beginning.

Basic reading texts contain nothing that is new to the child, and hardly ever anything of inherent interest to him. Even if it were possible truly to interest the child in the text's content as expressed in such a limited vocabulary, the level of thinking is far below that of an average child, so that the text in effect talks down to him. All these are reasons why it is impossible for the child to involve himself personally in the act of reading, unless he does so for his own reasons entirely.

Youth is when man's active-manipulative tendencies are at their highest, and the child is most desirous of making something his very own by giving it a personal imprint. We all are much more, and much more deeply, committed to what we actively shape or reshape than we are to what we must accept exactly as offered; and this is more true for the young child than it is for the adult. Thus, whether a child will develop a deep and lasting commitment to reading will be strongly influenced by whether he views reading as something imposed on him from the outside, or as something in the creation of which he actually participates.

It is a strange fact that in our teaching of reading to beginners we neglect their active manipulation of reading, which would and could make it a significant personal experience for them. We involve only the child's intellect in the process of learning to read, and we exclude his unconscious life from participating in it. It stands to reason that we would be much more successful in arousing a commitment to reading in the child if, from the very beginning, we involved his total personality in the process of reading. Which simply means that, following Dewey's precept, we would teach the whole child.

Some reading difficulties *are* due to neurological disorders. Children who suffer from such disorders need special help, which in most of the more serious cases the classroom teacher is unable to provide. But even for these children, it makes a great deal of difference whether or not the teacher meets their failures in reading with sensitive understanding of what they reveal, with compassion, and with respect for their efforts. If she does so, even these children will develop a positive attitude to reading and the desire to become literate, which is of considerable help to them in being able to cope with the consequences of their disabilities.

Since what the average teacher can do in a normal classroom is insufficient to overcome reading problems that are the result of real (as opposed to merely assumed) neurological disorders, the reading difficulties that are their consequence are disregarded here, because our concern is what the average teacher could do for the average child to prevent reading retardation.

Fortunately, the number of children who actually suffer from neurological disorders that make it difficult for them to learn to read is quite small. Regrettably, reading retardation and the other reading difficulties of a great many perfectly normal children are ascribed to neurological causes, although no valid indications are found that such causes exist. In a triumph of circular reasoning, the fact that a child has certain types of reading difficulties is considered proof of the presence of some neurological impairment. Dyslexia is the "disease" that is assumed to cause most reading difficulties. In 1965, the World Federation of Neurology defined dyslexia thus: "Dyslexia is a disorder in children who, despite conventional classroom experience, fail to attain language skills of reading, writing and spelling commensurate with their intellectual abilities." This definition begs the all-important question of whether these "conventional classroom experiences" are not the cause of the children's failure to attain the required skills which, according to their intelligence, should be quite within their reach. In fact, the National Advisory Committee on Dyslexia and Related Reading Disorders, appointed by the Secretary of HEW in 1968, found the concept of dyslexia so fuzzy that the committee, specifically appointed to study this so-called disease, decided not to employ the term in its report.

In the vast majority of children who have reading difficulties, these are due to those "conventional classroom experiences" alluded to when efforts were made to define dyslexia. Of course, a child's home background exercises a significant influence on his attitude to reading, and with it on his
ability or inability to learn it well. In Sandy's case, mentioned
in the first chapter, one must assume that his parents did not
motivate him to be interested in reading and that the schools,
as he asserted, failed to counteract this influence. The home
influences that interfere with a child's ability to learn to read
can be of a great variety. Often, a child's negative attitude to
reading is the consequence of parental disinterest in intellectual matters, even a subconscious aversion to them, to
which the child responds without quite knowing it. Refusal to
become literate can also be due to quite opposite causes: too
much home pressure to achieve academically can induce a
child to refuse to learn, either out of resentment of the pressure that makes life unbearable to him, or because he feels
there is no point in trying because he will never be able to
come up to parental expectations. A child may also refuse to
learn in an effort to assert his independence from his parents,
or he may court academic failure to defeat his parents where it
hurts them most.

Much depends on how the school deals with these negative
attitudes stemming from home influences. The right approach
will overcome the influences. But if a child meets with a
critical attitude to his failures—or with what he experiences as
a critical attitude—this will greatly increase his aversion to
reading, and so will texts that for one reason or another annoy
him. If a teacher views errors in reading as due to the inability
to decode—which it very well may be—this is also likely to
increase a child's already negative attitude to reading. If a
teacher, on the contrary, regards an error the child makes as
meaningful—as revealing an underlying thought or feeling of
importance to the child—then her attitude will be pleasing

even to the child whose reaction to reading is basically negative. And it may arouse some interest in reading, because his
teacher's concern with what is going on in him will induce the
child to look favorably on what the teacher wants him to learn.

It ought to be mentioned also that error-free, smooth
reading aloud is unfortunately not proof that all is well. A child
can have mastered the technique of reading, yet find it so
empty an experience that he avoids it whenever possible. He
then has acquired a skill that has no use for him.

Error-free reading can also occur when the child submits
passively to the dominance of the external stimulus of the
printed word and the demand that it ought to be read. The
child reads correctly if this is easy for him, because of the
degree to which he has mastered the requisite skills. He ac-
commodates, purely and simply, to the task of reading because
the teacher requires it, but no assimilation takes place because
there is no meaning ascribed to the text nor any derived from
it. Reading then is an empty gesture; it has no purpose. The
child feels that reading has no relevance to him personally or
to any of his concerns, and that it does not benefit him in any
other way than to get the teacher off his back.

In later years, such a child may not go to books for ideas,
since from the very start they did not communicate any to him,
and all his teacher cared about was that he should make no
errors in decoding. As an adult, since reading holds no technical difficulties for him, he may readily read the newspaper
headlines, the weather reports, the sports pages, or the stock
market reports—that is, he may read for information, but not
for enjoyment or to enrich his life. The fact is that such complete indifference or an entirely passive attitude to reading
seems to be typical for the majority of the population. When,
as children, they were asked to accept what the text said,
chided not to make any mistakes in reading, and criticized for
making them, these people learned to submit passively to the
dominance of the printed word, and for them reading became

and has remained an "ego-alien" experience, something in which they remain uninvolved. But true literacy—the enjoyment of reading and the meaning one gains from it that enriches one's life—requires that reading should be an experience in which the total personality is fully involved in the messages conveyed by the text.

This was all brought forcefully to our attention during our years of working with severely disturbed children at the Orthogenic School. Only by taking cognizance of how the child's unconscious was involved in reading (or, often, in his refusal to learn to read) were we able to induce nonreaders to learn to read, and make reading attractive to children who had before determinedly refused to be interested in it. By appealing to these children's unconscious, we succeeded in making reading not just possible but desirable to former nonreaders, many of whom afterwards became avid readers.

It was then often revealed that these children had become nonreaders because the way in which they *had* personalized what they read had been completely unacceptable to their teachers and other significant adults. Learning to read had been made into an imposed task that was alien to their interests. When they were forced to read in ways that contradicted the needs they had tried to express in their misreading, reading became inimical to their vital interests—something not only to be avoided but actively fought against. But once we succeeded in personalizing reading for these children—and particularly when we could help them recognize that through their reading they could gain a better understanding of themselves—then they sought to make their own what before they had shunned, and they became eager to learn to read.

CHAPTER 3

The Magic of Reading

Being able to read well is of great practical use in our society and the world. Unfortunately, however, this is the main reason teachers give children when announcing that they must learn to read. Reading is taught in ways that not only completely obfuscate what the art of literacy consists of, but prevent the child from guessing that it *could* exist. Even teachers who themselves are committed to literacy stress reading's practical value when teaching beginners, neglecting the more elusive but much more important value literacy can have for one's life. Earnest teachers, anxious to secure a better economic life for their students, press them to apply themselves more assiduously to learning reading skills so that they will be able to "get ahead in the world." But the child is not strongly motivated by distant future rewards; he is not firmly convinced by this reason.

We must not be led astray by the fact that everybody claims to know that to be able to read is profitable. The fact that people give lip service to such knowledge does not mean it has become part of their outlook on life or gives direction to their behavior; it can remain inoperative knowledge, which they file away in the far recesses of their minds and to which they pay no attention in their everyday lives.

A few segments of this chapter and of chapters 12 and 13 were first published under the title "Janet and Mark and the New Illiteracy: Reading and the Emotions," in *Encounter*, 43, 5 (1974).

Maybe this can be seen more clearly when considering the teaching of mathematics. Mastering basic mathematical skills is obviously useful; these are taught to all children. But despite this usefulness, most children drop their study of mathematics as soon as they have acquired the minimal smattering needed to get by. The reason is that with the emphasis on the practicality of the rudimentary computing skills, nothing in the way the children have been taught mathematics has made them aware of the fascinating world of numbers, or of how mathematics offers the key to a deeper understanding of the world. Only the few who for some special reason have become sufficiently entranced to penetrate beyond its practical uses comprehend what mathematics is really all about. I do not know whether this higher and truer concept of mathematics is potentially available to everybody, but there is no doubt that it could be opened up to a much larger number of students, were it not stressed that mathematics' main merit rests in its practical application.

What is required for a child to be eager to learn to read is not knowledge about reading's practical usefulness, but a fervent belief that being able to read will open to him a world of wonderful experiences, permit him to shed his ignorance, understand the world, and become master of his fate. For it is faith that kindles one's imagination and gives one the strength to undertake the most difficult tasks, even though at the moment one does not quite understand how, for example, reading will provide one with all these marvelous opportunities.

We would teach reading very differently if we viewed it as the initiation of a novice into a new world of experience— the acquisition of an arcane art that will unlock previously hidden secrets, open the door to gaining wisdom, and permit sharing in sublime poetic achievements. When learning to read is experienced not just as the best way but as the *only* way to be transported into a world previously unknown, then the child's unconscious fascination with imaginary events and magic power will support his conscious efforts at decoding, giving him strength to master the difficult task of learning to read and become a literate person.

Our thesis is that learning, particularly learning to read, must give the child the feeling that through it new worlds will be opened to his mind and imagination. And this would not prove difficult if we taught reading differently. Seeing how a child is lost to the world and forgets all his worries when reading a story that fascinates him, how he lives in the fantasy world of this story even long after he has finished reading it, shows how easily young children are captivated by books, provided they are the right ones.

Literature in the form of religious and other myths was one of man's greatest achievements, since in them he explored for the first time the meaning of his existence and the order of the world. Thus literature began as visions of man, and was not created to serve utilitarian purposes. All children are fascinated by visions, by magic, and by secret language, and the beginning of school is the age when the child is most desirous to partake of the secrets of adults. Satisfaction of these desires was historically contained in religious texts, so that children usually learned to read well from such texts. Mastering reading not only permitted access to superior powers but was the instrument through which we received their messages—those of God in religious writings, of superior minds in the writings of philosophers, poets, and scientists. When learning to read is experienced in this way, it involves not only the cognitive powers of the child's mind but also his imagination and his emotions—in short, all reaches of his personality. Learning to read then appeals to the highest and the most primordial aspects of the mind, involving simultaneously id, ego, and superego, our whole personality.

So there are the two radically different ways in which reading (and the learning of it) can be experienced: either as something of great practical value, important if one wants to get ahead in life; or as the source of unlimited knowledge and the most moving aesthetic experiences. Which of these two ways or in what combination of them the child will experience being taught reading, depends on the impressions he receives from his parents and the atmosphere of his home, and on how reading is taught to him in school. The image of literacy impressed on him by those who significantly shape his views of things during his most impressionable years is decisive, for during these early years when the child's basic personality is forming, he does not yet perceive matters on the basis of a rational and critical evaluation of their objective merits.

There is reason to believe that only those for whom reading was early endowed with some visionary qualities and magic meaning become literate. Reading and what it can contribute to one's life is not something that pertains only to the ego and the conscious mind; it is also deeply rooted in the unconscious. Those who retain all through life a deep commitment to literacy harbor in their unconscious some residue of their earlier conviction that reading is an art permitting access to magic worlds, although very few of them are aware that they subconsciously believe this to be so.

Consciously, most of us take pride in our rationality, and are correctly convinced that more than anything else it is literacy that lifts us out of irrationality into rationality. That an earlier, childish idea of literacy's magic power may still be at work in us is suggested by what we experience when we are deeply affected by art, poetry, music, literature, for then we feel touched by magic. It is an irrational attraction, but one that continues to move us throughout our entire lives.

The special fervor with which the astronomer engages in his scientific studies is imbued by remnants of the childish awe that overwhelmed him when first beholding the beauty or the immensity of the sky, if not also its eternity. While he does not look for the answers the astrologer sought—whose work was certainly a magic enterprise, but nevertheless the origin of astronomy—the astronomer still seeks to discover what created the universe, and how. Maybe in the development of the human mind from childhood to maturity, ontogeny parallels phylogeny in some measure or fashion. Magic belief in astrology slowly evolved into the science of astronomy, and alchemy into chemistry.

The good biologist as much as the good physician retains somewhere the feeling of wonder inspired by the miracle of life. However rationally the good physician proceeds when trying to relieve the physical and mental distress from which we suffer when we are sick, however much he relies in his work on his medical knowledge to help us, in our experience of him as a healer he must be tinged in some measure with the magical qualities with which past generations endowed the medicine man.

The more our rational abilities weaken, the more powerfully our emotions can impinge on us and the more dominant magic thinking becomes. As the child enters school, he is at an age when his rationality is as yet poorly developed, and his feelings dominate his thinking. So when something is really important to him, he is apt to invest it with magic; and the more he does so, the more important it will become to him emotionally. But if he fails to see some magic in what he is doing, he will be little interested in it.

If literature—irrespective of whether it is, depending on our interests and sensitivities, of a literary, philosophic, or scientific nature—had not been originally endowed with qualities that made it attractive to our unconscious, and if it did not still retain for us some of these qualities, we would not be fully committed to it, because an important part of our personality would remain uninvolved. For literature to affect us beyond what can be put easily into words, our response to it must continue to contain traces of the feelings and irrational ideas we projected into so many of our childhood experiences.

To the modern educator, who views learning to read as the acquisition of a particularly important cognitive skill, it may seem a far-fetched idea that this can be mastered well only if initially and for some time to come reading is experienced subconsciously by the child as a magic art, which potentially confers great and in some ways unknown power. Yet it is the child's wish to penetrate what he believes to be the important secrets adults possess that makes learning to read an exciting adventure to him—one so attractive that he is eager to expend the requisite concentration and energy on mastering it.

Here it might be worth remembering again that literature began as poetry, which was part of religion, as in invocations to the gods or rhymes to which magic properties were ascribed. Literature originated in poetry recited and transmitted orally. It often served magic rather than ordinary utilitarian purposes. Even when script became more common, much of the now recorded literature was still devoted to issues connected with religion—so much so that it could be said, and universally believed, that "In the beginning was the word, and the word was with God, and the word was God." For millennia, writing and reading were arcane arts that conferred special powers and privileges. It required a long and difficult struggle before the average man was permitted to read the Scriptures, and printing began with the printing of Bibles and other religious texts. It was from the Good Book that children were taught to read, and only after man was permitted to read the Scriptures did education become universal.

Today, too, for literacy to be a really desirable goal for the young child, it must be endowed by him with magic meaning. Only then will it become fully attractive to his unconscious, which will consequently support the child's conscious efforts to master reading. Later, the irrational aspects of literacy can become safely reduced and the rational ones gain ascendancy. But if this divestment of magical connotations occurs too soon and too radically, reading will not be strongly invested emotionally.

It is not objective merit, but high parental valuation, that makes reading so attractive to the child. This appeal does not emanate from the rational and utilitarian purposes parents may satisfy through reading; rather, the child responds to the parents' emotional absorption in reading. What makes it attractive to him is that it seems to fascinate his parents. It is their secret knowledge that the child wants to be able to share. The more parental devotion to reading and the child's belief in its magic propensities coincide, the easier time a child will have in learning to read, and the more important and enjoyable reading will be to him.

It is rare that we find a chance to compare the impact of two different methods of teaching reading—that typical of our schools, and that where reading is being taught immediately from a difficult text which carries deepest meaning for the child as it does for his parents—on one child's reading ability and interest in reading. But once in a while one hears about such an experiment *in vivo*:

A boy was educated simultaneously at the local public school and at an orthodox Jewish school, or yeshiva, where children are taught reading directly from the Hebrew Bible and have to translate what they read into the vernacular, exactly the way it has been done for hundreds of years. There, "none of the texts presented to young children are expurgated or bowdlerized. It is in fact forbidden by Jewish Law to abridge, expurgate or, for that matter, even to skip over what might be considered controversial passages. Thus children even in the early primary years read unabashedly about the attempt of Potifer's wife to seduce Joseph, of the twins fathered by Judah upon a woman he thought to be a prostitute, and of the rape of Dinah by Schechem."[1]

One day when his father wanted to demonstrate the child's ability to deal with sophisticated material, he asked this six-year-old boy

> to translate from the book of Genesis for a visitor in our home. The guest would call out chapter and verse, and after a pause to locate the passage, the young boy would provide a quite accurate translation in his own words. Our amazed visitor asked if by chance he were not dealing with a bilingual edition, and if he were not stealing an occasional glance at the English. To my embarrassment, I found that I had indeed given him a volume replete with a literal English rendition of each line. I began offering assurance that the boy was not using any crutch, but was in fact reading only the Hebrew original. Groping for a quick proof of my contention, I asked Steven to look at the English text and read it to me. Obediently, he focused his attention on the other side of the page, stumbled pathetically over the phonics, and with a grimace exclaimed, "I can't."

Here is a situation which is not at all uncommon among yeshiva students: children who can paraphrase the book of Genesis, provide an account of creation . . . and grasp such concepts as a vacuum, yet cannot understand the same material in their mother tongue. These same children are pursuing the secular curric-

---

[1] This and the quotations that follow are taken from Leonard R. Mendelsohn, "Sophisticated Reading for Children: The Experience of the Classical Jewish Academy," in F. Butler, ed., *Children's Literature: The Great Excluded*, Journal of the Modern Language Association Seminar on Children's Literature and the Children's Literature Association, Storrs, Conn.: University of Connecticut, 1973. The author is professor of English at Sir George Williams University, Montreal, and teaches also at the Rabbinical College of Canada.

ulum required by state law, and standardized tests
show that their achievement is at the very least equal
to their counterpart in the public school system. . . . .
Secular programs, even those of the more enlightened
school districts, such as the one I live in, are not keeping pace either with the concepts or the language skills
which are being taught in the Jewish schools.

Comparing the texts with which his son was taught in the
two schools he attended, this father commented:

I know of no parent who would open a primer today
with any intention other than to discover what his
child is reading. . . . The texts of the first grader in the
yeshiva, on the other hand, are the identical readings
explored daily by his parents and teachers. As a result
of this perpetual and subtle set of reminders of the in-
finite depth and potential of the subject matter he is
pursuing, the phrases "I have read" or "I have already
learned" are never used, since finality is neither possible nor desirable. Study is an ongoing process. The
objective is to be continually involved with the text, not
to outgrow it, because the material can never be fully
mastered.

The boy, having been taught Hebrew for meaning and with
complete disregard of whether some word by itself was easy
or difficult, read it for meaning and was carried along by his
understanding of it so that he could translate a difficult text.
In public school he had been taught to decode laboriously
simple English words in meaningless sequences. Since what he
was made to read there had nothing to awaken his interest,
he could read only the words he had learned in class. He knew
that no adult could possibly be interested in what he was read-

ing in public school, so he could not work up any interest in it either. Well aware that adults were as interested as he in what he was reading in Hebrew school, if not more so, he found learning to read there a challenge which he met to the best of his ability.

The significance of the text of the Bible invites every reader to seek his own meaning in what is written. From the moment he learns to read, the child is impressed that his teacher reads the same book innumerable times and always finds some new meaning in it. This challenges the child to do the same, and suggests to him that whatever meaning he finds in it is legitimate for him. What the text conveyed—as much as his teacher's and parents' attitude toward it—put the boy just mentioned under its spell as soon as he began to learn to read. With it, reading and literature attained magic connotations.

By comparison with the truly unlimited and deeply engrossing vistas the Bible opens up to the child, as Mendelsohn says, "the public school system employs various elementary reading series which for all their claims to linguistic and literary advancement really amount to little more than an updated Dick and Jane." What vistas, indeed, are made available to the child who is asked to develop interest in reading, not to mention literature, by learning to read: "Janet. Mark. Janet and Mark. Come, Mark, come Mark, come. Come here, Mark. Come here. Come here, Mark. Come and jump. Come and jump, jump, jump. Here I come, Janet. Here I come. Jump, jump, jump"? This is the entire text of the first seven pages of the updated *Janet and Mark* preprimer, which continues in the same vein.

Because of its central importance, reading should be the paramount example of what education in the deepest sense is all about: a progress from irrationality to rationality, starting with the id's irrational purposes, which become gradually controlled by the ego and thus changed to meet in a rational manner the challenges of both external reality and the inner life. If education equips students in this way, it enriches their personality and makes life more manageable and more worthwhile. But modern education—believing it can do away with the slow and tortuous development from irrationality to rationality—tends to deplete the ego of its natural resources and leave it weakened, subject to domination by an irrationality that has not been sufficiently transformed by the process of education.

A boy with the intelligence of genius (an IQ of over 160) had failed first grade repeatedly because he was thought to be unable to learn to read, despite special efforts to teach him. In our first meeting he engaged me in a highly sophisticated and involved, albeit idiosyncratic and somewhat delusional conversation on the nature of the heavenly bodies and their movements. The conversation left no doubt that he was brilliant, but as far as academic performance was concerned, he functioned as if he were truly feeble-minded. It took a couple of years of intensive therapeutic efforts at the Orthogenic School to free him of his complete blocking in respect to all subjects taught in schools. Given entire freedom in how he wanted to learn to read when he finally decided to make an effort to do so, he chose to teach himself from a book that explained how man developed the alphabet, a book for adults.[2] From it he learned easily and with only minimal help to read fluently. He chose as the next reading matter with which to increase his reading proficiency *The New York Times*, which he then read fairly regularly with great understanding.

Once he became able to read—that is, had decided it was worth his efforts to do so—he let us in on his view of the secret of why he had so determinedly resisted learning it: Both his parents were scientists; intellectual achievement was very

---

[2] O. Ogg, *The Twentysix Letters*. New York: Thomas Y. Crowell, 1948.

important to them, and they pushed it on the boy at the expense of his emotional life, which had remained completely barren. When he entered school, he had hoped that things would be different there—that learning would not have to be something abstract, devoid of all human contact and gained at the expense of the satisfaction of his emotional needs.

And so it had seemed at the beginning of his school experiences. He took hope, particularly since he had liked his first-grade teacher, who seemed to be "a warm person." But when she, on whom he had rested his hopes, waxed all excited about "See Spot Run," his desire and hope to combine true emotions with intellectual activities were completely destroyed. Reading—or rather, what he was directed to pay attention to in order to learn it—was simply too asinine to commit his emotions to it, while he had come to shun and hate intellectual endeavors that were not invested with emotionally satisfying aspects. The only escape from a life that had become insufferable was to withdraw entirely into himself and an inner fantasy life that excluded all reality—because at home, reality was devoid of the feelings he needed for emotional survival, and at school there were emotions, but they were so misplaced and perverted that the experience was an insult to his intelligence.[3]

In juxtaposition to this, let us consider the early memories of a famous poet who was equally convinced that his first

[3] There were, of course, more important and deep-reaching psychological reasons for his unwillingness to become educated, having to do with his relationship to his parents. He had been the object of very early emotional neglect; his mother had had no time for or interest in the baby, and soon pushed him intellectually, as did his father. This was more reason to hate intellectual activities that were emotionally barren, but he came to understand all of this only later.

He could then also realize why he had decided to give the Orthogenic School a try. In our first meeting he had tried to impress me with his erudite discussion of astronomy. I remained uninvolved and remarked instead that, as interesting as heavenly bodies are, I was much more concerned with human bodies. My concern at the Orthogenic School experiences with learning to read strongly affected his life. In *Aftergrowth and Other Stories*,[4] Chaim Nachman Bialik reflects on his first experience with learning to read:

> To tell the truth all they had to teach reached me only behind my ear, so to say, through the left earlock, as folks say in Yiddish. My right ear was busy listening to quite a different subject which rose from the prayer book between the lines, and united with what was already in my heart. The lines themselves, and the actual letters which made up those lines, were only faint intimations of this other wisdom. From the first day on which the teacher showed me the letters of the aleph-beth [these and the following are the names of the letters of the Hebrew alphabet] set in rows, I saw leaping forth the measured ranks of soldiers like those who at times passed in front of our house, with their drummer, rattling tum tararum tum, at their head. Those that most resembled this were the *alephs*, all arms swinging and legs striding, and the *gimels* with their boot moving off to the left, particularly when they had the kubbutz vowel beneath them, its three dots like a ladder. . . . My eyes began to search the sides and flanks of the book. "Whom are you looking for?" asked

---

was that they should be very well taken care of. I said that the relations of human bodies to each other are much more important and interesting than those of the heavenly bodies to each other. At that time he gave no intimation that this remark had penetrated his mind. Nevertheless it had been crucial in his decision to come to the Orthogenic School, upon my offering this opportunity to him.

But all this does not detract from his assessing, correctly, children's reaction to teachers who assume that such strings of words as "See Spot run. See Spot jump, jump, jump," amuse children, or are able to hold their attention through a boringly simplistic message.

[4] Philadelphia: The Jewish Publication Society of America, 1939.

the melamed [teacher]. "For the drummer," said I, my eyes searching. . . . All day long I daydreamed about armies and soldiers. . . .

When I reached the point of combining letters, I found a vast medley of weird creatures; they came in bands, back to back, the simple *nun* and the squash-nosed *pe* always jumping ahead on one leg. The *lamed* strode erect with outstretched neck. . . .

Out of the blurred little letters in these old books . . . all those book bits of which I learned in turn, with great jumps . . . out of all these there came towards me confused and incomplete fragments of generations . . . tales and stories. . . . Here I was, conversing with all these ancients, and participating in their life and deeds. . . . In a pinch, one of these ancient wise men would come and make a remark, and everything would clear up beautifully and happily.

With this kind of learning one can readily understand that "It became unnecessary to translate the words; translation was almost a defect. The words poured out and out from the heart, their meaning being part of them. The gate of understanding opened of its own accord."

It is because of experiences such as these that one learns to read all on one's own. As a result of what one reads, and what it evokes in one, it seems as if spontaneously the "gate of understanding" swings open all by itself, and what pours out enriches one's life so much that one chooses to become a literate person, whatever serious application this may require.

Traditional Hebrew teaching is by no means alone in being based on the deepest meaning literature can have. There was a time, not all that long ago, when if there was any book in the house at all it was the Bible, and it was read and listened to by people of all ages; it was the source of their deepest thoughts, whether they were the youngest child or the oldest adult. Many a Christian child then learned to read from the Bible, as do orthodox Jewish children in their yeshivas today.

The first sentences of the *New England Primer* of 1727 read: *"In Adam's fall—We sinned all—Thy life to mend— This book attend."* Reading this, there could be no doubt in a child's mind that learning to read had to do with the first and last things: with our human condition as symbolized by the fall from grace, and the hope for salvation. This book promised that if only we learned to read it, we could mend our life and earn eternal bliss. With such rewards held out, learning to read surely appeared, despite the difficulties involved, to be the most worthwhile thing anybody could do.

Given a chance, average American children today, including underprivileged ones, would be as receptive to the magic propensities of literature and respond to it as readily as did American children of the past. The poet Kenneth Koch taught third- to sixth-grade students of P.S. 61 in New York poems by Donne, Shakespeare, Wallace Stevens, Lorca, and so on, and found his students ready to comprehend the real values of literature and to be fascinated by them, eager to make their own what poetry has to offer, provided it was real poetry.[5] But their regular readers had left them uninterested in reading.

Speaking of the poems in today's primers, Koch maintains:

> The usual criteria for choosing poems to teach children are mistaken. . . . These criteria are total understandability, which stunts children's poetic education by giving them nothing to understand they have not already understood: "childlikeness" of theme and treatment, which condescends to their feelings and intelligence; and "familiarity," which obliges them to go on reading the same inappropriate poems. One aspect of "child-

[5] Kenneth Koch, *Rose, Where Did You Get That Red? Teaching Great Poetry to Children.* New York: Random House, 1973.

likeness" which is particularly likely to work against children loving poetry and taking it seriously is a cloyingly sweet and trouble-free view of life.[6]

It is hardly surprising that the minds of children respond most readily to true poetry, and that it motivates them best to learn to read. It is simply one more proof that children ought to be taught from texts that they find worthy of their attention and most determined efforts. Their reading material should not only be new and interesting, appealing to all layers of their personalities (the conscious as well as the unconscious ones) but, most important, it should open up new vistas which the children find captivating.

In line with Huey's suggestion, the child should be taught to read from "chosen classics of literature," so that from the very beginning of his introduction to reading he has a chance to appreciate literature. Good literature has something of meaning to offer any reader of any age, although on different levels of comprehension and appreciation. The child who reads one of the classics will ponder what it tries to tell him about himself and his world, and he will feel that there is more to it than he got on first reading. Whether or not this induces him soon to reread the story or poem, it promotes the attitude most important for becoming literate: that there is much more to be gained from further reading, from intellectual growth, and that what he is reading now starts him on an undertaking which, when consistently pursued, will increase his knowledge and appreciation indefinitely.

[6] Kenneth Koch, *New York Review of Books*, XX, 4, September 20, 1973.

CHAPTER 4

Observations and Principles

In exploring what a psychoanalytically oriented approach may contribute to the understanding of the problems encountered in the teaching of primary-grade children, we kept encountering the same vexing question over and over again: Why do so many children fail to learn to read as well as they could? Given our psychoanalytic bias, it seemed important to understand what the child brings to the learning situation: how he responds to it; what it does to him; how it feels from where he sits. In essence, we tried to concentrate on the child's concerns rather than those of the teacher and the educational system, whose main concentration is on what the child ought to learn. Given the limitations of what we could do, we studied children's responses to being taught reading, and tried to discover what the child thought of the books from which he was taught; how, deep down, he reacted to how he was taught; and how he responded to the way in which his difficulties in learning to read were handled.

Our observations and explorations suggested that many difficulties children encounter in learning to read, and many errors they make which are either corrected or for which they are taken to task, are due not to an inability to decode or understand the text, but often rather to their understanding the text quite well, sufficiently so to reject it for what seemed to them valid reasons. We also came to understand that the way the children's errors were corrected, more often than not, not only failed to improve their reading, or to encourage them to continue with reading, but actually set them against reading.

It is a psychoanalytic principle that the analyst must be ready and able to see the world through the eyes of his patient, considering his feelings and actions valid, taking his perspective on things, however much all these may be out of step with what is considered the norm. When this is done and the patient feels truly understood and (more important) appreciated and accepted, he then becomes open to experiencing things and responding to them as the rest of the world does. This principle suggested an exploration of what the consequences would be if we gave credence to the child's view that what he was reading needed improvement, or was worthy of rejection; that is, if his mistakes were viewed as meaningful. The results of our exploration of this theory proved fruitful.

Since later attitudes are conditioned by our first experiences, the teaching of reading to primary-school-age children of five to eight is particularly important. So we concentrated on studying what goes on during the first years children are taught to read in public schools. We tried to observe carefully what seems good and what questionable in the methods used, and what might be done to prevent children from becoming defeated by the difficulties they encounter as they try to learn to read. We also tried to explore how reading could be made more attractive to those who were uninterested in it. In this task we were helped by the six co-workers mentioned in the Preface.

The eight of us observed classroom teaching in eight schools, seven public and one private, located in three cities in California and two in Massachusetts. This is a small sample, although observations were made on the reading performance of some 300 children, over a period of four years. We decided that the type of errors made by them, and their reactions to their readers' contents, were by and large typical for this age group, and so was the teachers' handling of them. To check this assumption we also made observations in a number of other schools in different localities.

The eight schools in which the main observations were made were the best in their respective systems, according to school administrators and knowledgeable members of their communities. We began by explaining in some detail to principals and teachers what we intended to do, and exploring their reactions to it. We proposed to observe what went on in the classroom with as little interference as possible, and to talk occasionally with a child, or a group of children, about what they had been reading in order to elicit their spontaneous response to it; and further, to discuss with the teachers afterwards their motives in teaching as they did, to share our observations with them and explain to them why we took some action, if we had done so.

We did *not* say that we planned to concentrate on children's reactions to the texts they were using or on their mistakes in reading, for the simple reason that, initially, we were not sure what would be most worthwhile to study. We did say that our approach to making sense of our observations would be guided by psychoanalytic insights, since we wanted to study what contribution, if any, psychoanalytic understanding could make to primary classroom teaching. But we also made it clear that we were not in the least interested in trying to psychoanalyze children or teachers. That is, while among many other things we wanted to try to understand the role the unconscious may play in classroom learning, we did not intend to explore unconscious content, unless it revealed itself in what passes for normal overt behavior in the classroom.

Our observations took place in the system's best schools, and, further, only in what each school considered its best classrooms, taught by the best teachers—we were not interested in studying the entire educational process, nor in what went on in an average classroom taught by average teachers. Superior teachers and classrooms in a system do not so much represent what goes on in the typical classroom as suggest what the system is striving for—they reveal what is considered to be desirable teaching. If there were shortcomings in the teaching of reading in these classes, one might assume there would be even greater ones in the other classes. If an approach based on psychoanalytic thinking could contribute something to these superior classes, it could do even more in others.

Teachers volunteered their participation—understandably so, since the best teachers are also those who are most interested in educational problems. They were willing to spend some of their free time each week discussing with us what we had observed in their classes. It was understood that the teachers cooperating in this research would receive no extra compensation for doing so. We wanted to make sure that no ulterior purpose but their own interest would motivate their participation in the study. (A great deal of educational research by outsiders goes on in the three systems where most of our observations were made, since each of them is located in a town dominated by one of the leading U.S. universities; this, in part, explains the high quality of much of the teaching done in these schools.)

After some exploration and experimentation, most observations were concentrated in eight classes.[1] Overall, some thirty teachers were involved in the project, but some changed classes, others took a sabbatical, and a few left the system, so that, over time, we worked most closely with about fifteen teachers.

The children whose reading we observed were of varying

[1] At any one time we did not observe more than 200 children. But since the observations stretched over four years, children left the classes we observed, and new ones entered, which explains the total of 300 given above.

ethnic origins and socioeconomic backgrounds. Quite a few were children of university faculty members; all were students in schools that are trying hard to integrate white middle-class children with those belonging to ethnic and socioeconomic minorities, and that try to apply advanced methods of teaching. Their populations are completely integrated, both staff and students. The integration, moreover, is neither routine nor resented—at least not consciously so. On the contrary, it is consciously welcomed. Sincere efforts are made to gear all teaching toward promoting better relations among people of different backgrounds. The children are encouraged to discuss their feelings on subjects other than classroom topics, although not necessarily their feelings about other ethnic groups. Understandably, with such emphasis on integration, ambivalence about dealing with ethnic differences is sometimes quite intense among the children. The teachers have a conscious commitment to working through the children's ambivalence; this is apparent in the way the teaching staff approaches the problems, and it spreads to the children, so that following the lead of their teachers, children often interact with one another in mutually beneficial ways despite differences in background. Outsiders are frequently invited to visit these classes and to provide special experiences from the area of their competence for the children. Thus the children are accustomed to dealing with visitors and usually welcome them, which considerably facilitated what we were doing.

In order for the students to become comfortably acquainted with us, we spent several hours a week for a few months in just being with them in their classrooms before attempting to observe their reading, read with them, or begin speaking with them as to how they felt about what they read. The children needed to know who we were before they could freely volunteer their thoughts about what they were reading, and the teachers, too, had to become accustomed to having us present as observers while they were teaching. Observation was continued only in those classes where teachers responded positively to the project, for their attitudes communicated to the children that this was an acceptable and interesting enterprise.

After everyone had become comfortable together, we tried to observe the interactions that took place when a child read with a teacher, and then we talked with the child about his thoughts or feelings concerning the material he had just read. Eventually we also read with the children ourselves. All our conversations with children, and those we had after class with the teachers, were very informal, if for no other reason than that, at first, we did not know what to volunteer or what to ask. In line with psychoanalytic method, we tried to elicit ideas from the children and the teachers, and we made conscious efforts to avoid influencing their responses by any preconceived ideas on our part.

The children were free to shape the discussion in any way they liked. We tried very hard to make it possible for them to react spontaneously to their classroom reading materials. We preserved the setting as we found it, so that the child could reveal his thoughts without feeling that the normal classroom procedures had been altered or interrupted in any way. The examples used here to illustrate beginners' reactions to what they were reading are thus based on careful observations made in a casual manner.

In line with our stated purpose and our promise to the administrators who permitted, and the educators who cooperated in our research, no attempt was made to penetrate a child's unconscious. We only observed carefully what the child did during the time he was reading and what he said to the teacher who corrected him.

After a considerable period of observing children's reading in this way, it became apparent to us that misreadings, in addition to being personally meaningful, may also be in the nature of a message—more often than not unconsciously motivated—to the adult who is listening to the child read. So then we would talk casually with a child who had misread something about what seemed to us to be the implications of the way he chose to read some word or sentence. We did not mention possible unconscious needs or anxieties to which the misreading may have referred; we simply took seriously the way the child had read something, viewing it as an interesting statement about which we wished to learn more so far as the child's conscious understanding of the matter went.

We took this approach because we started with the assumption that not all errors in reading are due to a lack of skills, knowledge, or attention, but that they may reflect important processes going on in the child's mind which deserve our serious interest. When we show such respect to what is important to the child, he becomes much more inclined to pay attention to what is also of concern to us: his ability to read without making errors.

We came to feel that children's mistakes in reading may have much to do with their preoccupations of the moment, or, as Piaget would say, with the nature of the present system of meanings in use at the time of reading, although he has only conscious meanings in mind. But a system of meanings includes also preconscious and unconscious thoughts. A text that taps a system of meanings thus arouses reactions on more than one level of consciousness.

Freud describes how a mistake may anticipate something that is becoming conscious in the person who makes the error.[2] If so, then a misreading could reflect an interaction between several levels of meaning. The person makes the error because, subsconsciously, he is already occupied with the thoughts that account for the error. Other errors are often in the nature of a

---

[2] Sigmund Freud, "Psychopathology of Everyday Life," *Standard Edition of the Complete Psychological Works of Sigmund Freud,* Vol. VI. London: Hogarth Press, 1960. "Psychopathology" was first published in German in 1901; the first English translation appeared in 1914.

challenge, made in the unconscious hope of provoking a reaction. Sometimes they are made in order to enlist the aid of another person in resolving an impasse. Children's errors in reading may be attempts at solving conflicts that preoccupy them in general, or that are created by material they are asked to read.

We knew it wouldn't help to try to elicit a clarification by means of a pointed question, such as, "Why did you read 'can't' for 'can'?" Such a direct question is experienced by the child as a criticism of the way he read the word, or as a challenge to correct himself. It means to him that in his conflict, we side with the printed word against his rejection of it, or his effort to make the sentence more acceptable to him. Asking a child why he misread something is also a pointless question: if he knew and could state the meaning of his substitution, he would already have mastered the problem lying behind the misreading, and therefore probably would not have misread.

But neither would it help if we *sided* with the child's rejection or changing of the word as printed, for then we would be encouraging a solipsistic attitude toward reading that is also inimical to the acquisition of true literacy. We wanted to promote the spontaneous efforts of the child's ego to make his reading experience a meaningful one; any imposition of our opinions about how he ought to proceed in doing so would only tend to disturb him more.

We felt it would also be an error to tell the child that we thought he misread something out of preconscious or unconscious reasons—it is always extremely hazardous to make such guesses. While it is feasible to assess fairly correctly from a person's behavior (such as from his misreading) that the workings of his unconscious may have led to the misreading in a general way, it is very difficult to be sure about the specific emotions or unconscious thought processes involved.

So all we attempted in our investigation was to involve the

child in a conversation about what the misreading conveyed to us, within the context of the story as printed. Although we had expected that such an approach would provide verification for our speculations about the causes of misreadings, it was a serendipitous finding that this approach led in most cases to the child's spontaneously correcting the misreading; often he would correctly reread the pertinent part of the text all on his own.

It might seem odd that taking a misreading seriously and showing interest in what it could convey within the context of a story should have this positive result—learning theory would seem to suggest that rewarding such behavior would only reinforce it and promote a repetition of the misreading, not self-correction. The explanation may be found in the child's realization that we were not concentrating on his error, but on the meaning he gave to the story through his misreading. Through our response we emphasized meaning on two levels: that of the misreading itself, which we took to be a deliberate act, not an error due to incompetence; and that of the different content the misreading gave the story. Such an emphasis on meaning may have induced the child to devote renewed mental energy to comprehending the meaning of the text as printed. Since his efforts to project meaning into the text found positive acceptance, he then became more ready and able to accept the text literally.

The child's ability, in consequence of our intervention, to read correctly all on his own what before he had been unable —or unconsciously unwilling—to read, and the zest with which he continued reading, is seen as the result of his coming to understand in some measure why he had misread a word in the first place.

It might be thought that the child's rereading the text correctly was due mainly, not to our approach, but to the fact that our intervention made him focus on the text, while before he may have been daydreaming. Yet our observations showed that the teacher also brought errors to the child's attention, which equally would arouse him out of his daydreams and make him focus, but that this failed to produce a spontaneous correct rereading of the sentence.

In other cases our viewing his misreading positively may simply have fortified the child's ego to meet the task of reading the text as printed. Or it may have been that our acceptance of his misreading as deliberate though not correct had shown him that he was free to do in his reading what seemed best to him; with his interest and pleasure in reading as well as his self-confidence restored, correct reading became possible.

In the well-functioning person there exists at any given moment a dynamic balance between external demands and inner processes, and a comparable balance between id, ego, and superego—that is, between the conscious and unconscious forces as these struggle for ascendancy in the mind. Behavior is thus not just the consequence of how strongly any one of the several forces presses its demands; it also is affected by how much the ego has become involved in attending to the person's conscious interests. If reading in general and the book he is reading at the moment seem interesting to the child, and worthwhile to his superego, then his conscious mind will be much better able to assert itself successfully, even against fairly strong unconscious pressures. If, on the contrary, the material he is reading fails to stimulate the child's conscious mind, or does so only weakly, then even relatively weak unconscious pressures will be sufficient to overpower conscious attempts to read the words as printed.

The nature of the child's relations to those who are emotionally significant to him also exercises its positive and negative influences in this respect. If he is impressed by the teacher and wishes to please her, then this strengthens his ego and can keep in abeyance even quite strong unconscious pressures;

but if the teacher's demand to read well leaves the child indifferent because he does not think much of her, then his ego
will not be supported in its task by the teacher's impact.

The same holds true for parents—their values and their
desires. Other children, too, exercise influence. If they value
reading highly, the group climate supports a child's ego. But if
the child does not relate positively to the other children, then
the same group climate can have the opposite effect. If the
other children are negatively motivated toward learning and
school, then identification with their rejection of learning will
reduce the ego's capacity to hold its own against the assertions
of the id.

By and large the children we studied related positively to
their teachers and to their parents, whose values supported
academic achievement, although in varying degrees and with
some inner ambivalence. Since there was a mixture of social
classes and ethnic backgrounds, not all children were attuned
to learning in the same ways and there were, of course, a few
who were in opposition to parental values because of impaired
relations with their parents. But the majority of the children
had positive attitudes to learning, and received ample emotional support in this direction from both teachers and schools.
They were in public schools where optimal conditions for
learning were the rule—that is, optimal within the presently
prevailing structure of our educational system. So we felt that
the children's blocking or misreading was due more to inner
psychic processes and less to negative social motivators than
might hold true in a more ordinary classroom situation. These
are, of course, only impressions and at best rough estimates,
but they are all we can go by as long as we have no data on
what is the average positive emotional support (or its opposite) that the average child receives in the average class,
from teacher, parents, and peer group.

While children's positive and negative emotional relations
to others strongly influence their general attitude to learning,

blockings or misreadings result primarily from the impact of quite specific unconscious or preconscious processes.[3] With respect to their inner psychic causes, misreadings can be roughly divided into two quite different groups: those that are the consequence of unconscious pressures overwhelming the cognitive powers, and others that are the result of the ego not being sufficiently motivated. In both cases the result is a predominance of the unconscious or preconscious in the child's reading, expressed in either a misreading or a blocking. In misreading, one word is substituted for another; in blocking, the child stops reading, as if a curtain has suddenly been lowered, shutting off his mind, which becomes blank and makes continued reading impossible.

The child in his misreadings quite often comprehends subconsciously what the printed word is, and is more or less vaguely aware that he is altering it. Simple acceptance of this change with no comment can be felt as not taking seriously what he has done, although what he did is important to him. A mere correction of a misreading is also experienced as not taking seriously what was done by the child—that is, riding roughshod over what to him are significant matters. There is a world of difference, for the child's feelings about himself and his budding ability to read, between viewing his error as stupid and treating it as a significant act. For whatever the cause of a misreading may be—whether it is due to lack of knowledge, confusion, carelessness, inattention, rebelliousness, or dissatisfaction with the text—the word that is substituted for the one printed is chosen from many thousands in the child's vocabulary for some definite reason. For example, children often

---

[3] This is not always so, because under special conditions, refusing to do what teacher and the process of education (as represented by the system) require can be an assertion of the self, as when a delinquent deliberately and consciously defies the school in order to gain status with other delinquents. But this is more likely to happen when the child is older, and only quite rarely when he is beginning to read.

substitute a word beginning with the same letter for the one printed in the text. These children usually know many words beginning with this letter, which they decoded correctly; thus the question is why they chose this one word in preference to all others beginning with the same letter.

The reason why a word is misread in one particular way can be either entirely preconscious, or partly conscious, reflecting some association to an aspect or element of the word a child has chosen to read. Originally, such associations were called free associations, to differentiate them from directed associations—those with which, for instance, a person may be requested to state specifically what color or number comes to mind in response to a given stimulus. To retain this distinction, even when it became clear that associations are never entirely free but are always due to conscious or unconscious connections between stimulus and response, the term "free associations" was retained.

We know from the study of free associations in which a person is requested to say whatever comes to mind, that immediately after the stimulus (or after a period of blankness) some thought or association occurs to him. He either accepts the association that comes to his mind and reports it, or he rejects it as inappropriate, in which case he continues to respond to the stimulus until something comes to him that he finds acceptable and therefore says. What he chooses to reveal, as well as what he may reject, is relevant to the stimulus, whether he knows it or not; and sometimes he understands only a small part of this connection, which he assumes to be its entirety. The connection may be an obvious one, or it may be a highly idiosyncratic or most private one. It may seem senseless, entirely arbitrary, and pointless to others but most reasonable to the person himself; or he may be as baffled as everyone else by it.

Any association—and a misreading is an association in

which the printed word serves as stimulus—can be either conscious, preconscious, or unconscious; it can be a mixture of any two or three of these; and we can never be sure which it is from the association itself.

As there is always a reason why in free associations a specific thought comes first to our mind, so there is a reason why one word rather than another is substituted by the child in a misreading. Most "simple errors in decoding" simultaneously involve conscious and unconscious thought processes: all are involved when a child misreads, for example, "Tigger" for "tiger," as reported in the next chapter. What may have been at work in this misreading are conscious thoughts (such as "Tigers are dangerous, I love Tigger") as well as subconscious cognition that the word on the page is "tiger," which accounts for its being changed into "Tigger," and unconscious responses (such as "I am so afraid of tigers that in order to be able to function at all—i.e., continue with reading—I must prevent myself from thinking about them").

If the person does not block but misreads the word, this is the consequence of a compromise between what cognition conveys about the word and the pressures aroused in the subconscious by it, which interfere with cognition fully asserting itself. If the person blocks, then cognition had its role here too; otherwise there would be no reason to block—one would only have to ask for the information lacking to read the word correctly. In blocking there is no compromise between the conscious mind at work in cognition, and the forces of the unconscious (between ego and id); the id just overpowers the ego to the degree that it cannot even insist on a compromise but is rendered entirely ineffective.

At every moment in our waking life both conscious and unconscious forces are at work in us, and when we sleep, the latter continue to operate in our dreams. When the child blocks and is unable to read at all, his conscious processes continue to be active: they tell him that he is unable to read, a fact of which he is conscious; they assess what goes on around him, such as the teacher's reactions; and so on.

How does it happen, then, that most of the time we are unaware of the unconscious forces within us? The ego, as it stands for our self, erects something like a barrier between the conscious and unconscious processes, between the rational and the irrational aspects of our personality, which keeps the latter hidden from our consciousness and prevents it from taking over. This barrier permits us to attend to cognition undisturbed by unconscious pressure; to attend to the task of coping with reality—which is what we do when we read exactly what is printed. But when for some reason this barrier falters or breaks down, then unconscious content spills over into cognition, and we see, for example, what we want to see, rather than what is there to be seen, objectively speaking.

The younger we are, the less completely is this barrier established, the less effectively are we able to maintain it, and the more easily it gives way under pressure. But, as shown by the slips of the tongue and misreadings of very competent adults, there are always situations and moments when this barrier is less than perfectly effective. When we are tired or our attention wanders, we are more easily distracted; that is, cognition begins to yield to unconscious demands rather than attending only to reality. Further, this barrier *always* tends to give way to some degree or even entirely when our cognition brings something to our attention that, because of its disturbing nature, arouses strong unconscious forces to assert themselves much more urgently and effectively.

To use a crude metaphor: when we attend to cognitive tasks, our ego keeps the undisciplined dogs of the unconscious somnolent, or on a narrow leash. But when aroused, they break loose and run around wildly, barking so loud that they distract us from our cognitive tasks so that we can no longer think straight until such time as we again gain control over them.

This we do either by satisfying some of their demands, or by putting them on a stronger leash, in other words, by reinforcing the barrier between our conscious and our unconscious. How well the ego is able to achieve this depends on what help it may receive from the outside.

This may explain why our attitude toward a child's misreading or blocking is so important. If we are critical of it, this weakens the child's self-respect and with it his ego. If, on the contrary, we support the ego in its having attained a compromise with the unconscious pressures—for example, by reading the offending word in a somehow meaningful way, albeit not as printed—then our approbation strengthens the ego, giving it new courage to hold its own against the id. The child becomes able to control the unconscious onslaught and can afterwards read the word correctly.

We believe that the ability to read is seriously interfered with when purposeful behavior—as we assume misreadings to be— is regarded to be without deeper meaning, and is ascribed to ignorance, lack of skills, or neurological deficit, particularly when none of these is relevant. Second, we believe that teaching methods based on such erroneous assumptions are inappropriate and destructive to the enjoyment of reading. Finally, we think that learning to read can be facilitated, and the significance and enjoyment of reading greatly increased, when all aspects of the child's personal involvement with his reading, including the errors he makes, are viewed as interesting events, and when misreadings are not neglected but handled constructively. This positive attitude promotes reading, because it is based on a reciprocal agreement that enhances the child's self-respect around reading. We provisionally accept first what he does to reading, and with this attitude of acceptance, it becomes possible for him to accept what we *want* him to do with reading—namely, to read correctly what is printed on the page.

Quite the opposite process takes place when, in the context

of reading, we are made conscious that our abilities to cope with a task realistically are found wanting. This is always embarrassing, however gently and understandingly mistakes are pointed out. When I stumble and fall, it is of little comfort to be told that I have not yet learned to walk well, or that I slipped on a banana peel because I missed seeing it. Such explanations do not make me less annoyed with my lack of skill, with the banana peel, or with the person who dropped it in my way. As likely as not, I am angry at the banana peel—a projection of my annoyance with myself for not having been more careful.

Similarly, when a misreading is brought to my attention in ways that reflect on the shortcomings of my intellectual powers, annoyance with my failure to be able to read correctly makes me not only discouraged with myself but annoyed with reading, the teacher, and the educational system that gave me the book. It is quite distressing to the child when he slips and falls; the parent's implied criticism in his remark, "Why didn't you watch where you're going!" adds insult to the injury. And so does an implied criticism that the child failed to sound out the word, or to recognize the letter with which it began, and so on.

Beginning readers, naturally uncertain about their ability to read correctly and because of their age insecure in general (especially where intellectual tasks are involved), respond with great embarrassment when it is pointed out to them that they have blundered. The shame they experience adds to the discomfort of the conflict that provoked the error, and often makes spontaneous recovery impossible. It has been our experience that when the child's self-esteem was *not* weakened by his action being viewed as a sign of ignorance, but on the contrary was taken as an indication of an appropriate effort to cope with a difficult situation, then the child usually recovered, correcting his mistake on his own, without anybody having intimated that it *was* a mistake.

In sum, our observations and approach to misreading led us to conclude that the errors children make in reading can be reduced and even eliminated, and literacy simultaneously promoted, by proceeding in the classroom on the basis of three guiding principles. The first is the assumption that mistakes in reading are subjectively meaningful on some level, however wide of the mark they seem when viewed objectively; and that they often serve important purposes in respect to inner psychic processes, of which they are an expression. Therefore, to regard such mistakes as undesirable occurrences puts the child and teacher at cross purposes. Instead of bridging the child's mental gap between internal and external reality, the teacher's insistence on literal accuracy indicates that only the latter has validity in class and reading—setting the child against both reading and teacher.

The second constructive assumption is that a misreading often signals a reader's conflict between his conscious attempt to read what is printed and a subconscious need to give words to a quite different response that his reading arouses in him. Such a conflict interferes with his ability to read what the text says. The error is an unconscious attempt to express, solve, or escape the inner conflict. Occasionally, the error's unconscious purpose is to make the person who hears it aware of the conflict, to gain his aid in dealing with it.

A third principle follows from these first two: the child's misreading ought to be recognized and respected as an act of self-expression. Without accepting the misreading as an appropriate reading of the text (which it clearly is not), we ought to approach it with empathy for the child's predicament: his ability to read correctly has been temporarily interfered with by lack of skill, or the pressure of dominant thoughts, or unconscious processes. Such empathy suggests that we should treat the error initially with sympathy, or at least benign neglect, so as to permit the child some respite to recover himself from the conflict that caused the error. Often, then, he may be able to extricate himself from whatever is obtruding on his ability to read as printed, and do so. As the child reads on, he may become aware from the context that he has misread a word, and this may induce him to reread correctly. Or, once he has gotten the meaning of the story's content, he can on this basis read on with full comprehension, even if he is unable to read every word exactly as printed. After all, this is what happens frequently when adults make a slip of the tongue or an error in reading or writing. We soon recognize what has happened, and then in most cases recover ourselves and correct our error, or, understanding the meaning of what we are reading, we read on without our comprehension suffering in any way from the fact that we misread some words.

The educator's prime task is always to strengthen the student's ability to cope with the task at hand, *particularly* when it has become temporarily weakened. This is not achieved by bringing students' inadequacies to their conscious awareness; that only emphasizes the inability of the child to cope. But his ability is buttressed when our intervention implies that the child was *thinking*—albeit not so much about reading a word exactly as it is printed in the text as about important aspects inherent in the story he is reading, whether these are aspects of the story itself, personal meanings he has projected into it, or personal concerns aroused by it. After having been fortified, the child's intellectual abilities can frequently hold their own against subconscious pressures. Then the child can either reread the word or sentence correctly, or continue to read with renewed enjoyment of the story, which now makes better sense than before.

When an inner conflict aroused by a story we are reading comes to our awareness, and then comes to be resolved upon our realization of its nature, this is very satisfying, sometimes truly exciting. Our interest in our own reaction tends to be extended to the material we were reading that led to such awareness. Then a story that before had seemed uninteresting, maybe even frustrating because it aroused an inner conflict, takes on new meaning and we are glad that we are reading it.

School, and the process of learning in school, would be much more acceptable to many more children if from the very beginning there was a greater readiness on the part of teachers to recognize that in certain areas the child is right—namely, that in terms of his subjective experience, he has very valid reasons for his behavior. If this were accepted by teachers and schools, it would be much easier for the child to accept that in certain areas the teacher is right—on such matters as how the printed word reads, or what is the appropriate way to behave in class, or what must be done in order to achieve intellectually.

Given unavoidable uncertainty about a child's inner motivations, all that is often possible for us is a willingness to believe that the child has important reasons for his misreading (of which lack of knowledge may be one) and to show the child that we are sensitive to his need to block or misread, perhaps forming some tentative conjectures as to why he must do so. This is highly preferable to a determined probe for his motivations.

Our suggestions as to why he may have preferred to act this way must always be very tentative. First, such an attitude on the teacher's part gives the child a chance to correct himself, which is ego-strengthening. Second, to reveal to a child our guess as to his inner reasons for replacing a word (even when by chance or due to deeper insight the guess is correct) is intrusive, arrogant, and tends to create anxiety. What is necessary is that we convey to him that, although he has acted intelligently and with purpose, nevertheless as far as actual cognition is concerned, his effort has led him astray.

This, after all, was the real motive of our interventions: to convey to the child, with full respect for his autonomy and the processes of his conscious and unconscious mind, that there is a problem that demands attention—ours, to understand what may have motivated him; his, to reconsider whether his cognition had been commensurate to what is being demanded of it. In the last analysis, what has made our intervention effective in a positive way is that attention from both parties has been required; that we both had something new to learn: we, what may have motivated his alteration of the text; he, what the passage really means to say.

PART TWO

Misreadings:
Failure or Challenge?

CHAPTER 5

Misreadings:
Intuitions or Mistakes?

A small, very competent first grader was reading a story aloud smoothly, with interest and comprehension in her voice. She was reading about tigers in a book her teacher had assigned her. She made no mistakes in reading the story, except that she consistently read "Tigger" for "tiger."

One can imagine many reasons why a child would shy away from thinking about dangerous tigers in favor of contemplating the harmless character of Tigger in the *Pooh* books, favorites of most young children. Such a switch in thought may be particularly attractive when a child does not know what scary events may be brought to her attention as she continues to read about such ferocious beasts as tigers. But if indeed it was the dangerous nature of the animal involved that motivated the girl to seek refuge in pleasant thoughts about the *Pooh* story, it follows that she must have recognized the word "tiger" on the page; otherwise, there would have been no need to solve the problems the text created for her by the ingenious device of interpolating a *g* at just the right place, changing "tiger" into "Tigger."

In another class, a first-grade boy was reading a story about a man named Van and his dog Spot, who have been out hunting.[1] The man shoots five ducks, which the dog retrieves.

[1] "Van's Cave," in *Lippincott's Basic Reading*, Book B. Philadelphia: Lippincott, 1969.

They then return to the cave in which they live. The man starts a fire, on which he plans later to roast the ducks, but meanwhile he falls asleep. The text says: "Spot must not leave the ducks. He can see a wolf near the cave." This, inexplicably, is accompanied by a picture showing the dog asleep. Van then awakens, and the story continues: " 'The fire is hot,' said Van. 'I will roast the ducks now.' Van did not see his five ducks. And Spot was fast asleep." The boy in reading this reversed the meaning of the sentence about the dog seeing a wolf by reading: "He can't see a wolf near the cave."

It is possible that the boy did this simply because the picture showed the dog asleep; but it is more likely that the boy's knowledge of dog behavior made it appear unreasonable to him that a dog would sleep when it saw a wolf lurking nearby. A first grader may also wish to believe that his dog would safeguard him, another reason why he might be unwilling to consider that a dog would sleep when it ought to be protecting its master against a dangerous animal.

So the misreading of "can't" for "can," seemingly so simple an error, may well have been the result of quite complex conscious and subconscious thought processes. On one level, it reflects the child's attempt to mesh word and picture, to bring what the text said into accordance with the picture. On another level, it articulates the boy's mental reaction to the story—a protest that the story describes such a lazy or inadequate dog, one that sleeps when its master needs protection. Finally, the misreading is a statement correctly describing normal dog behavior.

In another class, a highly intelligent first grader puzzled his teacher because throughout the year he consistently refused to read, and on the occasions when he tried, soon gave up; all this although she believed he was able to read quite well. On the day we observed him, when he was forced to read and tried to comply, the boy as usual made numerous errors, for example, reading "stick" for "chick." This, the teacher told him, showed that he had not mastered word beginnings and endings, and that he therefore should continue with his exercises. The boy refused.

Knowing of our interests, the teacher suggested we read with him. The boy had previously been able to observe that we were not so interested in children's errors as in their motives for making them; so when we encouraged him to continue his efforts with us, he strenuously protested that the reading workbook the teacher had assigned to him was boring. The book, *Sullivan Programmed Reading, No. 4* (New York: McGraw-Hill, 1973), as is typical for this series, requires that the student fill in letters that are missing. The aim is to have the child learn about vowel sounds—in this particular lesson, the short vowels *a*, *e*, and *i*.

With our encouragement the boy made one more attempt, but again he read "sticks" for "chicks." But this time, before the teacher or anyone had time to react, he corrected himself and immediately thereafter angrily blurted out: "Fill in the blanks, that's all I get! Witch, witch, witch . . . ditch, ditch, ditch . . . stick, stick, stick . . . chick, chick, chick!" And that was it. Although we tried to let him know that we were in sympathy with his angry rejection of being expected to work on something that was objectionable to him, he would not do any more reading with us on that day.

This boy had made error upon error, in this way giving vent to his negative feelings. But by pairing "witch" with "ditch," and "stick" with "chick," he conveyed that he understood quite well which words sound alike, and that his substitutions were not due to ignorance.

A couple of days later when we again asked the boy to read, he refused the Sullivan series but was willing to try something more interesting. We settled on *The Bear Detectives*, by Stan and Jan Berenstain, a Dr. Seuss book (New York: Random House, 1975). The story tells how the small bears (bear children) together with Papa Bear hunt for a missing pumpkin, using a detective kit in the process. The bears' inability to find the pumpkin is described on many pages, although the small bears discover various clues to its whereabouts. After having read the story quite eagerly for some thirty pages, the boy substituted "defective" for "detective" in the passage: "He's in the barn. This is it! Hand me the detective kit." This happened even though earlier he had read "detective" correctly, demonstrating that he was well able to read the word, that he knew what it designated and how it fit into the story.

It seemed as though after having read for so many pages that the detective kit was no help in the search for the pumpkin, and carried away by the excited wish of the story's characters to find it, the boy was once more expressing his frustration with a text—this time by calling the kit defective, that is, not commensurate to the task for which it was designed.

In his previous reading, the boy had given vent to his feeling that the book from which he was supposed to learn to read was in his opinion defective, because all he got was the filling in of blanks, i.e., exercises in decoding a text devoid of any intrinsic meaning. In this text, all the bears got was a kit which, up to this point in the story, had also failed to help them gain a meaningful goal. Viewed in isolation, it may seem far-fetched that in the boy's mind the two defective instruments (the text with the missing letters, the kit that did not seem to serve any purpose) became merged, and that, without being consciously aware of what he was doing, he was expressing his displeasure with the defectiveness of both texts through his misreading. But a few days later, once more this boy's workbook required him to read a list of words out of context which, when read one after the other, made no sense. He then read "dump" for "jump." Responding to the feelings this misreading expressed, we asked: "Who wants to dump this?" referring to the workbook. The boy immediately reread "jump" correctly. He nodded a pleased assent to our remark that it seemed he wanted to dump the workbook. And when we asked him why he wanted to dump it, his unhesitating reply was " 'Cause it's garbage."

In the first example given in this chapter, in all likelihood it was the girl's unwillingness to hear about tigers that made for the substitution; in the second case, it was probably the boy's knowledge of facts, in this particular case of how dogs are apt to behave. In the third case, the emotions aroused by frustration with boring reading materials led to the substitution. Yet in the first two examples, the child's substitution was treated by the teacher only as an error due to an inability to decode. There is every reason to believe that the same would have been true in the last example, had the boy read with his teacher and not with one of us; that is, the meaningful change the substitution achieved within the context of the story would once again have been disregarded.

It requires considerable ingenuity on the part of first graders to make such radical alterations in meanings by only the slightest change of letters. In the first two examples, the children retained all the letters of the printed word, adding to them only a single letter. By adding a *t*, a boy substituted correct animal behavior for an incorrect description of it, and by adding a *g*, a girl replaced an animal threatening danger and destruction with one symbolizing safety and pleasure. In the third example the child, by exchanging only one of the letters of a nine-letter word, expressed his dissatisfaction and frustration both with the defectiveness of an object that played a central role in the story he was reading, and with the material from which he was expected to learn to read.

When a child in his reading does not make such a minimal change, but instead reads something quite unrelated to the text's content by substituting entirely different words for those printed in the book, then good teachers are likely to assume correctly that the child's attention has wandered, that he has been thinking of something else, or that he may have been turned off by what the text said or wanted the story to be different.

But when what the child reads is only minimally different from what is printed, even though this may radically change the meaning of the sentence, then teachers are convinced that faulty discrimination between letters is the child's problem. They assume this despite the fact that the child has already read most letters as printed, suggesting that he was paying attention to the page and could recognize the letters correctly. After all, we do not reject thoughts, or turn them into their opposites, unless we have first gotten a pretty good grasp of what these thoughts are. The fact that a child's substitution of one —or a few—letters makes good, albeit altered, sense within the context of a story indicates that he correctly perceived what the printed word signified, decided that it was unacceptable, and found a solution that met his purposes.

While the teacher thinks the child's misreading reflects his incompetence, the child may view it all quite differently. To test this hypothesis, we presented the story about the sleeping dog and the wolf to a bright third grader, asking him what he thought of it. He immediately and spontaneously picked out as problematic the sentence about the dog seeing the wolf. "Why does it say he can see the wolf?" he asked. "He's asleep, he can't see while he's asleep." Since the boy, on his own, focused on this sentence, we told him how the first grader had read it, and added that since he was able to read so much better, he hadn't made such a mistake. The boy's reaction was: "But it makes no sense!" referring to the unlikely dog behavior the story projected.

Good third grader that he was, convinced that teachers do things only for reasons, he added after some thought: "Oh, I know, they want to see if you really can read it the way it is printed. But I still think it's [the text] wrong." Thus what the teacher views as an instance of a child's inability to read, the child may regard as a trap, deliberately set to catch him making an error, since both the picture and the text that follows tell that the dog is asleep and contradict the statement that he can see the wolf.

Such stories, and teachers' viewing a reading that makes better sense than the text as erroneous, leave some children with the conviction that the purpose of reading is not to gain meaning but deliberately to mislead the child, so that he can be found at fault, if not also lacking in intelligence. The end result is an impasse not only between the teacher and a child, who feels the teacher does not respect his efforts to make good sense out of what he is reading, but also between a child and reading, which could seriously impede his ability to learn to read, discourage his interest in reading, and prevent its future enjoyment.

We can never be sure what motivates a child to misread unless he tells us; but even if he tries to do this, he may be unable to do so, or he may be able or willing to reveal only some part of the reason. Adults, too, find it difficult to identify or recognize the subconscious motives behind many of their actions, particularly their errors; and even when they can identify such motives, more often than not they are unwilling to reveal them to others.

The findings of psychoanalysis made it impossible for us to accept that children's errors are due only to inexperience, inattention, or lack of knowledge—although each may be a contributing factor. Since we could not be sure what went on in a child's mind as he misread some words, all we could do was proceed on the assumption that whatever may have caused them, such misreadings were meaningful. We tried to convey this conviction to the children appropriately.

When thinking of children just learning to read, we must remember that they are at an age when they are likely to be carried away by their emotions and are inclined to react sub-jectively to their experiences, very much including what they read. At this age the child is unable to separate himself from the figure, event, or situation he reads about, and he needs to make these conform to his view of things, gratifying his wishes and not arousing his anxieties. He projects his emo-tional preoccupations upon the printed word. Having much less experience with self-control in general, he has not yet learned to separate the printed word from the feelings it arouses in him.

There is another way in which the young child experiences words differently from the mature adult. Words are symbols; they signify objects, actions, feelings. The child, like primitive man, is convinced that words have magic power, and that by manipulating words one can manipulate simultaneously what-ever these words symbolize. The child about to learn to read is at a stage in his intellectual development where the separa-tion between symbol and what it symbolizes is still a tenuous one that tends to break down in moments of emotional in-volvement. Even in adults, unconsciously, a signifier and what it signifies always remain much more closely related than they are in conscious thought; that is why in dreams, for example, symbols so often stand in the place of real objects.

The primary-grade child still occasionally plays with words as if they were objects and enjoys putting them together in new and unexpected ways; he is convinced that words can and do hurt as badly as sticks and stones, despite what the nursery rhyme tries to teach. When deeply emotionally involved, the child subconsciously thinks that by changing some word for another he may possibly be changing the reality to which they refer. For example, by reading "Tigger" for "tiger," the girl not only avoided thinking about an anxiety-creating animal, but on some subconscious level she may have felt that she actually turned the ferocious beast of one story into the cuddly toy animal of another. For these and many other reasons suggested by this example and those to be presented later, in evaluating misreadings we ought to consider the possibility that a child reads one word for another because he wants to change the object to which the word refers.

For just as we tend to see what we want to see and often distort or fail to see what we do not wish to see, maybe children make mistakes in reading (which depends so much on seeing) because they want to see a different word on the page than the one printed there. So an error in reading could be due to a desire to read differently, not to an inability to read correctly.

Since there is no literature specifically devoted to the psychological meaning of children's errors in reading, we have to rely on the investigation of errors made by adults. Basic for this purpose is Freud's essay *Psychopathology of Everyday Life.* In pointing out that mistakes in reading and writing are subject to the same principles that govern slips in speech and errors in action, he suggests how errors in reading can best be understood. He further stresses in this connection the close relationship between all uses of language: "[T]hat the same viewpoints . . . should hold true for mistakes in reading and writing as for lapses in speech is not at all surprising when one remembers the inner relation of these functions," namely, that speech and oral communications preceded writing and with it reading.[2]

To clarify our reasons for making such mistakes, Freud describes why we repress thoughts that are unacceptable to us, and how what we repress continues to be represented in the unconscious and to press for expression. In talking about what is involved in repression, Freud also explains what is involved in forgetting. What often happens is that a related or compensating thought takes the place of whatever has been forgotten. Such substitution, when it occurs, is neither a com-

---

[2] Freud, *op. cit.*

plete success nor a complete failure. While it conceals that which has been forgotten, since the word or words that replace the forgotten ones in some (more often than not, unconscious) way are related to them, the substitutions at the same time in some measure also reveal what has been forgotten.

As far as reading is concerned, Freud stresses that, particularly in reading aloud, the reader tends to be distracted by matters preoccupying him at the moment. A mistake reflects this preoccupation but may also hide its meaning; therefore it often requires considerable perspicacity and mental effort to discover the (usually unconscious) underlying thought that caused the error.

When children are taught reading in class, they are made to read aloud. For some time to come, even if the child is not voicing what he is reading, he forms the words with his lips, as if reading aloud but suppressing the sound. When we are reading something aloud to someone or to ourselves, what we produce is very much like oral literature. And here the speaker feels free to take all kinds of liberties with the received text to make what he says suit his aesthetic criteria and better captivate his audience.

Scientific discussions of the teaching and learning of reading neglect to take into account that reading a story aloud creates a setting and psychological conditions similar to those characteristic of oral literature. They also pay no attention to the important fact that while the new reader has hardly any experience with reading, he has a great deal with speaking. As a matter of fact, this has been his lifelong experience with language; that it has stretched over only a few years does not reduce its having made an imprint on him as great as that which all lifelong habits make on us.

Reading aloud feels to the child as if he were speaking to his teacher, or whoever else is listening to him. In speaking to another person, we use the words most familiar to us, selecting those that will most closely convey our meaning. In a conversation, we wish to hold our listener's attention and impress him with what we have to say. But the teacher is oblivious to the fact that reading aloud feels somewhat like a conversation to the child. Instead, she listens carefully to make sure the child reads the words as they are printed in the book, and to correct him when he does not.

We all know how frustrated we feel when the mind of the person to whom we are talking is on something entirely different. We want our listener to be interested in what we are saying, and it is very distressing to realize that he or she is only checking whether what we say is exactly in line with what he thinks we ought to be saying. The child experiences the teacher's attitude as a rejection, which certainly does not make reading more attractive to him.

We might hark back to Freud's remark that, particularly when reading aloud, the reader tends to be distracted by whatever happens to be occupying his mind. In silent reading, our experience is that the author tells us what he wishes us to know; he speaks to us, as it were. When reading aloud, our experience is not so much that somebody else—the author—is speaking to us, but that we are talking to the person who is listening, or whom we imagine as our listener. What we say to another person is what we wish him to hear, and this is based on what we think, feel, fear—in short, on what is going on in our mind at the moment.

This is characteristic of oral literature, in that it addresses itself much more actively than most printed literature to the listener. It implies a more intimate, personal relation between the two. The person who reads aloud is not just reciting a story, he is telling it directly to the listener, using both the content and the way he is conveying it to establish a common bond between them. In their reading aloud, children spontaneously act in line with this second characteristic of oral literature. When called to task for doing so, they feel deeply disappointed and frustrated.

With the outlawing of variation, children are forced to go against a literary principle: when criticized and prevented from personalizing what they tell—in reading to their teacher—they are asked not only to transgress an aesthetic law but also to depersonalize the experience. They are thus forced to violate a basic principle of oral literature and destroy the very foundation on which its aesthetic impact rests: its essentially personal nature.

Another rhetorical device typical of oral literature ought to be mentioned in the context of discerning reasons behind misreadings. This is the device of alternating repetition and variation of verbal expression. Repetition is needed for emphasis; but to prevent the resultant lag in interest, material to be emphasized and impressed on the hearer is conveyed also by a variety of expressions each of which, while carrying the same essential meaning, has somewhat different connotations. Such variations hold the listener's interest, which would otherwise soon be apt to stray—apart from anything else, the listener's eyes are not necessarily riveted on the person who is speaking, as they must be on the page when he is reading, so the listener may look around and let his mind grow distracted.

The stories in primers from which the child is required to read aloud abound in repetitions of the same words. As he reads aloud and thus becomes a speaker, the child's feeling for what is needed in oral literature to hold attention—or rather, in truth, to turn the material more into literature—induces him spontaneously to supply the complementary principle of variation to the repetition. But should he do this, he is told he did wrong, and is either corrected or asked to correct himself. Most children will obey, because of the teacher's authority and her prodding. But as they do, they violate an important principle of oral literature. As a consequence they become discouraged with themselves, with the teacher, and with literature, because their correct feeling for it is labeled false. Due to the teacher's insistence, the child gives up varying words to make what he says conform to his aesthetic feelings. His earliest attempts at applying literary principles in his (oral) reading are thwarted—his efforts at being literate end in frustration.

If a child has great inner needs, it is natural for him to state them to an understanding and sympathetic listener such as his teacher. Since reading aloud tempts the child to tell the teacher what oppresses his mind, if the pressure of his feelings is great, the child cannot help misreading into the text what so deeply preoccupies him.

For example, a very bright, somewhat overeager six-and-a-half-year-old boy was reading aloud *Harvey's Hideout*, by Russell Hoban. In this story an older sister and a younger brother, barely camouflaged as muskrats, are trying to make each other jealous by pretending to have many friends for whom they give parties in their separate hideouts. At the end they learn the true state of affairs, discovering that each of them is in reality very lonely. The sister, angry at being found out, challenges her brother by saying: "I would like to know just who you think there is for me to have a party with, Mister Nasty Little Brother." The boy read this line as: "I would like to know you . . ." and stopped himself.

Two aspects of this situation are common to oral literature: the boy's reading to us, and his reading aloud what one of the figures in the story said to the other. His transformation of the story through the skipping of two words was an appropriate response to its essential content, which is loneliness and the wish of the little muskrat to form a much closer bond to her brother, to whom she is speaking. The boy makes this desire his own as he expresses his wish to form a closer tie to the person to whom he is speaking, i.e., reading the story. In doing so, he acts just like the muskrat whose feelings he is voicing as he reads the story.

He was thus giving expression to his own longing, strongly aroused by the story: he was responding to what he read with deep feeling and empathy for what the story characters were experiencing, just what is required if literature is to become personally meaningful to us. But in his skipping of two words, he may also have been influenced by his sensitivity to what is necessary for oral literature to be effective: to establish a bond between speaker and listener, to which he gave expression by saying, "I would like to know you." His stopping himself at this point clearly indicates that he realized he had deviated from the text, which he could not have realized had he been unable to read it.

Since the boy was reading with one of us, when he read: "I would like to know you," she reacted by saying with feeling: "I am glad to know you." At that the boy smiled broadly at being understood, and immediately went back to read the sentence once more, but now exactly as printed, and with feeling for the muskrat's anger and anguish due to its loneliness. This he could now afford to do, because our answer that we were glad to know him had taken the sting out of his feeling of loneliness. His action was further proof that as far as reading skills were concerned, he could have read the full sentence correctly all along.

One can imagine how disastrous it could have been for the boy if his reading, "I would like to know you," had been criticized as wrong—which indeed it was, on the level of mere word recognition. Through his misreading he had stated his desire to get close to the person to whom he read; if his reading had been deemed deficient, the boy would have thought that the feelings which had induced him to read the sentence that way were also wrong; that his desire to get more closely connected to the person to whom he read was rejected. If it happened that way to a child already insecure in his human relations, this experience would be tantamount to proving that reading makes one even more miserable than one was before.

It is often overlooked that the reader sometimes wishes to return a thought or share an emotional reaction, because to do so is part of the communicative process. The more meaningful a text is to the reader, the more it engages his emotions and personal responses, the greater will be his desire to respond to what he has read. When given the freedom to do so, young children in particular like to interrupt their reading and talk about what they are reading and their direct and indirect reactions to it. Just as an adult may jot down in the margin an opinion that differs from the text, the child when reading aloud may correct the text by reading it differently from the way it is printed.

In responding to the text, the reader digests some of its meaning in an individual and sometimes idiosyncratic manner. Piaget's concept of assimilation describes well the tendency to make the text's content meaningful according to what the individual thinks he knows or what he feels. While often the content and what the reader makes of it seem far apart, upon scrutiny a connection can always be found. A misreading thus represents the person's response to the text and his attempt to communicate this response to himself, to the author, or to anybody listening.

Older children and adults have the freedom *not* to read something that may arouse emotional difficulties for them; they can skim or skip a passage in a text if something gives them the impression that taking it in would be too much for them. They can misread some words, completely changing the meaning of a sentence, and nobody—not even they themselves —is aware of it.

The child who is learning to read is not given such freedom; he is expected to read every word as printed. The child therefore is denied the self-protective measures available to an older person when some word or sentence seems upsetting. If he thinks reading the words as printed would be threatening to him, the only methods of avoidance available to him are to block and declare himself unable to read; to change some word, and by so doing make the material nonsensical or incomprehensible; or to make only a slight change in word meaning, as in the examples cited earlier, if this is sufficient to render the material acceptable. The child who is called upon to read aloud in class cannot tell the teacher: "What I just read brought to mind some serious difficulties I am having in life, or with myself. I must first deal with these before I can go on reading."

Most teachers would not accept such an excuse—they would consider it a cover-up for an inability to decode a word. But even if they did accept it, things in the child's mind are not so clear that he can verbalize them so exactly; in fact, he is not ready to reveal to anybody those matters that disturb him most. When his inner pressures are warring with the demand that he read what is printed, the result is often a compromise between the two that expresses itself in some misreading.

Given prevalent American classroom settings and practices, it is hard to imagine how reading might be taught without requiring the child to read aloud. However, reading aloud creates the impression that the purpose of the text is to convey its content to a third person, the one who listens to what is being read aloud. Most children think that the author has committed to print something of importance, which he wishes to communicate to the reader. So, far from under-investing the text with meaning, they tend to over-invest it. In fact, kindergarten and first-grade children often think it is their teacher who has written the text, in order to impart special messages to them. This is their way of investing the text with a special and personal meaning it would not otherwise have.

Reading for meaning is anything but passive, even when the content is absorbed exactly as presented. The more intent a reader is on taking in the meaning, the more active he is in his reading. There is no automatic or "natural" response to a word, so the child sometimes fashions it according to his own needs.[3] David Elkind, following Piaget, maintains that both written and spoken words are given meaning by the reader or listener, "who interprets them within his own storehouse of knowledge. The richness of meaning that he derives from his reading will depend both upon the quality of the material he is reading and upon the breadth and depth of his conceptual understanding. Satisfaction in reading often derives, in part at least, from the degree of fit between the material being read and the conceptual level of the subject who is reading it."[4]

Frequently, in order for the child to maintain the minimal interest necessary for reading a story, he tries to invest it with some personal meaning by a misreading: it is precisely the boring nature of the reading matter that tempts the child to project meaning where there is none. And sometimes the meaning thus imputed touches upon far-reaching problems. If the texts dealt with important issues, it is doubtful that children would have to go to such great lengths to keep themselves interested in reading.

Her teacher described a certain first grader as brilliant and quite a competent reader. The child was told that she could pick whatever story she wanted to read in her book, which was *Round the Corner* (a Bank Street Reader). She chose "Blue Jeans, the All-American Pants." (The girl almost always wore blue jeans, which is perhaps why she chose this story.) Although she read easily such difficult words as "rivets" and "thread," she confused "were" and "wear"—possibly because she was reading quickly in order to glean meaning out of a text that disappointed her. She read the sentence: "In 1848, gold was discovered in California—and so were jeans," as if it

[3] P. A. Kolers, "Reading Is Only Incidentally Visual," in K. Goodman and J. T. Fleming, eds., *Psycholinguistics and the Teaching of Reading.* Newark, Del.: International Reading Association, 1969.
[4] David Elkind, "Cognitive Development and Reading," in *Claremont Reading Conference,* 38th Yearbook, Claremont, Calif., 1974.

contained the command, "Wear jeans!" Told that this might indeed convince people to wear jeans, she then read "were" as printed.

The story explains how the pants were called "levis" because this was the name of the man who invented them. After finishing the story, the child wondered about the derivation of "jean" in blue jeans. Thus she was responding intelligently to what the story had said. She remarked that while "Jean" is a girl's name, it's also a boy's name—"Gene." In considering how it was possible for boys and girls to have the same-sounding name, she revealed how creative she could be in elaborating the theme of the text to make it more interesting, and to understand better the nature of language.

Discussion ensued about the fact that while "Jean" and "Gene" sounded alike, they were different names—"Jean," a girl's name derived from "Joanne" or "Jane," and "Gene," short for "Eugene." She was praised for having listened carefully to her teacher, who had been explaining synonyms, antonyms, and homonyms, and for having understood what had been taught to her. She was given the feeling that her pair of homonyms ("Jean" and "Gene") was a clever use of this teaching, since homonyms one of which refers to males and the other to females might be especially interesting to a child of her age. With this she heartily agreed.

The teacher did not probe for further reasons underlying the misreading of "wear" for "were," or for her interest in "Jean" and "Gene"; and since the girl did not volunteer any more information, the matter was left at that. Asked to read another story, she chose "My Father Is a Terrible Shot." In reading, she began again to impute meaning to the text, whose theme she disagreed with, and which aroused in her a conflict of supreme personal importance.

The teacher noticed that after every discussion of misreadings, the girl spontaneously corrected her errors and also ceased making that particular error—with one exception. Instead of "terrible shot," she read "trouble shot" or "trouble shooter." The story is told by a son who is amused by his father's clumsiness in aiming coins at a toll basket—he misses frequently whereas the son's aim is accurate. The son gets out of the car to retrieve the father's quarter, discovers many other quarters, and reassures his dad that lots of fathers are terrible shots. The story ends with the boy using the quarters he has found to buy ice cream for the family.

When the girl read "trouble shot" for "terrible shot," the teacher said that the father was indeed in trouble, not being capable of getting the quarter into the basket. The girl immediately corrected her mistake and asked what "terrible shot" meant. Told that "shot" had a special meaning when used this way, the girl indicated her understanding by imitating someone aiming a gun.

At this point, she began to substitute "trouble shooter" for "terrible shot," as in the passage: "But my father said he had the exact change. When he got to the basket, he flipped out the quarter. But he is a terrible shot." It seemed that the earlier misreading, which implied that the father was in trouble, led to the second error, which stated its opposite—that the father was someone who deals effectively with trouble. The teacher wanted to find out about her understanding of the colloquialism "trouble shooter" and so asked her what it meant. The girl replied, "It means getting rid of trouble." She thus obviously recognized the different usage of the verb, as in shooting with a gun and in solving or removing trouble.

All this began to make sense when the teacher remembered that the child's father had recently left the family. Instead of acting as a "trouble shooter," as the girl wished, he actually had *caused* trouble—as did the father in the story, by delaying the family and other cars while he aimed unsuccessfully at the toll basket. Since the story's content centers on an inadequate father, this had reminded the girl of the ways in which her own father was inadequate.

The girl continued to read "trouble shooter" for "terrible shot," but now corrected herself every time she made this substitution. Finally she explained, "Oh, it's terrible shot . . . [meaning he or the story is terrible]. Why can't he do it? . . . I could do it." It made no sense to her that the text portrayed adults as less proficient than children; in fact, this idea aroused her indignation. Her desire to protect adults (particularly beloved parents) prompted her to assert that if adults cannot perform skills better than children, they have no business instructing them (as in asking children to read such stories). As if to make her message absolutely clear, she said: "That's stupid . . . the father is not very smart." In this way, she criticized a text that made no sense to her and, at the same time, her father's recent behavior.

The girl had been reading a story about an inadequate father, a phenomenon with which she was only too painfully familiar. To her, a father's inadequacy in being unable to shoot a quarter into the basket at a toll booth seemed trivial compared to a father's inadequacy in keeping a family together, and a story that made so little of such weaknesses, treating them as a funny matter to be enjoyed by a son, was irritating and offensive to her. Her unhappiness that her father had "shot" the family full of trouble, and her deep wish that he might still turn out to be a trouble shooter, showed how much she was trying through her misreadings to bridge the gap that separated her inner world of troubles about a father and the silly father the story depicted. When her teacher showed some understanding and acceptance of her need to change certain aspects of the story, which she had to do to actively master the emotions the story aroused, she could do justice to the objective reality of the story as printed, although even then she pronounced it "stupid."

Although this girl was so very critical of the text and tried to correct it through her misreadings, it did permit her to come to grips with her feelings about her father, which consisted essentially of anger and disappointment, but also tremendous hope. If the teacher had only corrected her misreadings, thereby not accepting them as valid, it would have meant to the girl that in school no attention is paid to what is most important in life. And if the school doesn't take the child seriously, the child can't take seriously what school is all about, including reading. Fortunately, this girl had the experience that, contrary to her expectations, reading even a "stupid" story had helped her to understand better what was going on in herself, because she had been encouraged in her efforts to endow the story with personal meaning. Although previously she had strongly preferred recess to reading, she now wanted to continue reading, even though it was time for recess. Reading had become a highly significant activity—something deeply meaningful in terms of her personal life.

CHAPTER 6

Taking Reading Seriously

The authors of American textbooks are fully aware of the importance of making reading attractive to children. The trouble is that their views of what captivates children are very narrow and simple-minded. They seem to believe that all that is necessary is to evoke pleasant thoughts and feelings of an essentially shallow nature. In consequence, their stories tell (and in a superficial manner) only about the good things that go on in the lives of children and parents, in their relations to each other, their siblings, and other children; and about pleasurable events that elicit images of parallel occurrences in the child's own life.

This would not be so bad if these stories, in addition to emphasizing the light, also painted some contrasting shadows to give the light its brilliance. But by rendering an entirely monochromatic picture of what the child from his own experience knows to be most complex relations, feelings, and events, the stories are robbed of all deeper significance. Completely absent are the ambivalences, jealousies, anxieties, exaggerated and frustrated hopes that are the inseparable accompaniments of all deeply felt attachments and all truly important events. These complex feelings are very confusing to the young child, particularly because at his age he cannot distinguish adequately between the true facts of his life and his fears about them.

The beginning reader has an incomplete grasp of many aspects of reality, and of what others think and feel about things that are important to him. Therefore he needs some affirmation that what he thinks and feels about himself and others is valid—and not only in respect to his positive feelings, which are so comforting to him and so acceptable to others. The child's darker emotions are problematic to him and confuse him, especially because adults tend to make little of them—further reason that in his reading he should find confirmation that these problematic emotions are very much part of life, as well as suggestions for possible ways of coping with them. If only the inner struggles—the ambivalences, the fears, the angers from which children often suffer more acutely than do adults—were reflected in the stories children are asked to read, they would be convinced not only that these stories were true to life but that reading them could help them to understand themselves better. Like all good literature, such stories would make the child ponder life and his own role in it, would teach him that while life is always complex, his own is not necessarily more difficult than that of others, and that however difficult it may seem at the moment, there is no need to despair, because there are ways of coping with it successfully.

The child has been encouraged by parents and teachers to expect that through reading he will come to learn how to deal with what is most important in life—such matters, for instance, as his relations to those closest to him. But when he reads the stories in primers about children like himself, and *their* relations to their parents, siblings, and friends, he realizes to his disappointment that they speak only about things that are unproblematic, the very matters with which he needs no help.

The reason textbook writers present such one-sided and untrue pictures of children's lives is that they know that when children's deeper feelings about those closest to them and about the important events in their lives are brought to their conscious attention, irrespective of whether these feelings are ambivalent or negative, they are apt to so preoccupy the children's minds that they become unable to attend properly to the abstract task of correct decoding. And since skill in decoding is the primary purpose of these texts, great care is taken to prevent the child from becoming involved in such difficult personal thoughts and feelings as might distract him. Yet because these stories completely neglect children's deeper feelings and their negative counterparts, they seem not only untrue to life but lifeless. Thus the stories defeat their most serious purpose: to make reading seem a desirable activity to the child. By depicting only the good times children have, and suggesting in the rare stories in which some small problem arises that it is always easily and pleasurably resolved in no time, the stories seem vacuous, if not outright objectionable.[1]

There are few words acquired as early in life as those which designate the child's parents, and few which remain as meaningful emotionally. So it is understandable that the child has a particularly difficult time giving up using these terms when thinking, talking, or reading about parents, and accepting instead words that carry none of these highly personal, most significant connotations. For this reason, tales that have parents as their main figures provide telling examples of the child's need to perceive a story first in an egocentric way, particularly when the story makes a strong emotional appeal. When a child has to read a story in which parents figure prominently, and in which there occur situations that remind him of his parents, it may become necessary for him to express first and foremost how affectionately he feels about his own parents and how intimately he relates to them, by substituting "mom" and "dad" for the printed words "mother" and "father." Only after he has done so may he become ready to

[1] For a discussion of the so-called fun morality that dominates our textbooks, see Martha Wolfenstein, "Fun Morality: An Analysis of Recent American Child-training Literature," *Journal of Social Issues*, 7 (1951).

think of parents in an abstract manner, as parents of others rather than as his own parents; and only then is he able to read about them in the form presented in the book.

Another reason certain children find it difficult to read the words "mother" or "father," apart from being accustomed to calling their own parents "Mom" or "Mommy" and "Dad" or "Daddy," is that the story's content strongly activates their feelings for their parents, which makes it hard to think of them in the unemotional way the story refers to them. But when the child reads with feeling about "mom" or "dad" where the printed text says "mother" or "father," he is criticized by his teacher, or at least asked to concentrate and pay attention —this, when the child's reading should have revealed to the teacher that he has paid very close attention by investing the story with personal meaning.

The teacher's attitude reflects what is most important to her in the child's reading, just as the child's reading reflects his conviction about what makes reading worthwhile: to understand a story on the basis of how he can experience its meaning. Because of the depth of the child's feelings for and about his parents, nothing epitomizes better the disparity of attitudes —the real conflict—between teacher and child around the teaching of reading than what happens when a child misreads "mom" for "mother." This disparity explains why all too often the child's original excitement about learning to read is replaced by deep and frequently lasting disappointment in reading, even though the motives of both teacher and child are the very highest: hers, to teach the child to read well; his, to make reading as meaningful to himself as he possibly can.

As we observed it, the insistence of teachers that children read about parents as printed and not as they felt was particularly ironic in view of the fact that this was happening in schools whose avowed policy was to bridge the gap between home and school. Everything possible was done to encourage

the parents' active participation in all school activities, to induce them to be present as often as possible in class, and to
know about everything that went on there; the idea being to
merge home and school as much as possible so that the child
would come to feel that there was no divergence of opinions
or values between the two.

Children of all ethnic groups and social classes, irrespective of whether their home background was barely literate or
highly educated, reacted with equal dismay and, not infrequently, with stubborn resistance to the idea that they should
read about parents by using the formal terms "Mother" and
"Father" when they had been accustomed all their lives to
thinking of parents as Mom and Dad.

One child of ethnically mixed background, whose reading
had remained blocked and undeveloped for three years, was
given some very simple exercises to help him. To make it easy
and to make the lesson meaningful, the teacher wrote five
sentences about a child and his mother, about how the child
left for school and the mother for work (as was true in this
boy's life, since his mother often dropped him off at school on
her way to work). The teacher then asked the boy to point to
the words he knew in these few, short sentences. He pointed
to all the words with the single exception of "mother." The
teacher was puzzled and asked him what the word was, to
which there was no answer. Exasperated, the teacher said:
"You know it: the lady who takes care of you." The boy immediately said: "My mom." Subsequently, whenever the word
"mother" appeared, he consistently read "mom," although he
had been repeatedly corrected and knew that the printed word
was "mother." He simply refused to refer to his mother by a
word that failed to connote his feelings for her. As in so many
other cases, the teacher agreed with the boy's view of his
mother in every context but that of reading. In talking about
what the boy was to read, she stressed the importance of the
mother's taking care of the child. But when it came to reading,

the teacher insisted that he use the more distant term just because that was what was printed.

The same boy on another day was given some simple sentences about a father who is a mailman and at the end of the story comes home to his son, who says: "Hi, Father." The boy persistently read "Daddy" for "Father." Such misreadings are obviously synonym substitutions, as K. Goodman has called them,[2] but this designation fails to pay attention to the underlying motivation. To carry Goodman's analysis one step further requires asking why one particular word is chosen for synonym substitution. In his substitution, the boy showed that he could read, because he substituted a word that means the same thing as father. At the same time, this "nonreading" boy improved the text to suit his needs, as well as those of many other children in the class whom he had heard make similar mistakes.

Another child in the same class, who read much more fluently and at grade level, came across the word "mother" in a story about a cat that visits several families in an apartment building ("Mr. Charles," *Uptown, Downtown*, a Bank Street Reader). He recognized the word "mother" but instead read aloud something that sounded like "mo-ver", substituting a "v" sound for "th," although he made no such letter substitution in any other context. Since the theme was of a mother feeding a small child sitting in a highchair while the cat was being fed as well, one might think that the boy had regressed in his pronunciation of the word to a time when a much younger child might, in the boy's mind, need this kind of care and be unable to speak correctly. In answer to the teacher's remark that he had mispronounced the word, but without her saying what it was, he answered: "But I call my mother 'Mom.'" In his speech, there was no peculiar and regressive substitution of "v" for "th," indicating that he could pronounce

[2] Kenneth Goodman, ed., *The Psycholinguistic Nature of the Reading Process*. Detroit: Wayne State University Press, 1968.

the word very well when he wished. The implication was that he could read the word too, but thought it would be better if the text had told of a "mom" feeding a small child rather than a mother.

Reading the same story, two other children had difficulty with the words "first floor" and "house." The story relates how the cat visited each floor of the building where different people lived, either to get food or attention. One child read "family" for "first floor," and another "home" for "house." In reading, these children, too, made what they read more personal, and in so doing captured the text's meaning much better than the printed words did: the cat liked to visit families and homes. It visited first floors or houses—the words used in the story— only because these were the locations where families had their homes. To children, their own families and their own homes are matters—and concepts—that rank next to their parents in emotional importance; hence in reading about them, children are induced to read words that correspond to the feelings they have invested in them.

A boy who had demonstrated his brilliance repeatedly in science and math projects, which interested him, often declined to read because, he said, "Reading is boring." He was reading a story about a child who wanted to get bigger and whose mother marks lines on the wall to show him that he is in fact growing. In this particular story, no father is mentioned. In reading the story, the child made substitutions. He also inserted words to make the text more interesting or to satisfy needs. One particularly telling example was his adding "and father" in the sentence: "Willie's mother said, 'After awhile we'll make a new line.'" The boy thus created an additional story figure, a father. It was an especially revealing use of the text as he had lost his father as a result of his parents' divorce and his mother's unwillingness to let the boy see his father. The child, by way of this insertion, was stating that for his growth he needed both parents.

The other children in the reading group reacted to the insertion with an understanding and sympathetic giggling, recognizing the importance of the addition and what it signified. Since these children had been together in the same class for two years, they knew the boy's mother because she was actively involved in the school curriculum, and they knew, too, that the father had left the family. The teacher also noticed the boy's insertion of father, but instead of appreciating how meaningful it was, she told the child to concentrate on his reading. She failed to recognize that the insertion showed just that—concentration. He had concentrated well enough to know that there was no father in the story, as there was none in his life, and he wished to correct the story accordingly—and by implication the conditions of his own life.

Obviously not just "father" and "mother," or words denoting homes and families are full of significance, but also those that refer to any kind of family relationship. Some bright children try to protect the personal meaning with which they endow the story they are reading by refusing to read aloud, so that the teacher will not interfere with the importance the story has for them—a sad reflection on their feeling that to preserve the meaning of reading, they must exclude the teacher.

A very bright girl claimed to be better able to read silently than aloud. She was reading a story about Zorro, a boy who is a poet, which disappoints his father, who wants his son to become a fighter. The girl consistently read "Zero" for "Zorro," and talking about the story, she spoke of "Zero" as well. Our first remark—that Zero was an interesting name for a boy— seemed to fall on deaf ears as she continued to misread the name; but she did reiterate, now somewhat aggressively, that she read better silently. When asked why, she said that she only made mistakes when reading aloud, revealing that she knew quite well that her reading "Zero" was a mistake. In reply we said forcefully that reading "Zero" was not a mistake, but that on the contrary it showed a very good understanding of how the father felt about his son.

If we had not experienced many similar situations, we would have been very surprised when in reaction to our appreciation of the meaningfulness of her misreading, she revealed her reason for it by telling us that her father was a poet.

We did not know exactly what she was expressing by calling a poet "Zero"—whether she was perturbed by what she knew was an unusual occupation for a father, or whether some significant member of her family thought little of such an occupation for a man, as had the father in the story. One can well understand why a girl would not like to read this story aloud when she knew that her reading would reveal that she thought of a poet as a zero, and that her father was a poet. But whatever her reason for reading "Zero" for "Zorro" may have been, in her opinion saying that her father, like the boy, was a poet constituted full explanation. We respected it as such by thanking her for the information without making any further inquiries.

In this case, appreciation of the intelligence and meaningfulness of a misreading did not lead to its spontaneous correction, because such a correction would have denied what the girl wished to assert—that in some respects, a poet seems to her to be a zero, as the boy in the story seemed to his father.

Just because the child knows very well what takes place in the daily life of his family, he feels like a liar if he has to read aloud stories that describe family relations in ways he knows are not true to fact. And if a child feels forced in his reading to tell some other person things he knows from his own experience are untrue, the moral dilemma of being caught between the obligation to speak the truth and the need to read a printed word accurately can be quite acute.

A very bright first grader, a superior reader, was reading "Jack and Jim," a story of twins in *Land of Pleasure*. He read the story easily and smoothly, although he made one error on the second page, where he read the sentence, "Jim looked just like Jack," as, "Jack looked just like Jack," even though he had read their names before and had no difficulty in reading them later on. The identical appearance of the twins was clearly something of a problem to him, since through his mis-reading he was stating that Jack looked like himself, by implication denying that the twins looked alike. But he must subconsciously have realized that he had distorted the meaning of this sentence, because after he had nearly finished reading the next page, he suddenly turned the page back, looked at the sentence again, and read it as printed.

Without having commented on the misreading at all, we asked the boy—after he had corrected himself—what he thought it would feel like to be a twin. He answered: "I don't think it would be fun . . . cuz I have two brothers and they're a pest." It turned out that these brothers were twins, and he spontaneously remarked on one of the experiences that makes twinship difficult, particularly if the twins look alike. He said, "I wouldn't want to be called the wrong name. If you call one the wrong name, you better run cuz he doesn't like it and he pinches."

After this exchange he read well until, three pages later, he encountered the sentences: "In the morning the boys said, 'Hello Jack.' 'Hello Jim.' This is how the twins began a good day together." After he had read it, he added in a forceful and angry tone: "No way!" He was clearly demonstrating both his annoyance at being forced by the text to tell a lie and his need to correct it by telling the truth. Asked how he thought the twins really began the day, he replied: "By one getting up and getting someone like me up, and then Mother, too."

Overconcern with certain meanings owing to special per-sonal problems can also trigger misreadings, in addition to those elicited by texts which are experienced as unreal or bor-ing. A rather mature black third grader was reading a story about a girl who visits a land where everyone speaks "opposite language"—that is, the people say the opposite of what they really mean ("Ann Visits the Roundabouts," *Sullivan Programmed Reading Book 15,* New York: McGraw-Hill, 1973). The girl in the story talks with an elderly gentleman who understands that all the people are saying the opposite of what they mean, and like an indulgent father, he helps the girl realize what's going on and come up with solutions to their various dilemmas in the strange land.

Four times during the reading lesson, the girl had read correctly and without any hesitation the word "castles," so it was not lack of familiarity with the word that could explain her reading "casteless" for "castles" when the fatherly figure says: "But I have a feeling for castles, my dear. I'm quite sure this is the right way."

Since she had read "castles" easily before, her changing it to "casteless" this time had to be understood from the context in which the word appeared. Most likely she had read ahead to "the right way." To her, this phrase referred to the right way of ordering society; so where certainty was being expressed about "the right way," she changed "castles" to "casteless." After all, a casteless society is the opposite of one in which a castle dominates the life of the inhabitants. Since the story tells of a country in which people say the opposite of what they mean, making contradictory statements was encouraged by the text, and this may have induced the girl to a misreading that changed the text into the opposite of what it meant to convey. For castles, surely, suggest a society opposite to one that is casteless.

That the girl had read ahead in her mind, although she was behind with her voice, is hardly remarkable; on the contrary, this is normal in oral reading, where the existence of an eye-voice gap is a well-known phenomenon. With adults, the eye is often a full line ahead of what the voice is saying; otherwise we could not read with the proper emotional emphasis, which is possible only if we know what is to follow. While the eye-voice gap for children learning to read is shorter than for the adult, the print of basic readers is much larger and stands out much more clearly on the page, which facilitates reading what lies ahead.

That misreadings are based on a previous correct understanding of what is being distorted has been known since the beginning of this century, when Freud wrote:

> In a second group of cases the part which the text contributes to the misreading is a much larger one [when compared with a series of misreadings Freud had discussed previously]. It [the text] contains something which rouses the reader's defenses—some information or imputation distressing to him—and which is therefore corrected by being misread so as to fit in with a repudiation or with the fulfillment of a wish. In such cases we are of course obliged to assume that the text was first correctly understood and judged by the reader before it underwent correction, although his consciousness learnt nothing of this first reading.[3]

The teacher thought that this misreading had to do with the school's, her own, and the girl's deep conviction that a classless society was much to be preferred to one dominated by castles. After having made a remark to this effect, the teacher, wishing to increase the girl's linguistic skills, suggested that while the first syllable in the two words sounds alike, actually the root words of the two are different, even though they have "cast" in common.

In consequence of this comment, and much to the teacher's surprise, it turned out that the error was over-determined, as so often happens with misreadings and slips of the tongue.

[3] Freud, *The Psychopathology of Everyday Life.*

The girl's error, in addition to its social meaning, also had a very personal one. She said that her brother had a cast on his leg. Thus "casteless" may also have expressed the wish that her brother be rid of his cast.

But that would not explain why the misreading took place in the context of this particular passage, because the wish that the brother be free of his cast could equally well have been expressed in all the other passages where the word "castles" appeared. So the explanation has to be found in the particular context of this passage, which refers to knowing "the right way." A cast makes a person infirm and restricts his movements in space, as racial discrimination restricts a person's movements in society. In times and places where castles are important, their rulers restrict the movements of their inferiors, as a cast restricts the movements of a person. In the imagination of a third grader, the concept of freedom is understood as being free to move at will, both physically and socially, and the desire for this double freedom probably was what the girl expressed in her ingenious misreading.

It may seem far-fetched that a nine-year-old would know the meaning of "caste," which she would have to know to make this substitution at just the appropriate point in the text. Actually, it would be more surprising if she had not known it, attending a school that makes great efforts to teach the evils of discrimination and how these are related to social and economic issues, and living in Berkeley, a community that is alive with discussions about issues of caste and class. Fortunately the teacher, from her many discussions with her children of class and caste issues, was aware that these problems might explain the misreading. But it is worthwhile contemplating what it could have done to the girl's sense of her own intelligence, as a child in a self-consciously integrated school, if the teacher had assumed that she did not know this word.

It really doesn't matter whether children possess the knowledge or intelligence to know a word like "caste" at the age of nine. The point is the damage that results if adults believe they don't know it, whether they do or not. It is this belief, and the actions which spring from it, that get in the way of teachers' handling misreadings constructively. The belief is a reflection of the intellectual discontinuities existing between adults and children about which Piaget wrote so extensively—that because the child views the world differently from adults, he is viewed as being wrong, or unintelligent. This same discontinuity can also lead to a different misunderstanding of what Piaget said. When we accept that children are more intelligent than was formerly thought, we sometimes then impute to the child the ability to understand, for example, "caste" in all of its many ramifications as an adult would. This would be clearly untrue, and is not what Piaget had in mind. But that does not negate the fact that the development of the child's intelligence at the age of nine is sufficient to permit a concrete understanding of a concept, such as caste, especially as it relates to her everyday life, as caste did for this black girl, who heard almost daily of frictions between blacks and whites, what causes them, and how these were or were not resolved, and not just in abstract history lessons or talks at home but in the much more immediate reality of the playground.

Another girl, worried about her severe myopia, reacted strongly to the title of a poem, "What I Can Do" (*My City*, a Bank Street Reader). This first grader was very much concerned with what she could not do, as a result of her visual impairment. The poem begins:

I'm not as tall as my friend Ben.
I'm not as smart as John or Ed.
I cannot spell as well as Will.
I cannot catch as well as Ted.

After reading the first two lines correctly, the girl read the last two:

I cannot see as well as Will.
I cannot watch as well as Ted.

It was probably the highly personal form of the poem that forced her to state what she could not do, since these were facts of greatest concern to her, while for her grade level the girl was a very good reader and speller.

It may well be that having comprehended what the third line actually said, preconsciously the girl had thought: "Spelling is not my problem, so why say 'I cannot spell'?—But I cannot see as well as other children; seeing is my problem." Her anxiety about not seeing well may have combined with the inner demand to be honest when talking about herself (as the way the poem is written almost forced her to do) and made her replace the text with a truthful statement about what she could not do as well as others. Having done so in the third line, she continued in the same vein with the fourth.

Another, or an additional, explanation may be found in her having correctly perceived and understood the first two lines. At the beginning it was clear to her that she was reading a poem somebody else had written. But as she went on, she may have been carried away by the content, which is a comparison the speaker makes between himself and others like him. So she moved from an objective view of what she was reading to a highly subjective one, which forced her to think more intensively about herself as she read on. Reading the lines aloud, she made statements about herself; as she proceeded, she became ever more drawn into the spirit of what she was reading and ever more tempted to speak truly about herself.

Just before she began reading this poem, she had read the story preceding it ("Smarty-Arty Finds Out") without error. But it is a story that does not solicit the same personal involvement, since it is not written in the first person, nor did it touch on an immediate and pressing concern. Here is another illustration of how much and in what various ways reading is an active process. If the content permits, reading is experienced in an abstract manner, and it is the person's cognitive powers that are primarily involved, while the rest of the personality (its subconscious aspects, the id and superego) remain relatively uninvolved. But when the text touches on important personal issues, then the total personality becomes active, and a process begins in which the text's meaning is partly comprehended correctly by the cognitive powers and partly assimilated to the person's preoccupations—"I cannot see as well as others." The girl had correctly perceived and retained the essential meaning of the poem: it presents a comparison between the speaker and others in respect to some skill in which he is deficient by comparison. It is not at all essential to the poem's message what particular skill this is, which is why the pressure of anxiety about myopia could easily obtrude. In an active process, the girl made the poem much more meaningful to her than it would have been had she not manipulated the text. While retaining everything essential to it, she replaced something nonessential with something very essential to her.

Without referring to this girl's misreadings, or implying that she had read differently from what was printed, we observed aloud that the beginning part of the poem spoke about what someone could not do, rather than what someone could do, contrary to what the title suggested. The child responded by continuing to read, to find out what the subject of the poem could do. She read without error the last stanza:

I cannot run as fast as Ben.
I cannot sing as well as Fred.
But I can whistle through my teeth
While I'm standing on my head!

The text had become meaningful to her as she "did something to it"—assimilated it to her anxiety about her eyesight. She could then read the rest of the poem correctly and with great interest, even though two lines continue to speak about an inability to do things. Talking about what she could do, running and singing, did not provoke anxiety as had the earlier spelling and catching, because our intervention had helped her over her anxiety about seeing and watching. She could now openly state that she could run and sing as easily as other children, where before, though she knew she could catch and spell, she needed to express what she could *not* do as easily as other children. Once given help with her feelings about seeing and watching, she was free to enjoy reading about activities that came easier to her.

A common worry of children is whether they perform well enough academically. Even some of the best students, however good their performance, are anxious about this, thinking they ought to do better. This is in part a reflection of parental ambitions and anxieties concerning their academic success, so that sometimes the brightest students feel under the greatest pressure to achieve, independent of whether the classroom is conducted along progressive or traditional lines. In the traditional classroom, the anxious child feels supported in his need to attain academic excellence by the more definite demands made by the teacher and the more clearly defined learning tasks. In a progressive setting—where the child has much greater freedom whether to learn, and if so, has a say about what and when to study, and is in some sense more comfortable with the curriculum—he often is more anxious about his performance, missing the reassurance that comes from knowing the teacher will insist that he learn.

A very bright first grader, taking advantage of the freedom

to choose his activities, preferred roughhousing with his friends to schoolwork, despite the fact that achievement in reading was important to him, as indicated by his fear that he could not read well enough. His teacher did not insist that the children read, and so he often refused to do so, choosing to play with some favored classmate.[4] But he then concluded that he was unable to read because he had in the past chosen not to.

The teacher was worried because the child, who generally read well for a first grader, nevertheless made numerous substitutions, which she thought reflected a careless attitude. She wondered if things were on his mind that interfered with school learning, and she asked us to try to find out by reading with him.

When asked to read with us, he was resistant because it meant giving up having fun with some other boys. At first it seemed that he might refuse to read altogether, as he had done with his teacher so many times. Finally he agreed to read a story but gave up very soon in the middle of it, saying as was his custom that he didn't want to read this story, and then choosing another story that was below his reading level. Soon he gave up on this one too and picked still another story in a book even easier for him to read. It was as if he wanted to make sure that his reading would be a success by choosing books that were very easy. When he then read "fast me" for "first me," it seemed that part of his resistance to reading was either anxiety that he wasn't good at it (that he could not read

---

[4] The schools in which these observations were made were (as mentioned) the best in their systems; however, teacher style varied greatly between schools and from class to class. Many teachers were not as progressive in their manner of conducting class as the one who taught this boy; she permitted her children to choose whether to read, for how long, and which books. It was rather more typical for teachers to insist on a reading time during which they used standard texts, and to permit a choice of books during the rest of the reading period, after the assigned work had been completed.

fast enough), or that he wanted to be a fast reader so that he could quickly return to playing with his friends.

Since this was merely a hunch, we waited to see what else the boy would do. He volunteered that "Magic Doors" (*Uptown, Downtown*, a Bank Street Reader) was his favorite story, and immediately began to read it. He substituted "little" for "long" in the sentence, "He looked for a long time because he couldn't find the cheese." Assuming that he wanted to be finished with the reading lesson, we said that it is indeed hard to read if one looks for a little time. The child relaxed, and continued reading. He could do so following this comment because it implied that it was not his reading ability that was deficient (nor his intelligence), but that he didn't look at the text long enough—in other words, that he gave up too soon. For the first time while reading with us, he read a story from beginning to end. Then all on his own he began talking about its theme and what it reminded him of, which turned out to be an accident that was preoccupying him deeply.

The story tells about a little boy and his curiosity about the magic doors of the grocery store—doors that work automatically by electricity. This detail reminded the child that he had recently received an electric shock. He told how it happened, and showed us the sore that still remained. Then he went on to talk about his brothers and sisters, a topic suggested by the story, which was about an older brother taking care of a younger one. He complained about his younger sister, who continually interrupted his play with friends—in this way explaining one reason for his resistance to reading when *this* interrupted his play. After having talked about all this, he wanted to read a story entitled "Too Little." We said that it was obvious who was too little. The boy smiled with understanding, and said wryly: "Yeah, my sister." He read the entire story from beginning to end with lively interest and without error.

Originally, his approach to reading had been colored by thoughts of playing with classmates. When he chose to read

"Magic Doors," he was not consciously aware why it was his favorite story, he just felt it was. There are three good reasons for assuming that he did not know why he liked the story. First, if he had known why, he would probably have revealed it. Second, as long as the connection between unconscious thought and reading had not been established, he made errors in reading (such as reading "little time" for "long time"), whereas after it had become established, he made none; thus had he been aware of his reason for liking the story, in all likelihood he would have read it error-free. Third, after unconscious reasons for acting in a certain way (misreading some words) had become conscious, he spoke about his reasons for wanting to read "Too Little"; hence one can suppose that if he had known the reasons for his wanting to read "Magic Doors," he would also have explained his choice beforehand. But the most convincing demonstration that he had not known why he wanted to read "Magic Doors" is that it was only after coming to understand his reason for reading "little time" for "long time," and how this unconsciously made error reflected his inner attitude to reading, that his emotions suddenly became invested in reading and talking about it.

What happened here illustrates that by doing no more than teaching reading the way all teaching should be done—with a positive, accepting attitude to what the child is doing in his learning—unconscious phenomena can be brought, or can come, to consciousness, so that the ego is strengthened and security replaces insecurity. The boy had been quite insecure about his ability to read, hence his rejection of a text on his real reading level and its replacement by an easier one, and then by an even simpler one. Since we did not help him to understand his reading "fast me" for "first me," nothing happened. But when we helped him to understand why he read: "He looked for a little time," and that his looking only for a little time had something to do with his difficulties in reading, then unconscious motivation became conscious. It may even have permitted this boy to reflect back to his previous misreading, since to look only for a little time is tantamount to doing it fast.

Since it had come to his awareness why he had read that the boy in the story looked for only a little time, and since with his (mis)reading he had personalized the story, he now also became conscious of why he had wanted to read the story—it was his favorite because it told about a boy who was curious about electricity, as he was. Once he knew that reading a story could connect with one of his dominant interests, he could consciously decide that he wanted to read a story that related to a central problem in his life: that his sister was too little, and therefore interfered with what he wanted to do. This story he could read very well because his ego had been strengthened, and he had gained greater security from an experience that demonstrated how his failures in reading were not (as he had feared) due to lack of ability but, on the contrary, made good sense.

Since the child had become interested in reading when it met his conscious or unconscious needs, there was no reason to insist that he read. Thereafter he often chose to do so on his own, and when he did, he got further assurance that his misreadings were not evidence of poor reading ability. The teacher reported that both his resistance to reading and his preference for other activities decreased. No longer convinced of his inadequacy, he no longer thought he ought to be able to read fast and well even when looking at the page only for a little time.

As some of these results were achieved in a very progressive classroom, it might be mentioned that in both traditional and progressive classrooms we found that misreadings were treated exactly the same—as meaningless errors, pure and simple, devoid of any deeper meaning. While there was no way of knowing in advance whether treating misreadings as meaning-ful performance would fit better in a traditional or a progressive classroom, it seemed reasonable to assume that a positive handling of misreadings would be more acceptable to teachers who felt free to experiment with new ways. This is in fact what happened. What mattered was the attitude of the teacher to-ward a novel idea, not whether her style was more progressive or more traditional.

Most important of all to the child is the seriousness of the teacher's commitment to his learning. What matters is that the child be given the conviction that he will learn to read, ir-respective of whether he is taught in the morning or the after-noon, whether he refuses at one moment or the next, whether he reads this book or that. Again, while the climate of a class-room can be more or less conducive to learning, what counts most is the teacher's devotion to, and enjoyment of, teaching. Such commitment to vocation can be found equally in class-rooms conducted along traditional and progressive lines. Even in the best-equipped progressive classrooms, using the most advanced methods of instruction, when this commitment is missing, the child—who may already be anxious about school learning—becomes more so because he realizes he has not sufficient emotional support from the teacher in his as yet tenuous endeavor.

It was gratifying to observe what happened when teachers spontaneously put to use what had been demonstrated to them. Not only did the child receive credit for what he had done, but the teacher came to feel that her teaching had not been a fail-ure. The child was convinced that those who read with him viewed reading as very important, and further, that they as-sumed that his misreadings were due to his changing some words so as to express himself better. And the teacher felt vali-dated in her attempts to teach, which added interest to what otherwise was often a rather dull task.

CHAPTER 7

Misreadings and
the Teacher

The nature of a teacher's response to a reading error has a great deal to do with its consequences for a child: whether a teacher views such an error as an undesirable failure or as an interesting performance determines whether the child will feel discouraged or encouraged about his reading. Such feelings directly affect the child's attempts to become literate, and indirectly his general attitudes about learning and himself. Yet hundreds of hours of classroom observation and many long conversations with teachers proved to us that most teachers consistently view misreadings as the child's making either "a simple error" or "a silly mistake." Teachers believe the causes of such errors to be a lack of attention or an inability to decode the word correctly, a deficiency they relate to a variety of undesirable sources, from lack of experience to genetic defect.

It was only very occasionally, and nearly always under the spur of our questioning, that some other explanation of what might have caused the error was forthcoming. The nearly uniform interpretation of such mistakes as reading "Tigger" for "tiger" or "defective" for "detective" was that the two words contained almost the same letters so that the child, having recognized or sounded out most of the letters, merely guessed at the rest of the word instead of working it out. Other explanations, depending on the case, were that the word as printed and the one spoken by the child sounded alike; that the two words began with the same letter; that the child had difficulty in concentrating, paying attention, or focusing on words. The teachers did not concern themselves with the child's possible feelings about what he .was reading, or with the change in content and meaning that resulted from the replacement of one word by another.

We talked with teachers about all kinds of things we had observed during the day, and misreadings came up only incidentally in our discussions about the teaching of reading in general. The teachers generally thought that we were interested in the way *they* had handled an incident of misreading— hardly ever, unless we made it clear to them, did it occur to them that we might be curious about what the *child* had done. Even then, their replies indicated that they were convinced we wanted to discover what deficiency the child's error indicated, and what remedial work it required; they had never considered the possibility that the misreading may have been the deliberate result of some pertinent thinking on the child's part.

These conscientious teachers, viewing us as experts in reading, wanted to learn from us whether their approach to the child's misreading had been the best one. They explained, for example, that they had pointed the error out to the child so that he would not repeat it or fail to get the gist of the story; or that they had let it pass without comment in order not to discourage the child about his reading ability or interfere with his enjoyment of reading.

When teachers began to recognize from our remarks that we were interested in the specifics of what the child had done, they talked about what they considered to be the cause of his error, and what might be done to prevent it in the future, the two being closely related in their minds. All kinds of causes were considered by the teachers, with two exceptions: that the error may have been an appropriate reaction to the text's content as printed, or a response to the meaning of the text as ascribed to it by the child as he was reading it.

Yet in a study made in the late 1960s of the errors that first graders made in reading, it was found that out of 1,943 ascertainable errors, 1,675—or 86 percent—were substitutions that made equal or better sense than the original text. The example used to illustrate this is a child's reading "Spot can hear me," when the text has "Spot can help me." Spot is a dog, and a first grader knows that a dog can hardly help a child—but a dog can indeed hear the child, and respond appropriately to his command.

Next in type of error frequency were omissions, which made up a little over 6 percent of the errors. In these the child would skip a word that was part of the text, such as reading "the umbrella" for "the black umbrella." Insertions, such as reading "down to the creek" when the text was "down the creek," were encountered with the same frequency. All other errors amounted to 1.4 percent of the total.[1] So, according to this study, nearly all errors made by the child being taught to read—whether he substitutes, omits, or inserts a word—either make the sentence more colloquial and less stilted, or more sensible.

The texts of the preprimers and primers most widely used in the United States to introduce reading to kindergarten and first-grade children consist of words that are supposed to be easy for the child who is just learning to read. The intention is to facilitate the child's task by using only words that can readily be sounded out, repeating them frequently, and combining these easy words into very short sentences. Actually, all this makes it harder for the beginner, because the text just doesn't sound like anything anyone would ever say.

For example, because the child usually learns early to recognize the words "store" and "man," one widely used basic

[1] Rose-Marie Weber, "First Graders' Use of Grammatical Context in Reading," in Harry Levin and Joanna P. Williams, eds., *Basic Studies in Reading*. New York: Basic Books, 1970.

text (*People Read,* one of the Bank Street Readers) refers to a "store man" when meaning a salesman. Neither *Webster's* nor the *Oxford Dictionary* contains the phrase "store man"; one finds instead: storekeeper, salesman, salesgirl, saleswoman, clerk. Thus, in order to make learning to read easy and attractive, in this story children who have a vocabulary appropriate to expressing what the text means to convey are asked to recognize and use in their reading words that exist neither in their vocabularies nor in English or American dictionaries. To compound the irony, this happens in a book entitled *People Read,* which by implication promises to tell how everybody reads and what they do when they read. The result is that children are provoked to errors by the discrepancies between the way people ordinarily talk and the way the characters are made to talk in these stories.

Teachers' inability to consider that children may have excellent reasons for their misreadings is hardly surprising when one realizes that in the books most widely used to instruct American teachers and reading specialists, the possibility that a child's misreadings may hold specific meanings is not even mentioned (not to speak of the possibility that they may be due to preconscious or unconscious thought processes). As far as the "experts" on reading are concerned, it does not seem worthwhile to consider either the role of the unconscious in reading nor the findings of Freud (and psychoanalysis) on errors in reading.

To mention only two recent scholarly publications: in neither Harris and Sipay, nor Gibson and Levin,[2] is Freud or the unconscious mentioned. In the latter it is called "interesting" that "about 90% of the substitutions were words that the children had encountered elsewhere in their reading." But

---

[2] Albert J. Harris and Edward R. Sipay, *op. cit.* Eleanor J. Gibson and Harry Levin, *The Psychology of Reading.* Cambridge, Mass.: MIT Press, 1975.

this did not suggest to the authors the possibility that children may have substituted words which to them seemed more suitable than those printed in the text. Instead, they implicitly accuse children of acting mindlessly, as they continue: "The tactic seemed to be, if you are going to guess, try a word you have seen before. Could this be due to the frequent repetitions of a small vocabulary in first-grade reading books?" If the *scholars* in the field of reading do not contemplate the possibility, not to mention the likelihood, that children's errors in reading may be meaningful responses, how can classroom teachers be expected to do so?

Only when they realized that we were concerned with what a child actually did with the words, as opposed to what class of errors the mistake fell into, did some teachers begin, however hesitantly, to pay more attention to what specifically had happened. Even then, it was not the substitution itself on which they would comment (such as the reading of "defective" for "detective"), nor the change in meaning that was brought about by it. Instead, they would talk more about the child: his level of intelligence or attention; his interests, or home background; other mistakes he had made in reading; or the difficulties he had in school. Unless we carried the conversation further, it would stop there. It did not occur spontaneously to a single teacher that what the child had done might have meaning, so deeply are teachers committed to their obligation to teach children to read words exactly as printed on the page, and so convinced are they that it is the child's task to do this.

Some explanation for this may be found not only in the teachers' complete concentration on teaching word recognition but in their own inability to keep themselves sufficiently interested in the content of the textbooks to notice how the meaning may be altered by the substitution of one word for another. The vacuity of the texts of American primers, with their mind-dulling repetition of words, has a near-hypnotic effect. Since there is no worthwhile content to the primers' stories, the only way a teacher can keep herself interested in the children's reading is to make sure that they read the words exactly as printed.

Others, too, have reflected on what they view as the strange behavior of teachers as they teach beginners to read. Courtney Cazden, for example, writes: "Normally, in out-of-school conversations, our focal attention as speakers and listeners is on the meaning, the intention, of what someone is trying to say. Language forms are themselves transparent; we hear through them to the meaning intended. But teachers, over the decades if not centuries, have somehow gotten into the habit of hearing with different ears once they got through the classroom doors. Language forms assume an opaque quality. We cannot hear through them; we hear only the errors to be corrected."[3]

But it is not true that teachers "hear with different ears" in the classroom than in life. Such a widespread contention is most unfair. Teachers do this only while teaching reading; once they stop teaching it, they immediately revert to hearing the child's intended meaning, whatever language form he may use. Nor is it correct to ascribe such strange behavior to "habit" acquired over time. Habits develop for reasons, and are maintained only if the causes for their acquisition continue; otherwise they extinguish themselves. It is the inane content of the basic readers that makes it impossible for the teacher to find any meaning in what the child is reading, always with the exception of the meaning she sees in correct word recognition.

Here it ought to be remembered that modern teaching methods force the teacher to read and listen over and over again to the same essentially senseless chain of words, while working with individual children or reading with children in small groups. The minimal meaning a so-called story may have had on first or second reading becomes completely eradicated

---

[3] Courtney B. Cazden, "How Knowledge About Language Helps the Classroom Teacher—or Does It: A Personal Account," *The Urban Review*, 9, 2 (Summer 1976).

when it is read and listened to time after time, year after year. In order to be a good teacher, one must involve oneself in what goes on in class. As the teacher cannot involve herself in any meaningful way in the content of what the child reads, because to do so would be offensive to her intelligence, she disengages herself from the content and concentrates instead on single words, one at a time. It then becomes difficult to recognize how the change of one word, or a change within a word, may relate to the child's feelings about a story. But it is not only the teacher's experience that leads to this result. Again, the prevalent literature on the teaching of reading, on which the readers themselves are based, induces the teacher to proceed as if "language forms" were "opaque" for the child, and to "hear only the errors to be corrected."

So what Cazden calls the "habit" of teachers are methods developed for reasons perceived by them as valid. Unfortunately, these "habits" are detrimental to the child's enjoyment of reading and his ability to extract meaning from it—the very experiences that would make becoming literate most attractive to him.

Had we approached our observations with a similar commitment to the importance of correct word recognition for learning to read, we would not have behaved much differently from the teachers. As a matter of fact, one of our most difficult tasks was to change the thinking of our co-workers, who were not classroom teachers but educational researchers specializing in reading. They had to free themselves of their entrenched commitment to the importance of correct word recognition before they could open themselves to observing and recognizing the meaning and importance of other factors in children's reading. Only then did it become possible for them to remain fully interested in the content of what the child was reading, despite the interest-dulling repetition of words. Only concentration on how the children reacted to what they read—with boredom, anger, or lack of interest, as though desiring to be done with an onerous task, or as though they were discouraged with themselves—and on their spontaneous reshapings of the text, permitted *us* to remain interested in the pseudo-content they were supposed to be taking in.

Disregard of meaning and concentration on the single word seem to be imposed on teachers and children alike by the extremely limited vocabulary used in books designed for the first, second, and third grades. Graded readers are generally used as the basis for reading instruction by 98 percent of first-grade teachers, and by 92 percent of second- and third-grade teachers on "all or most of the days of the year."[4] As mentioned before, the four preprimers of one highly popular series use altogether only 78 words, to which the first basic primer adds another 104 words.[5] The most frequently used first readers contain only from 285 to 340 words.[6] Anyone restricting himself to such an extremely narrow vocabulary in conversation would be interpreted either as very limited in intelligence or as regarding the person to whom he was speaking as infantile, or both. Yet there is nothing the beginning reader hates more than the feeling that he is being degraded to the level of an infant.

Not only do these books contain but a few hundred endlessly repeated words; they often use words and word combinations that do not conform to common language usage, and children rightly object to this unusual and stilted language. One first-grade girl, for example, complained about a story that told of a ball falling into a tar patch.[7] She thought it should

---

[4] Allen Barton and David Wilder, "Research and Practice in the Teaching of Reading," in M. B. Miles, ed., *Innovation in Education.* New York: Teachers College, Columbia University, 1964.
[5] Harper and Row Basic Reading Program, 1966.
[6] Harris and Sipay, *op. cit.*
[7] *Sullivan Storybook No. 6B, The Red Ball.* New York: McGraw-Hill, 1966.

have said that the ball fell into a puddle. The teacher, knowing that this phonics-based text used "tar patch" in preference to "puddle" because the first two words are pronounced as printed, while "puddle" is pronounced "puddel," said that perhaps the author of the story thought children would have difficulty in recognizing the word "puddle." By this, she meant difficulty in decoding and reading the word. But the girl fastened on exactly the words the teacher had used: that it might be difficult for her to recognize the word "puddle." This made her truly indignant, and she angrily exclaimed, "I know 'puddle' when I see it." We do not know if her remark was due simply to the fact that "puddle" was a word of her active vocabulary, while "tar patch" was not. But the way she expressed herself suggests a much more subtle reason why "tar patch" insulted her: she made it clear that what she sees—that is, what she encounters as part of her everyday experience—is puddles, not tar patches; and her reaction suggested the wish that teachers and those who write for children should show respect for the child's experience of the world.

What happened here is but one example of a situation that occurs over and over again in schools, and not only where beginners are taught to read: abstract ideas on the part of the educator about how learning must proceed, in this example the importance of correct recognition of phonemes, clash with the emotional reality in which the child lives. The teacher neglects the child's ideas about the correct way to deal with the material at hand, being thoroughly convinced of the modern methods of teaching reading. The teacher's insistence on accuracy often barely hides that what is involved here is also a power play, in which the teacher uses her superior knowledge and her authority within the system to gain her point. The child consciously (or more often subconsciously) reacts to being the victim of such a power play and becomes antagonistic. Many children manage to defeat the teacher's power by refusing to learn—a Pyrrhic victory that robs the child of his chance to become fully educated, and with it deprives society of a well-educated citizen.

The average first grader comes to school with a large vocabulary of commonly used words.[8] Yet teachers, as they read with the child, somehow seem to disregard this fact and proceed as if the child knows only the words he has learned in his reader, and not even those well. The consequence of this attitude is the assumption that the child who misreads does so because he does not know the words involved. But when freely conversing with the child about his reading or any other matter, the same teachers clearly demonstrate their recognition that the children have quite a rich vocabulary at their disposal. These frequent, sudden switches from using a wide and expressive vocabulary when talking with the child to a boringly limited one when reading with him are an important factor making reading so unattractive to both teacher and children, when compared to the good times and fascinating conversations they have with each other when not engaged in "learning to read."

Aside from the implication of stupidity inherent in using such a limited vocabulary, there are also technical reasons why reading ought to be taught for meaning, using a vocabulary closer to that which the child would use on his own, and not emphasizing single word recognition. Concentrated attention to letters or even specific words distracts from meaning and thus seriously interferes with the reading process. As Frank Smith points out:

The reason that reading has to be fast we now know. The processing of visual information is not instantaneous but takes a significant amount of time, during which losses always occur. Information is very quickly lost in reading, especially if it is not condensed into

---

[8] Chall, *op. cit.*

"meaningful" form and put into long-term memory. A child who has to read letter by letter, or even word by word, has very little chance of comprehending.[9]

The child's attempt to grasp meaning, even when it some-times takes the form of misreadings, ought to be the basis for the teaching of reading. Smith suggests this by saying that when a child is reading for meaning, he "may not be in need of feedback that a particular word is 'wrong.'" Smith views mis-reading as an unintentional error, a misfiring of the child's attempt to identify the distinctive features of letters and words, but not as meaningful behavior. Not recognizing the uncon-scious processes at work in reading, he fails to note that subconscious recognition of the text may occur (through cor-rect decoding) and spark a rejection and subsequent change of the text.

To encourage reading in the face of misreadings it is not necessary that we recognize the relationship between what the child does with the text and what the text purports to say. To comprehend the unconscious reasons why a child may misread a word is obviously beyond the teacher's task—and is not necessary for dealing more constructively with misreadings. Teachers with no familiarity with psychoanalytic thinking or unconscious processes can learn to recognize that misreadings are due to conscious or preconscious reactions to the text, and can apply such knowledge with most desirable results. This was demonstrated by several teachers whose classes we ob-served and with whom we discussed our experiences over some time. Once they accepted our thesis, reading even a simple text with a child became alive and full of interest for them. They then had fascinating conversations with their children about their reading—and misreadings—just as they had had before about other things taught in class. Reading became an

[9] Frank Smith, *Understanding Reading*. New York: Holt, Rinehart and Winston, 1971.

exciting enterprise for both teacher and child, as teachers assumed that real intelligence and a well-developed vocabulary (albeit different from that used in the text) were being brought to bear by the child on the task of reading, and that misreadings also reflected the application of these faculties.

One of the teachers who had become familiar with our method of approaching reading realized that a third-grade pupil about whose reading she had been worried had actually made very intelligent substitutions that sometimes preserved the meaning of the text, but more important, usually reflected the girl's sophisticated vocabulary, which was much in evidence during free conversation. The teacher then became interested in separating the mistakes that improved the text while preserving its meaning from those that changed the text but made it more meaningful to the child, because it made the text say what the child for personal reasons wished it to say. The teacher's renewed interest in reading in turn sparked a greater interest in it on the part of her student.

This girl was reading a difficult text for a third grader, a book called *A Dog on Barkham Street*.[10] The first substitution the child made was to read "extinguished" for "exhausted" in a sentence that told about how the bully, Martin, chased Edward, the main character. The sentence sums up how Martin taunts, teases, and bullies Edward, with whom the girl identified: "This time Martin had chased him for blocks, and then, when Edward was absolutely exhausted and fell down, Martin sat on top of him, and pulled his hair and said over and over, 'Uncle, say uncle.'" The teacher told the girl that if Edward were extinguished, he would be finished, all right, by which the teacher meant to imply that by reading "extinguished," the child had not only preserved the meaning but imputed deeper meaning than the text intended to convey.

Although we cannot be sure what motivated this misread-

[10] By M. S. Solz. New York: Dell, 1960.

ing, it is reasonable to consider the possibility that the girl's eyes had moved ahead of what she was reading aloud and that she had taken in the danger that Edward might give in and indeed say "uncle." Giving in out of exhaustion, as mentioned in the text, would be a sign that Edward's will to resist had become extinguished. But it would also threaten to extinguish him as an independent, self-respecting person. The girl may have seen this inherent danger of giving in to a bully as the central problem presented by the story, while exhaustion was only the condition that could lead to it.

We cannot be certain how the girl interpreted the teacher's agreement with her that Edward would be finished if he were extinguished. However, in response to it, she immediately re-read the sentence exactly as printed, although nothing the teacher had said suggested this to her, nor had she been given any clue that the printed word was "exhausted." All the girl may have gotten from what the teacher said, in addition to the feeling that the teacher agreed with her interpretation, may have been an inkling that the text was somehow different from the way she read it, in particular as far as the word "extinguished" was concerned.

The story continues to tell how the bully Martin called Edward names, such as "Weird One." The first time the bully called Edward that, the girl substituted "worried" for "weird"; and the second time, "wary." The teacher now remarked that the girl had an excellent vocabulary, implying that the mis-readings reflected an understanding of the printed word "weird," while the particular words chosen as substitutes sug-gested mature use of the English language insofar as these terms expressed the hero's feelings at being called such names. The teacher further said that it was clear that Edward was both worried and wary because of Martin's bullying. At that the girl looked again at the word "weird," and now read it correctly.

As the story develops, Edward wishes to move to Alaska to escape Martin. At this point, the girl made another mistake, not one that more or less preserved the meaning of the passage but one that reversed it. In so doing she once more gave precedence to expressing Edward's—and by proxy, her own—feelings, namely, her hope that Edward would be spared further torture. The story quotes Edward's mother telling him, didactically, that: "—even if we did move somewhere else, it wouldn't be much help, probably. I understand there's a bully on every block. I expect even Alaskan blocks. It's what the other mothers tell me, at P.T.A. meetings, and all." The one substitution the girl made in this quite complicated passage was to read "except" for "expect." Contrary to what the text said, she had the mother reassure Edward about Alaska, rather than tell him that he would have to learn to deal with bullies anywhere he lived, even in Alaska.

This time the teacher told the girl that she must agree with Edward that it would be a big relief if there were no bullies in Alaska. Once more the child scrutinized the text, and reread it correctly. Given credit by the teacher that her way of reading made sense in voicing the hero's (and her) hopes, the girl became able and willing to read correctly, although inwardly she probably continued to disagree with what she was reading aloud.

This extended example illustrates that it is quite possible for teachers to understand that a child's substitutions are not haphazard performances. Yet the universal practice is to assume that when one letter, for example, looks like the mirror image of another, this sufficiently explains the child's mistake, even though the word he read differently from the text produces the most significant change in meaning. If appreciation for the meaning—and also for the often subtle cleverness—of children's misreadings replaced their being viewed as pointless errors, the child's feelings of inferiority over his reading ability would not be increased but reduced, and the teaching of reading to beginners would attain additional interest for both teacher and student.

Kenneth Goodman, in defining a miscue as "an oral response that differs from the expected response," correctly emphasizes that the child's mistake fails to conform to the expectation of the teacher or the text.[11] But is everything a student does that is contrary to the educator's expectations therefore wrong and to be rejected? Does such a belief not justify the student's abiding conviction that in school the only thing that counts is what goes on in the teacher's (or the text writer's) head, while what goes on in the student's mind counts for nothing? If we approached the child's performance not with the expectation that he will make meaningless mistakes, but rather with an open attitude toward his efforts, then children's attitudes to learning would be very different. While it is not very exciting if things go as expected, the unexpected always is a surprise which, when we can accept it positively, stimulates our interest.

In the same publication, S. Nieratka advises, as an effective remedial strategy, asking the student whether what he read "makes sense."[12] But to respond to a misreading with the question "Does that make sense?" is both inappropriate and insulting, because the way the child reads the text makes sense in some context, even if only he understands it. Thus, when the teacher is further instructed to help children make "better miscues,"[13] one wonders how it is determined that one miscue is better than another. A better miscue from the teacher's perspective might seem much worse from the student's

[11] Kenneth Goodman, ed., *Miscue Analysis*. Urbana, Ill.: Clearinghouse on Reading and Communication Skills, National Council of Teachers of English, 1973.

[12] S. Nieratka, "Miscue Analysis in a Special Education Resource Room," in Goodman, ed., *op. cit.*

[13] Yetta Goodman, "Miscue Analysis for In-Service Reading Teachers," Kenneth Goodman, ed., *op. cit.*

viewpoint. In fact, the student considers his reading as the right and best one, otherwise he would not have rendered the text in this fashion, and he will resent the adult's implication that some other misreading makes better sense. What is required is an acceptance of the child's version without, however, pretending that it is what the author intended.

Since our approach to misreadings is derived from psychoanalytic insights, it might be mentioned that even in psychoanalysis it would be erroneous in most cases for the analyst to interpret, for example, a patient's slip of the tongue. This the patient ought to do himself in his own good time, when doing so is constructive for him. On the other hand, it is usually best to bring to the patient's attention that he did make an error, because if the analyst failed to do this, the patient would come to feel that his actions were of little importance to his analyst; also, it would prevent the patient's learning important things about himself. But making him aware that he committed an error is appropriate only after it has been established that such mistakes are made for important reasons, and that they have great psychological significance.

In psychoanalysis, too, the analyst by no means always knows why the patient made an error, what caused it, and what meaning it expresses. And in those cases where he thinks he does know, he would usually be wiser to keep his knowledge to himself. After the analyst makes some remark indicating that the slip has been recognized by him and encouraging the patient to consider it, it is up to the patient to decide whether he wishes to make this effort. Whether or not he does so, bringing the slip to his awareness in a way which conveys the conviction that he did something clever, however idiosyncratic, nearly always permits the patient to *recognize* the slip and to correct himself, saying what he had consciously meant to say —even without any clear recognition of what caused the slip, or any grasp of its deepest meaning.

Similarly, in most cases it is sufficient for the teacher to convey to the child that she knows he has cleverly, and for important personal reasons, manipulated the printed word. It is by no means necessary for her or for the child to understand the cause of his having done so. When we accept that in his error the child has made a (to him) important point, and when this recognition has sunk in, the inner pressures that had prevented the child from reading the word correctly may subside, often allowing him to read it correctly thereafter.

When teachers asked us to explain why we proceeded as we did, and how the efficacy of our method could be understood, we had to fall back on insights derived from psychoanalysis. At this point they would object that they were teachers and not psychoanalysts, as though a mere acceptance of the fact that there are unconscious aspects to our behavior required knowledge of psychoanalytic theories and the ability to set them into practice. There is an unfortunate but widespread misconception that recognizing the role unconscious processes play in our lives is equivalent to engaging in psychoanalysis. And moreover, recognizing these unconscious factors is perceived as being linked to neglecting the importance of the conscious cognitive endeavors that are the business of education. But such a separation of the cognitive and conscious realm from the emotional and unconscious one clearly runs counter to the educational principle of "teaching the whole child." Since his unconscious is very much part of him, an education that disregards it does so at the risk of failing in its purposes. Yet despite certain commonalities, the disciplines of education and psychoanalysis, although sharing an ultimate goal, are quite different in their intermediate goals and in their methods.

Both education and psychoanalysis aim to equip a person to cope with the vagaries of life by strengthening his or her ego. Psychoanalysis tries to achieve this by concentrating on our inner life, hence Freud's remark that "where there was id, there ego should be." In psychoanalytic therapy the person's attention is deliberately turned to his inner life, to the dark world of the unconscious and the chaotic realm of the emotions, so that it will neither destructively interfere with his ability to love freely and in ways fully satisfying to him and those he loves, nor prevent him from working successfully at self-chosen tasks he deems socially constructive and personally important. Thus psychoanalysis approaches the task of making the ego as effective as possible by freeing it from enslavement to the irrational tendencies of id and superego. As far as knowledge of the external world and skills for coping with it are concerned, it may be said that psychoanalysis improves these only incidentally, in a roundabout way. Any increase in cognitive powers that may accrue to a person as a consequence of his increased ability to cope with his unconscious is incidental to psychoanalysis' main purpose, which is to enable a person to understand and control his unconscious.

Education, by contrast, concentrates directly on developing a person's cognitive abilities—his knowledge, the skills and attitudes he needs to deal best with problems not in his inner life but in the external world and society. Whatever better understanding and mastery of his unconscious may accrue to a person through the increase in his cognitive powers, and with it his better mastery of the external world, is but an incidental consequence of his growth along cognitive lines. Of course, in all we do, a dynamic interplay takes place—on the one hand, among ego, id, and superego, on the other, between ego and external world; and also among conscious, preconscious, and unconscious aspects of the personality. So, in a deeper sense, any attempt at a clear-cut, definite separation between what education and psychoanalysis each tries to achieve will be somewhat arbitrary. Certainly, psychoanalysis ought to be a significant educational experience, albeit of a very specific nature, and any truly meaningful educational experience cannot fail to have its impact on a person's unconscious.

Given the radically different settings, methods, and intermediate goals of these two disciplines, classroom teachers make unsuitable psychotherapists, while psychoanalysts are most unlikely classroom teachers. Witness the fact that some of the earliest child psychoanalysts were originally teachers, including Anna Freud, who was the first child analyst, and they all gave up teaching when they became analysts. Among the many causes for this is that the strongest commitment of the teacher ought to be to rationality and the intellectual virtues, while that of the psychoanalyst is to the irrational and the unconscious aspects of the personality. If, for example, a teacher encourages her students to write down their fantasies, or even their dreams, she should do so to develop writing skills, not because she wants to help the child understand his unconscious. By contrast, a psychoanalyst should only suggest to a patient that he read some piece of literature in order to open up to him a better understanding of the unconscious, not to improve his reading skill.

The reason this study leans heavily on psychoanalytic insights is that we found them useful in spotlighting neglected aspects of teaching and of learning to read. Its purpose is to suggest procedures that facilitate learning to read, but these procedures do not require psychoanalytic understanding —only that we show as much respect for what the child is doing on his own as we want him to show for what we are trying to do in teaching him.

Viewing a misreading as due to the child's ignorance (regardless of whether it is ascribed to lack of attention, skill, practice, etc.) has many bad consequences. Being told—or in any other way being made to feel—that we did something wrong makes us insecure, the more so the younger we are and the less competent we feel. The more insecure we are, the more apt we are either to give up or to assert that we did nothing wrong, or both. The child, convinced the teacher knows better, is more likely to give up on reading, feeling "I cannot do it"; but his inner reaction of "I am right" is not absent, only suppressed. The censure is just too painful for him to simply accept it and go on with the task at hand.

If the child has the need, or at least the desire, to feel that "I am right"—as we all do much of the time—but is obviously wrong in what he has read, he can continue to support this underlying feeling by shifting the ground for it, as many a child does in such a situation. Not being able to maintain "I am right in what I read," the "I am right" becomes transferred and transformed into the feeling, "I am right in thinking that reading is just too difficult for me." Thus the child can maintain the inner attitude of "I am right," which he needs for his security and self-respect, particularly when he has to accept being corrected by a superior. With this inner conviction that in some essential sense he was right, the child can, without too much loss of self-respect, accept that in regard to how the actual printed word reads, the teacher was right. But the tragic result of all this is that the child who has many such experiences concludes permanently that he is right in his conviction that reading is not for him.

The readiness with which a child responds to a correction of his misreading with an "Oh, yes," or "I see," or "That's right," is his way of appeasing the teacher, and of trying to minimize in her eyes and those of others what she perceives as his blunder. Unfortunately, such a response is taken by the teacher as an indication that nothing untoward has happened. The child's purpose is to pretend that this is so; but the fact is that reading has inflicted another defeat on him, and has been instrumental in lowering his self-respect—yet another reason to avoid books and reading, which have become sources of his feeling deflated.

It takes not only courage but persistence to continue to

struggle with a problem after having experienced repeated defeat. Only those children who for reasons of their own are determined to learn to read, however difficult it may be and however many setbacks they may experience in the process, will continue the struggle. But these children do not present the problem. It is the ones who are lacking in such resolve who cannot afford to experience many defeats in their attempts to read.

In fact, the common view of misreadings as caused by lack of knowledge or skill has pernicious consequences, particularly for the insecure child, and doubly so for the child who already has learning difficulties. Typically, such insecurity is more prevalent among children who belong to groups discriminated against, or ethnic minorities, or those who come from deprived homes. But it is not restricted to them; it occurs also in children of well-educated, middle-class parents. Too-high parental expectations can make children worry about their ability to perform. Such anxiety, and many other pressures all pushing for expression, may take the form of blocking, or of reshaping the printed text to meet idiosyncratic needs, or, one might more correctly say, to permit ventilation of what is most important to the child at the moment.

Two examples may illustrate this. The first relates to a boy who had to contend with overly high parental expectations; the second to a boy whose background was culturally deprived.

In the opinion of his ambitious parents, an eight-and-a-half-year-old boy was not doing well enough academically, since he learned more slowly than had his sisters, with whom they compared him disparagingly. One day he was struggling with a Walt Disney version of *Cinderella*. He had reached the part of the story where stepmother and stepsisters do not permit Cinderella time off from her labors to prepare herself for the ball. They mock her: "You must learn to work faster." Finally she is able to put on her dress. The text reads: "Cinderella ran down the stairs. 'Wait,' she called, 'I can go now.'"

Instead of reading it as printed, the boy read: "Cinderella ran down the sisters," and stopped. So, as though it had been an unfinished sentence, we concluded it by adding "because she was so mad." At that, he spontaneously reread the line exactly as printed.

Pushed by his parents to work faster in school and teased because of his slowness by his sisters, he rightly felt they thought little of him, as Cinderella's family had thought little of her. So he identified with Cinderella. While the Cinderella story does not say that she was angry at being disparaged, we feel she must have been. The boy in his misreading made her give vent to her anger—and his own—in an aggressive act directed against those who behaved badly to her and him: the sisters. Our giving words to her anger—and with it, implicitly, to his—conveyed to him that we understood the motive for his reading the sentence the way he did, and that we accepted as valid the feelings he expressed through his misreading: his desire to run down those who seemed the cause of his being pushed to work faster than he was able.

Stating the wish to get even probably provided some relief for the boy; our accepting it in a matter of fact way did the rest. The pressure of previously suppressed inner rage was sufficiently reduced so that it no longer interfered with the cognitive task of reading the words as printed, and the boy could read the line correctly, clear demonstration that his misreading had not been due to lack of skill. Through his correct reading of the sentence, the boy may have rewarded us for having taken his side in his conflict with those who pressed him to work too hard, i.e., to learn faster than he could. Since we had sided with him, to please us he now sided with us, or rather, with the text he assumed we wanted him to read.

While this may have played some small part in his spontaneous rereading of the sentence correctly, much more important in the long run is that he was able to please himself by successfully mastering the cognitive task involved in reading the text correctly. That he was able to do so all on his own, without any prodding or help from us—such as asking him to take another look at the word, to sound it out, or to ask him whether nice Cinderella would do such a nasty thing, all interventions teachers typically engage in—demonstrated to him that if he wanted, he could read well, and that his first misreading was not due to his being incompetent. Such pleasure in himself and his achievement extends backward to the process of reading, because it was the experience of reading that led to it. The boy's misreading had invested the text with deep personal meaning. Through the correct second reading he gained pleasure in himself, and also in reading. It is many such experiences demonstrating that reading is both meaningful and pleasurable that eventually make for literacy.

What might have been the results of correcting the boy's misreading? In this particular case, an attentive teacher might have pointed out that the word in the text indeed began with the letter s, but that it was not "sisters." Doing this, she would only have been following what she had learned from the pertinent literature on common mistakes in reading: that when two words begin with the same letter, as "sisters" and "stairs" do, the beginning reader makes his mistake by correctly decoding the first letter of the word and then guessing at the rest.

But giving such help in decoding a word completely disregards what is actually going on in the mind of the child, which has nothing to do with guessing—on the contrary, he is projecting important personal meaning into the story. Had we corrected his error, as his parents, his sisters, and his teacher typically did, it would have reminded him of their criticisms. Not only would it have intensified his anger at them and his frustration with himself, but it would have made him additionally angry at us. It would have added new fuel to his wish to run down all those who pressed him to read faster and better, in which group we also now would be included. Vastly increased anger would have made it nearly impossible for him to read the sentence in any other way but one that permitted the discharge of his frustration and anger, as did his original misreading. He might have been so flooded with anger that his cognitive capacities would have become completely overpowered by it. Asked nevertheless to read what was printed, he probably would have blocked, as he often did in similar situations; he might just have stopped reading, claiming that he could not do it. The reason would have been that the overwhelming pressure of his emotions had blinded his vision, had reduced it, so to speak, to a tunnel vision in which he saw only his anger. The pressure would have made it impossible for him to recognize words that spoke of Cinderella's compliance, so contrary to the feelings filling him at the moment.

In order to appreciate why correcting a misreading such as this boy's may so overwhelm him with anger, one must remember that it is nearly always the teacher who, directly or indirectly with her insistence that the child ought to read, causes him to react this way. If what he reads arouses very strong, even unmanageably painful feelings in the child, it is the teacher who, with her demands, has subjected him to such an unpleasant experience.[14]

On a subconscious level, the child is likely to experience it as most unfair that his teacher first induces him to read something that arouses over-strong emotions in him, and then, when these feelings express themselves in some misreading, finds fault with him. Unconsciously, he grows even more annoyed with the book and with reading in general, because what he was reading projected him into a situation where his cognitive powers gave way under the impact of the emotions the text incited. And when these feelings forced him either to read the text inaccurately or to block altogether, then to him

[14] The psychological experience of the child who reads all on his own because he enjoys it, or for some other personal reason, is, of course, quite different.

the text becomes the cause of his being put down and criticized.

If one wishes to view all this within the theoretical framework of psychoanalysis, one might say that correcting his misreading would have added to the child's feeling of inferiority and with it to his anger at all those who forced him to consider himself inferior—an unavoidable consequence of having one's error pointed out, particularly when the error is considered a stupid one. Whatever mental energy was theoretically available to the boy's ego for correct cognition, after allocating some of it to containing the subconscious pressure of the anger stirred up by the story, would have become additionally depleted by the defeat his ego experienced when he failed to read correctly. His mental energy thus reduced, he would have needed most or all of it simply to control himself; and the greater amount of mental energy required to keep the subconscious pressures repressed would have left less available for the cognitive task of reading as printed. Lacking the energy required for it, his subjective experience would have been that he could not read. He would have acted accordingly, and when asked why he did not continue to read, would have had to say truthfully that he *could* not.

If such psychoanalytic ruminations seem far-fetched, perhaps recalling an occasion when some emotional upset has left us so depleted of energy that we felt too exhausted to perform even simple everyday tasks may help us to understand how a child may feel unable to perform when drained of all energy. That by the next moment, at recess, he may feel full of vigor does not invalidate the phenomenon; on the contrary, it may add credence to it. The boy may be convinced that on the playing field he can display his mastery—a demonstration of adequacy he needs particularly badly at this moment because of the defeat in intellectual matters he has just suffered. Thus the need to compensate for a defeat in cognitive activities combines with the conviction of success in motor ones and induces the organism to replenish the ego with energy so that it will succeed in the different endeavor. This energy had to be allocated previously to the repression of anger at the sisters, a repression that had to be maintained as long as the ego's activities were directed to something connected with them—i.e., reading about sisters. But as soon as the ego concentrated on other activities, such as sports, the boy felt equal to his sisters, if not superior to them.

Despite the desirable results of viewing misreadings with sympathy and understanding, and the unfortunate consequences of rejecting them critically, errors in reading are consistently ascribed to cognitive deficiencies only. It happens in every beginners' class, every school day, as the most casual observation of what goes on in the teaching of reading shows. True, it does not happen to each child personally, not every day. But it happens to him as an experience, since he is exposed many times each day to the teacher's correcting with a critical attitude the misreadings of some children. While he is taking this in, the child does not consciously understand all the psychological ramifications for him of what is going on. Subconsciously it nevertheless leaves an impression, because it was not so long ago that *he* was the one who had made some error in reading through which he expressed his dominant inner feelings, and the teacher through her critical behavior had demonstrated that what was truly important to him had no place in his reading. This by itself has a serious impact, which is further aggravated by the new reader's insecurity.

The worst aspect of all this is the monstrous degree to which teacher and child are at cross-purposes, whereas the development of his ability to read and, even more important, to enjoy reading, requires most of all that their intentions be closely aligned. By correcting what the child has done to project meaning into a story he is reading, the teacher convinces him that she disapproves of his investing a story with personal significance. Her correcting him not only makes him doubt, but in some cases makes him despair of, his ability to read, and it also causes him to lose hope that he can find something of personal importance in a story. And this happens when he is in a developmental stage in which stories can acquire meaning at first only on a personal, egocentric level.

As we have seen, positive acceptance of a child's misreading as meaningful can and often does lead to a spontaneous second reading of the text as printed. This happens in line with his developmental stage, which is one of transition from egocentric to abstract thought. After having first become able to appreciate a story through a highly personalized reading of it, he is able to move on to a more objective acceptance of the story's content.

Frequently it is not the personal interest a story arouses that leads to the error, as was true in the Cinderella example, but, on the contrary, the blandness of a text. A story that fails to hold the child's attention induces his mind to wander away from the text to whatever preoccupies it. If then, by chance, one word of such an uninteresting story connects with deep personal concerns, this may result in a misreading or, as in the following example, in blocking. The reason is that there seems no way for the child to connect the depth of feelings aroused by the word and the thoughts it evokes with the general vacuity of the story's content.

A boy, the son of a culturally deprived family, was notoriously difficult to handle, although when occasionally he concentrated, he read quite well. His explosive behavior often interfered with schoolroom learning, especially reading. At recess he performed dangerous feats on the play equipment, picked fights, or got into trouble in some other way. Yet once in a while, in class, he would settle down and conscientiously attend to the task. His teacher, recognizing his intelligence and that something was interfering with its operation, wanted to know how to deal with him better. She asked us to try to increase his attention span and encourage him to concentrate more. To this end, we decided to read with the boy in the hope of getting him to gain some pleasure from reading, assuming that he would then read more frequently.

From the start it seemed clear that it was not inability to decode that was the source of his difficulty, but rather that the boy found no interest in reading, which made it difficult for him to attend to it while satisfaction was easily available to him through his physical pursuits in the playground. Even when he read accurately, he did so slowly and laboriously, concentrating on one word at a time, rather than trying to comprehend a whole phrase or sentence. He seemed to pay no attention to the content of the text, but treated reading as a technical exercise that held no promise of interest or enjoyment. The value of reading, now or later in life, was not something he was able to consider. He gave the impression that while success as such was important to him, reading was not. In contrast, being the star of the playground held great attraction, especially on those days when he had done poorly during the reading lesson. Thus there seemed some connection between defeat in one area and need for success in another.

He was supposed to read a story in *Enchanted Gates* (a California State reader) about a dog named Hound-pup, a basset puppy whose ears are so long that he falls over them. By reading the story with the boy, we tried to make it a worthwhile experience. In the story, Old Red, an aging basset, tells Hound-pup to eat his dinner every day and then look at himself in the shiny dish and bark three times—then his ears will grow smaller. And indeed, as Hound-pup grows bigger, his ears don't look as big. Hound-pup asks Old Red how looking in the dish and barking made this happen. Old Red answers that it wasn't the looking or the barking that made Hound-pup bigger, but eating his dinner, and the barking helped him learn to bark like a grown-up dog. The implication is that the dog's ears only looked smaller because they were smaller in proportion to the rest of its body, which had grown.

This could be an interesting story, since it touches upon the problem of reality versus appearance—an issue of great importance in cognitive development that holds some fascination for intelligent first graders who at the age of seven (the boy's age) are beginning to master the difference between reality and appearance.[15]

Unfortunately, and typically for stories in basic readers, instead of elaborating on the issue of the size of the ears in relation to the rest of the dog's body, and with it on the problem of appearance versus reality, the story then drops what might have aroused the child's interest and in the most pedestrian manner tells that eating is necessary for the puppy to grow—something of which every first grader is boredly aware. That barking helps the puppy learn to bark like a big dog is simply untrue, as the child well knows. He resents being expected to believe that what in fact is the result of the maturation of a bodily function is due solely to exercise. In maintaining that this is the case, the story offends the child by assuming that he is less intelligent than he is, or that he may be amused at the idea that the puppy is so stupid as to believe this.

After he had finished the story, we asked the boy what it was all about. He answered that the dog's ears got smaller through its looking in the dish and barking, an answer probably due partly to the story's being too silly for him to pay it any attention and partly to make fun of us, who expected him to find something of interest in such a story. When he realized from our reaction that we did not expect him to believe such nonsense, he said that the dog got bigger by eating.

Having found out that we agreed with him that the way the

---

[15] See Karen Zelan, *Facilitation of Conservation in Atypical Learners,* unpublished doctoral dissertation, University of California, Berkeley, 1974.

story was written was an insult to his intelligence, he went on to answer correctly the questions asked in the exercises accompanying the text, and his reading became more fluent as he did so. His greater ease in reading proved the validity of teachers' conviction that comprehension of a story helps with its subsequent reading, or reading about it. However, teachers mistakenly define "comprehension" as understanding only the overt meanings that can be gained from a correct reading of a text, ignoring the kind of comprehension by which a child, drawing on outside information, finds a story untrue to facts, lacking in interest, or uncolloquial.

In talking with the boy, we missed the opportunity to find out whether his first reply had been made to mock us, who, obeying the teacher's request, had read such a ridiculous story with him, or whether he had been too annoyed by the story to pay it any attention or give any thought to what it told, and therefore had said whatever came to his mind. If so, his silly statement that the dog's ears got smaller by means of its looking in the dish and barking was a subconscious but appropriate reaction to the silliness of the story.

Fortunately we were better attuned to considering what inner processes could be shaping his responses when doing the exercises accompanying the text with him. He answered all the questions with one exception, where he blocked completely on a key word. The phrase, "What you may tie up your dog with," was followed by the choice of words: "rope," "rabbit," "kitten." While reading all other words correctly, including the three choices, the boy blocked on "tie." He then seemed to guess at the word and came up with "tease." So we said that if the word were "tease," either "rabbit" or "kitten" could be correct choices, meaning that these are "What you may tease your dog with." He continued to block. We then speculated aloud that perhaps the difficulty was that he would not want to do such a thing as the sentence said to his dog, phrasing our comment in a way that implied his blocking was deliberate.

In sudden reaction, he said with deep feeling: "My dog got run over." Now his blocking when asked to read about tying up a dog made sense, and we replied that if he had done to his dog what the sentence said, perhaps his dog wouldn't have been run over. As if in reply, he immediately read the whole phrase correctly and matched it up with "rope." All subsequent reading of "tie" and "tied," words that appeared several times more, was done correctly, without hesitation or difficulty.

It seems clear that the rather silly story about a dog getting bigger had reminded the boy of the tragic fate of his dog, which stood in stark contrast to the superficially happy view of dogs presented in the text. Talking about his dog having been killed—a fate that would have been prevented had it been tied down—released the feelings which this story about dogs had activated in him; freed to some degree of their pressure, the boy could do the exercises fairly easily and successfully. What was a more significant and highly gratifying consequence of this intervention was that the boy then spontaneously decided to continue reading and to make up his own reading exercise, probably to assure himself that he could control the content and therefore make it safe. His exercise consisted of a crossword puzzle using the names of musical instruments. He worked hard on it until recess, and when told he had done a good job, his characteristic frown melted, and he grinned happily.

What happened here shows that a positive intervention requires no information that is not readily available. Our intervention was the consequence of the supposition that there must be powerful reasons for a child's blocking on a word (or sentence), and that these are somehow always connected with what such words arouse in him. Our assumption is that subconsciously the word is recognized, because otherwise it could not produce a block. This was all we needed in order to respond to the boy's using a substitution in a way that freed him from what had been inhibiting his ability to read correctly. To experience relief of the emotional pressures that had led to the blocking was so gratifying for him that, all on his own, he began to find pleasure in improving his reading skills. Even more remarkable, he also acted on what he felt was necessary for making learning tasks acceptable to him: his great need to assert himself and his resistance to adult-set tasks, which showed in all his behavior, made it difficult for him to learn from lessons assigned to him. So he arranged his own exercise to develop his reading ability by constructing a crossword puzzle.

What is even more significant—suggesting that some important inner processes had taken place in the boy, which had strengthened his ego so that he could both work better and play more socially—was that right after finishing work on his crossword puzzle, he went out for recess and there for once engaged in neither hostile nor provocative behavior. Satisfied with his academic success, he could be at ease with himself in the playground. His prowess established in reading, he had no need to demonstrate his mastery defensively by bossing others.

CHAPTER 8

Errors That
Promote Literacy

Any reading difficulty—a blocking, neologism, or some other form of misreading—can either lead to a fuller comprehension of what is involved in literacy or become an impediment to achieving it. It depends on how the teacher handles the difficulties the child encounters as he tries to read. Neologisms are particularly instructive in this respect.

A neologism camouflages those thoughts and sentiments that a person feels he should keep hidden. But neologisms often show a fine, though idiosyncratic, sensitivity to the possibilities inherent in language for expressing one's true feelings. In a way, neologisms point both backward and forward—backward to the small child who has not yet mastered language sufficiently, and so makes up his own words and sentences, and forward to the poet's feelings for the subtleties of language, which convince him that no available words fully express his meaning, so that he too must make up new words or word combinations that often capture the reader with their originality, appropriateness, and succinctness, and thus enrich the language. In both cases, neologisms are original language creations.

There is a booklet in the SWRL (Southwest Regional Laboratory for Educational Research) series[1] that tells of a mon-

[1] This series attempts to teach reading in kindergarten; the assumption is that a controlled phonics text with humorous stories and pictures

key walking on stilts. The monkey eventually climbs a tree and sits on a branch from which the stilts (which have shoes on them) hang down. A lion and a snake sit under the tree, notice the stilts, become frightened, and start to run away. Suddenly their fear abates, and they watch the monkey fall from the tree; yet neither from the text nor the pictures is it at all clear why the animals became afraid and started to run away nor why their fear suddenly abates. Most children reading this story thought that the animals were angry, not scared. It gave them a feeling of frustration, because they knew that they didn't understand the story's content; their interpretations, in light of what they had read correctly, made no sense to them. The tragedy of this situation is that the children cannot recognize that the text is misleading and tend to blame their lack of understanding on themselves.

Part of the difficulty with the readers in this series is that their texts are so truncated and condensed as to introduce only a few words at a time to children who are beginning to read. But then the plot of each story should be equally simple, or at least very clear; there must be no ambiguities in the pictures that are not explained in the text—the text ought to support the story content as depicted in the pictures. When it doesn't, the child concludes that the written word is not really very important to understanding, since the pictures tell their own story.

One very bright kindergarten child was having difficulty understanding this so-called story about the monkey on stilts. The last sentence is "What fun!" Instead, the child read "What fail!" The word "fun" had appeared three times previously, and

---

offers an inducement to children to read. The series was used in "follow-through" programs designed to accelerate the learning of minority children who had been exposed to an intensive and carefully planned nursery school curriculum. These follow-through classes were typically heterogeneous, in terms of ethnicity and social class, as a result of the busing policy that had been introduced a few years earlier.

she had read it correctly every time; obviously she knew and could read it easily. The phrase "What fail!" not only isn't a colloquialism but makes no obvious sense and the child knew this, as indicated by her puzzled expression. Her puzzlement at what she had read aloud showed that as soon as she spoke the word "fail," she realized something was not quite as it should be. Having had many stories read to her, and having read some simple ones herself, she might have expected that the last sentence would sum things up. But as far as she could understand, there was no fun and nothing funny in the story, hence "What fun!" did not sum it up. "What fail!", though it didn't sound right, summed it up better. If she had been more sure of her ability to judge what she had just finished reading and better able to express herself directly, she might have added: "This is stupid!"

As happens so often in cases of puzzling misreadings and slips of the tongue, mixed emotions find expression in them. Clear and direct sentiments do not lead to misreadings unclear in their meaning. "What fail!" is a neologism that gives voice to very complex feelings, while at the same time it hides their exact nature. "What a failure!" for "What fun!", which also would be a misreading, would not be a neologism, since it would be using common idiom in grammatically correct form. When misreadings take the form of neologisms, it is often because unconsciously the person wishes both to reveal and to conceal, either from others or from himself, or most likely from both. For example, a five-year-old such as this girl would find it difficult to call the story her teacher has asked her to read a failure. She may find it easier to see herself as a failure, although she may not wish to say so aloud in front of teacher and the other children. Misreading "What fail!" reveals her feelings, while at the same time it conceals her thoughts about whose failure it really is.

In actuality, this child was truly confused and could not make up her mind: Is it the story that makes no sense, or is it me who cannot make sense of it? It takes a very determined person—much more determined than any beginning reader can possibly be—to try to ascertain through a rereading whether the story, or she herself, is the failure. To find herself in such a bewildering situation suggests to a beginning reader that giving up the enterprise is the easiest solution, because reading, instead of clarifying things, only confuses her; trying to read has only landed her in trouble.

These are natural responses unless the teacher assures the child that although what she read aloud was not what was printed in the booklet, it was a most appropriate response to what her experience had been; that her misreading shows not only that she is a good and intelligent reader but—what is much more difficult—that she is also a critical evaluator of what she is reading. The teacher in this case, however, gave no such assurance, and what actually happened was that this very bright child, who had approached her reading lesson eagerly, stopped reading altogether, puzzled and discouraged.

When handled positively, however, neologisms can encourage the child to explore language further and in depth, and so become a bridge to literacy. A somewhat older girl, a third grader, chose to read *Black Beauty* because, as she said, "I love it." Understandably, she much preferred it to all the textbooks available in her classroom. Her remark shows that reading a truly engaging story can arouse deep feelings, even in beginning readers. The girl could learn to read from such an attractive book because her teacher thought children ought to be able to choose the books they read, and so while textbooks lay on their shelves, most children went and borrowed books from the school library, or read books the teacher brought to class.[2]

The girl, who identified with Black Beauty, was very in-

[2] In this class, the children were required to spend an allotted period each day on reading silently as well as out loud to the teacher, although they were free to choose what they read.

terested in such matters as the horse's relationship to its mother when a baby and the kind way in which the owner of the horses treated animals. This story draws the reader into a whirlpool of events, each scene heightening the tension, until one chapter ends with a black horse (not Black Beauty) breaking its leg and having to be shot. In reading this chapter, the girl came to the following passage:

> Then someone ran to our master's house and came back with a gun; presently there was a loud bang and a dreadful shriek, and then all was still; the black horse moved no more.

The girl made only one substitution in what, for a third grader, was a difficult passage, as she read "deadful" for "dreadful." Asked what had happened, she answered: "The horse was shot because it had a broken leg." "Since the horse was shot," we replied, "its shriek certainly was deadful." In reaction to this, she looked at the text and said: "Oh, no, it says 'dreadful.'"

Completely engrossed in a story she understood well, the girl had spontaneously and without knowing it invented the neologism "deadful," which accurately sums up what she had just read. When given credit for what she had read, although "deadful" was a non-word, on her own she successfully brought to bear her good cognitive abilities to read what was printed. As a result, she was left with the feeling that her mastery of language was so good that she could even invent new words which—while not acceptable English and thus to be discarded—were more expressive than those used in the book she liked so much. All this made the girl feel good about herself and gave her a new view of language, and it would enhance (if that were possible) her interest in the story she was reading.

"Tigger" is not exactly a neologism, since it is known as one of the animals in the *Pooh* stories. Still, when the character

Tigger was so named by Christopher Robin, the hero of the *Pooh* stories, or rather, by their creator, A. A. Milne, it was a new invention—a neologism—signifying in one word the ferociousness of a tiger, the playfulness of a kitten, and the lovable harmlessness of a cuddly toy. It was used in this sense by the girl who through her misreading transformed a story's threatening beast into a harmless stuffed animal. The teacher, attempting to find out more about the error and to have the child recognize it, engaged her in a discussion about the story and tigers, but the child insisted that "Tigers are small." If she had said, "Tiggers are small," there might be some justification for the view that it was a phonics error—indeed, she might really have thought that the text said "Tigger," and that Tiggers are small. But she clearly *said*, "Tigers are small," though she *read* "Tigger."

The teacher, not recognizing the discrepancy between what the girl had read and what she had said, continued to think that the mistake was a phonics error—that the child thought the *i* in "tiger" was a short *i*, not knowing that the single *g* makes it a long *i*. The teacher was oblivious to the fact that the context in which the misreading took place made it most unlikely that the mistake had a phonetic basis. This mistake occurred in the passage: "On a tall weed, a mantis waits, too. He is as dangerous as a tiger to the other jungle insects."[3] Since the girl had read correctly all words in the sentence (including "dangerous") until the word "tiger" appeared, it seems reasonable to assume that it had been the dangerous character of the animal that prompted the change to "Tigger."

The teacher again went over the content of the story, say-

[3] The story ("City Park Jungles," *Round the Corner*, a Bank Street Reader, 1966) likens the animals in a city park to those in the jungle. Since, according to the story, the animals living in the city are insects, they are small as compared to those of the jungle, and so the girl may have been thinking of the small city "tiger" rather than of the real, large, jungle tiger. But in preferring to think of Tigger, she was also expressing the wish to read and talk about safe, undangerous animals.

ing that the city park animals were small, but that the animals of the jungle—tigers, for instance—were large. At that, the child again insisted that tigers are small. The teacher, growing annoyed at the girl's obstinacy, now said for the first time quite strongly that both the girl's reading and her statement about tigers were wrong. At this point the girl caved in, feeling that the teacher was no longer trying to help her make up her own mind but was insisting that she see things the teacher's way, no matter what. Defeated in her purposes by the teacher's authority, the girl sullenly repeated the teacher's words, saying, "Tigers are large."

The misreading, as well as the girl's insistence that tigers are small, did not reflect a difficulty in comprehension; on the contrary, they were the consequence of accurate comprehension. The story as written had aroused her anxiety. In order to be able to read most of the sentence without error, the girl had to deal in some way with the discomfort it had created. This she did by changing the animal from a dangerous to a lovable one. But when the teacher tried to force a correction both in reading and in comprehension by talking about tigers, the girl was no longer able to make the story safe by thinking of Tigger and had to distort reality by insisting that tigers are small animals. Rejection of the child's way of mastering her anxiety forced a stubborn denial of reality, which exasperated the teacher and prompted her to say the child was wrong.

This example illustrates once more the destructive discrepancy inherent in the way reading is being taught: when

---

And as far as she was concerned, she might take her Tigger to a city park, but a tiger would not be there.

It is equally possible that the idea the story was trying to convey— that a park is like a jungle—was scary to her; it might have made her fearful of going to the park. So she tried to deny it by maintaining in her mind that the story did not really mean to speak of animals like tigers, but of toys like Tigger.

the child gets really involved in what she is reading, she becomes torn between concentrating on decoding words and comprehending the story and reacting to it. The child is supposed to learn to read by immersing herself in a story, so that reading will be interesting and enjoyable, but if she does so, she is brought up sharply by the teacher's insistence on correct decoding. The tiger in this story was mentioned only as a stand-in for—or by comparison with—the real animal, the mantis, so what was compared with a tiger in the story was indeed small. While the child in her mind was still living in the story, the teacher paid no attention to what the story evoked in her and insisted on correct decoding. This yanked the child rudely out of the story world into the reality of school, with its insistence on correct decoding. Adults can switch easily from fantasy to reality, particularly when they don't seriously enter the fantasy world. But children cannot do that. Deep down, it makes them very angry with teacher, school, and reading that at one moment they are asked to enter the fantasy world of the story and take it seriously, only to be required at the next moment to ignore the fantasy and take nothing but the decoding of a word seriously.

When an error is brought to the attention of the person making it, whether child or adult, often his first reaction is to deny or doubt that he has made the error; and when such attempts fail, the second reaction is to deny the error's meaning. The girl who insisted that her reading the word as "Tigger" was correct, and then that tigers are small, had both these reactions. Schoolchildren, as soon as the teacher corrects what they have done, feel bad about not achieving—and every error implies a failure. But this girl's insistence was also partly a wish to conceal the meaning inherent in her error. Yet despite herself, even while supporting the error, the child revealed what was preoccupying her. In this case, her insistence that tigers are small had the purpose of defending her against the recognition that she might have read "Tigger" for "tiger" because she was afraid of large wild animals; nonetheless, it revealed the nature of her concern.

The girl was very satisfied with having read "Tigger" for "tiger," and it was indeed a clever solution. Not only did it permit her to read the rest of the text correctly, it also allowed her to enjoy the story. What might in the long run have been even more important was that her misreading, if accepted instead of corrected, could have convinced her of the safety of reading: "I have within myself the resources needed to make reading safe for me. Hence I do not need to approach new reading with anxiety about what fear it may create in me."

When the teacher, instead of merely correcting a child's error, gives recognition to the importance of the feelings that led to its being made, the result is usually that the child laughs, agrees, or in some way acknowledges that the error represents something of significance—often thus divulging more of his preoccupations. Having to some degree dealt with his feelings, the child is then freed to attend to the text. While questions or other interventions—such as asking the child to sound out the word in an effort to have him correct the error—are often met with resistance, a statement which indicates acceptance that the error was made for good reasons relieves the child. If a suggestion is offered as to why an error *may* have been made, often the child either agrees with the interpretation or amends it so that it becomes more accurate, and then proceeds to deal easily and realistically with the task at hand. This can happen even when it is not just a matter of misreading one word, but a total blockage of all reading.

In one instance, a girl found herself in an impasse that resulted in a combination of substituting and blocking. She was reading in *Sullivan Storybook No. 9a, Kitty and James* (New York: McGraw-Hill, 1967) the poem "The Fancy Dress Ball." The first two lines are: "In this forest a dragon lives. But let's not shake or shiver." The girl substituted "look" for "shake," but after the following "or," she could not go on; she blocked on "shiver," claiming to be unable to read.[4]

Without indicating that the child had substituted a word for the one used in the text, or saying anything about her claim to be unable to read, the teacher observed that when confronted with a dragon, most of us would not want to look at it. Although nothing else was said, in response to this remark the girl spontaneously reread without error the beginning of the second line, "But let's not shake." There she stopped, still unable to read "shiver."

Acceptance of her desire not to look at something scary was sufficient for the girl to be able to accept what was printed on the page. It was no longer important to change it, since she had received the assurance that her wish not to look in such a situation was readily understandable; far from being wrong, it was what most people would do. It seems reasonable to assume that the teacher's saying that most people would prefer not to look at a dragon—paraphrasing what the child had misread—not only established a common bond between teacher and child but clearly separated both of them from the hero of the story. With this separation, it became possible for the girl to read things about the child in the story. As the girl's behavior shows, this process of separation from the main figure of the story made it possible for her spontaneously to correct her misreading. All that was needed was a statement that implied: It is perfectly all right for you to feel differently from the way it is told in the story.

Why, then, did the girl continue to block on "shiver"? Since she did not misread this word, the teacher could not show ac-

---

[4] This, incidentally, may serve as an illustration (if one more is needed) of how easy it is to find support for one's preconceived notions if one explains a child's behavior in line with them. If we assume that a child becomes panicky and subsequently blocks solely because of having made a mistake, we could view the girl's inability to go on reading after having read "look" instead of "shake" as the consequence of her anxiety about having made an error.

ceptance of her substitution. When a child blocks altogether, one must consider the context in response to which the blocking happens, or certain characteristics of the child's experiences, and how these intermesh with what she is blocking on.

The teacher had observed that this girl was very timid, particularly in interactions with older or bigger children. In an effort to open up the subject, the teacher asked the girl what she did when scared. Fortunately, the girl had a good relationship with the teacher, whom she had known for nearly two years (she was in the first grade of a K-1 class), and so she felt free to be honest about her feelings. Her ready reply was: "Hide." In saying this, she made clear that to be told not to shake is of no help if one is scared; what is needed is some action that makes one safe, such as hiding.

She felt comfortable disagreeing with what was printed, because from the teacher's reaction to her misreading she knew that the teacher was concerned about her, and not solely about her temporary inability to decode. Her conviction that what the poem suggested was unacceptable (not shaking or shivering) proves once more that she had comprehended what was printed, but that the idea it expressed was experienced as unnatural and unacceptable.

Since the girl's response, "hide," suggested that she wanted to take some evasive action rather than stand and suffer, as demanded by the text's admonition not to shake and shiver, the teacher asked her what the two of them could do, now that she had been able to read the first of the two offensive words so well but was still unable to go on reading. Animatedly the girl answered, "Let's find out if it's a good dragon, or a bad one!" So they read a later part of the poem, from which it became clear that this was a friendly dragon. Reassured that she did not need to be afraid of what might happen later on, the girl could then read "shiver" and read well from there on.

This girl's behavior demonstrates what reality testing is all about. It is one of the most important ego functions, particularly when it deals with possibly dangerous situations. Since the content of the text is potentially threatening and the child does not know what else will happen in the story, the ego is called upon to deal with the problem. In this case, the teacher encouraged the child's ego to function spontaneously by asking her what she would like to do. In response, the girl came up with an entirely reasonable solution.

Teachers may find it hard to accept that the content of apparently bland texts can be threatening or cause anxiety. Year after year they have read stories to children about dragons; the idea of meeting a dragon in print has become an everyday event to them. But not so to children. They respond to texts very differently. If a dragon appears to the story's hero, the child feels that what to him is a real dragon is being encountered by a child just like him; so he might encounter one too. Only a very rare teacher, after reading such stories for years, can remember what her reactions to dragons were when she was a child; most teachers no longer respond to a story's emotional impact, and so forget how deep an emotional impression such texts can make on children.

Achieving such an insight is greatly facilitated by viewing misreadings not as errors but as carriers of potentially significant information. No speculation about why the child might be afraid of large creatures, or more specifically of a dragon, was necessary. It was only necessary to stimulate her to use her own resources to do something reasonable and appropriate about her reluctance to read. Since the blocking was intimately bound up with what she was reading, the most natural method of reality testing was through reading: because the dragon was evoked through reading, reading more about the dragon was the logical solution.

At first, the girl had not wanted to look. When she gave up the defensive maneuver of not looking and read, "Let's not shake," she accepted that a fear reaction might be appropriate. Then the only way to be safe was to hide—from the rest of the poem, which she did by declaring herself unable to read. She could not expose herself to what she feared might create unmanageable anxiety. Once she had made sure that there was no reason for such anxiety, she no longer blocked.

She then read the rest of the poem quite well, but continued to misread one word consistently: she always substituted "fantastic" for the printed word "fancy," which appears several times in the poem describing the costumes of the animals that come to the dragon's fancy dress ball. This was a misreading the teacher could easily accept and she conveyed her acceptance to the child by saying that "fantastic" described the events very well. At that the girl reread the lines correctly. Some need for reassurance may have remained, even after she had learned that the dragon was a friendly one. If so, she now may have tried to derive that reassurance from the idea that it was safe to read the poem because its content was a fantasy—fantastic, not real. Fancy costumes, about which the poem spoke, exist in reality, but something fantastic is clearly unreal. Reassured by the teacher that the poem was indeed fantastic, the girl no longer needed to express this through her misreadings and could read "fancy" as printed.[5]

Blocking is much more serious than a mere substitution of one word for another, because when he blocks, the child is giving up entirely: the material or what it arouses by association is so threatening that he must conceal his thoughts not just from others but, more importantly, from himself. If this happens, unless the teacher's intervention succeeds, the child cannot continue reading. However, if the teacher empathizes with the child so that he feels his inability to read is considered

[5] It is also possible that the child was thinking of the colloquial expression, "That's fantastic!", which connotes something outstanding, as in a "fantastic dress," clearly a thought in line with "fancy costumes." If this were the correct explanation of the misreading, then it would be similar to those described by Goodman as synonym substitutions—Kenneth Goodman, *op. cit.*

a significant expression of his feelings, the child can usually resume reading.

A very energetic, assertive, almost pugnacious boy was reading a story about a dog and cat fighting ("The Cat's Yard," *My City*, a Bank Street Reader.) This story is about a cat that lives alone in what looks from the pictures like a yard in the city. The cat guards its territory fiercely, especially against a dog, and there are some pictures showing vicious fighting between the two animals. The boy blocked on the word "fight," pronouncing only the "f" sound, and was unable to go on with the lesson after that.[6] He had come to the passage: "The dog barked. He turned to fight." The teacher tried to help him sound out the word—in fact, was pleased that he sounded out the initial *f*. The boy continued to block. She defined the word for him, all to no avail; he only became more stubbornly resistant. The teacher finally began to talk about the content, saying that perhaps the boy couldn't read about the two animals because it might remind him of what children do. Then the boy said, somewhat sheepishly: "It's what I do with my sister all the time." In saying this, he was suddenly able to read the word "fight." He did not substitute any word for "fight" because he could not think of any compromise between his need to fight with his sister and his anxiety about it—the anxiety having been aroused by a text with pictures vividly depicting a fierce fight.

[6] This particular story is atypical of the Bank Street Readers in that this series, unlike the Sullivan books, contains pictures that are generally quite bland. The pictures accompanying "The Cat's Yard" are suggestive of a wild, angry fight between the cat and dog. Since the Bank Street Readers were the only texts used in this class, the boy was not accustomed to seeing such pictures, at least not in school. The story probably aroused stronger feelings than usual in this boy, who was prone to fighting. His blocking on "fight" may thus have been due to a combination of the problem the child brought to the lesson—his tendency to fight—and the book's unusually vivid depiction of violently aggressive animal behavior.

The boy's blocking on the word "fight" is clear indication that subconsciously he had read it correctly; otherwise, the blocking would not have begun with this particular word. His being able to sound out the first letter, *f*—as in many similar cases—is tantamount to his saying: "It is not lack of cognitive ability that makes it impossible for me to read this word, but emotional blocking, because if I did not know the letters, I would not know even the first letter." This teacher fortunately did not react to the blocking as a lazy attempt to avoid reading; she assumed that the content had aroused something in the child. Once she showed that she understood his dilemma, he could read the word. The discussion had helped him to understand that what had blocked him was not the text, but his feelings about his fights with his sister.

The girl's reading "Tigger" for "tiger" and the blocking on "fight" occurred in the same classroom and with the same teacher. Why did she handle matters so differently in these two cases? In conversations with us she had said that she believed errors in reading were the results of faulty comprehension. She therefore used discussion of the text as a way to help the child correct his misreadings. In the first case, the girl's statement that tigers are small suggested to the teacher that discussion of the story had not worked, because the child was deeply confused about reality. Such a distortion of reality was a challenge to her as a teacher; she felt she had to correct what she viewed as the child's misinformation and insist that it be replaced by a correct view of things. This is why she called what the child did wrong.

The boy who blocked on the word "fight" did not substitute another word in its place, so the teacher did not think he had misperceived reality; hence there was no need to set him straight by telling him he was wrong. She correctly surmised that he needed help with what the word aroused in him, and her view was validated by the success of her efforts. This teacher's error was to believe that a distortion of reality is always a sign of miscomprehension. Often—as was true in the girl's case—it is the consequence, rather, of an emotional reaction to a correctly apprehended experience.

How easily even total blockage can be relieved when its cause is brought to consciousness is demonstrated by what happened when a vivacious but anxious child was unable to continue reading a story about a bear that was trying to get some honey from bees (Dr. Seuss's *The Honey Hunt*). The teacher made no effort to have the girl sound out words or guess at them. Assuming that she knew how to read the story, but for psychological reasons could not, the teacher asked the child directly why she could not read this story, even though she had read stories just as difficult before. The girl's immediate answer was that she was afraid of bees, because in the past she had been stung by them. She then indicated how the text should read to make it easy and comfortable for her. She said: "I'd rather find honey at the store, because that way you wouldn't get stung." After that, she was able to continue reading, and did an especially good job of it, as if showing how appreciative she was of having been helped to master her reading block.

In trying out our methods, teachers often claim that for various reasons they cannot estimate what lies behind a child's misreading. They believe they don't have enough information, or that they aren't skilled in understanding unconscious motives, or that they can't understand the misreadings of many children simultaneously. Teachers are both right and wrong about these matters. They are right that uncovering unconscious content in the classroom would be difficult and problematic—but in fact this is not necessary, and often not desirable. What *is* necessary is a provisional acceptance of the word the child substituted for the one in the text, or in the case of blocking, understanding that the word or the topic of the story may be creating problems for the child. Such a response takes no longer, nor is it any more difficult, than a discussion of textual meanings—a procedure obviously acceptable to teachers since all good teachers use it.

Teachers deal daily with what the child likes to do; they recognize and take account of his strengths and weaknesses in intellectual and social skills, his special interests, certain basic facts of family life, and so on. Knowledge of these matters is all that is needed to make a tentative but educated guess as to why a child might misread or block. Competent teachers have sufficient powers of observation to judge what may be attracting or repelling a youngster at the moment he is reading, and to use such knowledge in dealing with several children simultaneously. Since most teachers can do this quite well, they are wrong to assume that they cannot respond to reasons for misreadings.

In helping a child correct a misreading, the first step is a recognition of the emotional appropriateness of what the child has done. The second step is to talk with the child about some aspect of his daily life that may seem pertinent. Children in the early grades are eager (if self-conscious) to reveal such information, as can be seen by their frequent willing and interested participation in "show and tell," "chat time," and the like.

Much can be achieved when a teacher takes advantage of information that is readily accessible to her and that she is comfortable in using. One third-grade girl was deeply preoccupied by her recent adoption, and by an important event in her new existence, having been taken for the first time in her life on a big family trip, which happened to be to Washington, D.C. The teacher was quite familiar with these facts, as the child had talked about them for days. The girl was reading a book about the Revolutionary War (*Six Silver Spoons*, by J. S. Lowrey), which tells of the children of an early American family who plan to travel to a shop to buy some silver spoons for their mother's birthday, and who meet up with Red Coats along the way. The girl read "red coach" for "Red Coats" every time these words appeared. The teacher at first thought this was a comprehension error—that the girl didn't understand who the Red Coats were. So she explained that "Red Coat" was a name given to the British soldiers, pointing to a picture that showed them in their red coats. When, nonetheless, the girl still continued to make the same error, the teacher concluded that there must be some other reason for it.

The substitution of "red coach" took on meaning when the teacher remembered the recent trip the girl had taken. The teacher commented that she knew the girl had gone on a trip to Washington, and asked if the child had eaten at a Red Coach restaurant (a well-known chain on the East Coast). The girl said she had, and began to talk excitedly about eating there, describing in particular detail the salad bar where one could help oneself to whatever and however much one wanted —a marked contrast to the deprived conditions of her life before her adoption. The child, as revealed by her misreading, wanted to read (talk) about her positive experiences at the Red Coach Inn, not about the threat the Red Coats posed for the children in the story. Moreover, she wished to change thoughts about domination by strangers, such as by the English Red Coats, into those about the deep satisfaction of being part of a real family of her own, which she had experienced so pleasantly in the Red Coach Inn. The teacher noticed that this ordinarily quiet and reserved child came to life while discussing what to her was a very pleasurable and significant event. Thereafter, when "Red Coats" appeared in the text—which happened four more times—the girl read the words correctly.

CHAPTER 9

Reversals and Other
Perceptual Errors

Reversals, to teachers and reading specialists, have become the models of perceptual errors. But reversals, as much as any other type of misreading, are neither random performances nor mere technical errors. With the exception of the rare cases of true dyslexia, normally when children make even the most common reversals, such as "was" for "saw," or vice versa, these are substitutions made for important psychological reasons, one of which is complete lack of interest in what they are reading.

It is astonishing that students of such reversals have paid little attention to the fact that the same children who reverse letters in reading use them correctly when speaking. This is because there is no need for a child to make reversals in his speech; if, out of some inner need, he should not want to say either word, he simply does not say it and uses other words as substitutes. But when he is learning to read, he is forced to say particular words as he reads aloud from a book. Then one way he can assert his needs or preoccupations—if and when they exist—is through a reversal of certain letters.

It is thought that children when they are learning to speak make errors by reversing letters because they do not hear, or don't hear clearly, the difference between words that sound similar, and that such errors are analogous to those made by older children learning to read. It is assumed that these reversals in speaking, especially in very young children, have to do with confusion in hearing the beginning and the ending consonants of syllables, which is why, for example, they might confuse the words "lemon" and "melon." When a two-year-old reverses these words, frequently substituting "melon" when it would be correct to say "lemon," the supposition is that she found it easier to remember the *m* in "lemon," since it is the last consonant of the first syllable of the word, and so said "melon" instead, which begins with an *m*.

If this assumption were correct, the same two-year-old ought to make reversals in her speech by also saying "lemon" for "melon." But in fact although both words were part of her vocabulary, she never substituted "lemon" for "melon." The reason was that the little girl had sucked on lemons, found them sour and not to her taste, and had rejected them; but she loved sucking the juice from melons. To make sure that the child knew the difference between the two fruits, she was asked the color of each, to which she answered that lemons are yellow and that melons are orange, pronouncing the names of the two fruits correctly and without difficulty. What on the surface might seem simply a linguistic confusion was actually the expression of a preference for one fruit and the rejection of the other. This is mentioned here not so much to make a claim for the etiology of all such confusions, but to warn against assuming automatically that such reversals and substitutions are due to either aural or visual deficiencies. Sometimes they may be, but often such substitutions and reversals are motivated by preconscious predilections, concerns, fears, or wishes.

Reversals in speech tend to diminish gradually as speech develops. This is so because the child's speech grows at a rapid rate from the age of two on, and soon when she wants to state a preference for melons over lemons, she becomes well able to do so and no longer needs to imply her preference through a reversal. At a later age, she can say: "I like melons better because they are sweet, and lemons are sour." As language develops, the child becomes increasingly able to give her inner needs an ever clearer verbal expression, not just in stating what she wants but also in voicing objections against what significant other people—usually her parents—want her to do. With her rejection of verbal statements by her parents, speech comes to be experienced by the young child as a medium for communication over which she can exercise her control.

By the time they enter school, most normal children speak correctly, without engaging in reversals in spoken language. The child's error-free use of words in his speech shows that he must be able, on some level, to recognize immediately when words are used incorrectly in reading; that is, if he would read for meaning. But there is one critical difference in the child's mind between the spoken and written word. As a speaker of language, he is active, the originator of what is communicated. As a novice in reading, he is supposed passively to accept what is given to him by an outside source, rendering it exactly as printed.

As a speaker, the child is well able either to say or not say what he deems appropriate, since the thoughts that shape his speech come solely from him, or are at least shaped by his personality as he reacts to the outside world. But when reading aloud, he must speak the thoughts of another person—ideas that do not necessarily mesh with his feelings or thoughts. Moreover, in basic readers the text is usually so empty that it doesn't seem to the child that it makes any difference what he utters in reading it. If reading, like speech, was taught for the information and enjoyment that can be gained from it and not for word recognition per se, it would be impossible for the child to make most of the reversals normally ascribed to perceptual deficiencies, because he would not be in the position of having to say or read something nonsensical.

For example, one child who consistently read "saw" for

"was," or "was" for "saw," did so (as we shall describe) not out of inability to read the words, but out of the need to reverse past and present. In his mind, "was" stood for the past, and "saw" indicated the present. In his speech, no such reversal occurred. Since it was he who determined what he said, in contrast to what he was required to read, he had no need to say "was" for "saw" or the reverse. He simply expressed what he wished to say. True, insofar as reading was concerned, in some sense he behaved as immaturely as did the two-year-old who said "melon" for "lemon." But he could not state, while reading a text imposed by author and teacher, that he was struggling to separate past and present, and so had to express this desire by reading "was" for "saw."

Speech and reading aloud being so closely connected, it is not impossible that the child beginning to read may unconsciously in some fashion connect the two and, however dimly, remember that in his earlier struggle with learning to speak, he had often substituted one word for another, one letter or syllable for another. He may also recall the experience of acquiring mastery over these substitutions in speech as he became better able to say what he had in mind. Despite these parallels, adults' reactions to a slip in speech are entirely different from their reacting to an error in reading by the beginning reader. Except for those of the very young child, we reject slips in speech as meaningless if we are not psychologically oriented, or we may ascribe them to valid psychological processes; we never explain a slip in speech as due to an inability to speak. Slips in oral reading are often explained away, like slips of the tongue, as meaningless; but, in addition, entirely different categories of explanations are added, such as the inability to decode and the many technical reasons for it.

As a result, the two related linguistic functions of talking and reading are treated very differently by those whom the child views correctly as teachers of these skills. The child is taught in school to concentrate on word recognition and on decoding letters and not to pay attention to the meaning of what he is trying to read (mainly because it has none). As a consequence, while the child is used to listening to what he is saying, he does not try to make any sense of what he is reading, having learned that it has none. That is why children in their reading come up with statements, or rather sequences of words, which they would never utter while talking to someone. They would never do it in their reading either, had they not been taught similar senseless sequences of words in their readers. The readers induce children not to pay critical attention to whether what they read makes sense. But even should a child try to fathom whether what he is reading makes sense, many sentences he is asked to read make equally good sense—or equally no sense—whichever way he reads some word.

There can be, and of course are, much more important and complex reasons for what are generally thought to be simple reversals: as an example, we can take the boy whose reading of "saw" for "was" proved not to be a reversal due to a perceptual deficiency or an inability to decode correctly, as is always assumed in such cases, but a deliberate effort to reverse present and past.

This boy was intellectually blocked to the degree that for several years he had been diagnosed as feeble-minded. As a young child he had been most severely abused: his alcoholic father had threatened repeatedly to mutilate him, had attacked him sexually, had held him out of a fourth-floor window threatening to drop him. For his safety he was finally removed from his home. In consequence of the severe traumas he had suffered, none of the several foster homes in which he was placed could manage him, nor could he learn in school. At last he came to the Orthogenic School, but even there for a long time his learning block persisted. When he eventually began to learn to read, he often read "saw" for "was," and vice versa, reversals that could readily be explained by his reading disability, educational retardation, lack of attention, and so on. But in truth it was the result of his understanding very well the difference between these two words, which was of greatest psychological importance to him.

His past often haunted him, particularly when his mind was not actively occupied with matters of great interest, or when something reminded him even only remotely of his past trials. Then vivid and extremely painful images of the abuse he had suffered appeared before his eyes and seemed to warn of present danger. After he had begun to learn to read, this tended to happen as he was looking at the page if the text did not hold his interest sufficiently to prevent these visions from occurring. Trying to read, but trying even harder to ban the vivid memories of past miseries, which seemed very present at the moment, he attempted to convince himself that they belonged permanently to the past; that is, he wished to tell himself that what he *saw* (in his fantasy) *was* now part of the past. When at such a moment he encountered the word "saw," he had to read it as "was."

Both words consist of the same letters; only two of them are transposed to change the meaning. Yet by doing this, he could use language symbolically to turn what he presently saw in his mind's eye into a past matter. At such moments, the boy's misreading had the purpose of convincing himself that he could relegate to the past what presently oppressed him. Here, once more, it must be remembered that words are symbols that stand for objects and events; thus, words are particularly suitable for expressing desires in symbolic form, or performing symbolic actions. Young children—particularly when for some reason their emotions are strongly aroused—take the symbols for what they symbolize, and think that if they manipulate words, they are also manipulating that which the words signify. The boy's reading of the word "saw" had a double symbolic meaning: by reading it backwards he expressed his desire to change a present experience into a past one; and by reading "was" for "saw," he changed a word that referred to a present experience into one that signified a past one.

Our sympathetic acceptance of his need to make this change offered relief, and over time this particular substitution became less frequent. However, in a parallel development, he began also to read "saw" for "was." He did so to give us a signal that he once more was seeing as present something that in fact was past, and needed help in overcoming the anxieties this created. Once fully assured that we understood the need out of which he engaged in these so-called reversals, and that we considered them meaningful and important, he began to read correctly at the same time that he finally dared to speak openly of what had happened to him, and how it still persecuted him in his mind: how often he saw what once was, and how much he desired that he would not be forced to read that people "saw" what he wished "was" in the past and finished with. When he read "was" for "saw," and vice versa, it was because at that moment he was under the sway of inner processes that did not permit him to read something that was contrary to them.

Traumatic events in this child's past life had forced him to reverse these letters regardless of the content of what he was reading. More often, reversals or other types of misreadings are caused by feelings which the text itself arouses in the child, emotions which have their origin either solely in the text's content, as was true when the girl could not comfortably read about tigers, or in thoughts aroused in the child by the content, as when the boy who was reading about dogs being tied up was reminded that his dog got killed.

One boy we observed misread by reversing m and n as he read "mane" for "name." The story ("The Dog That Barked at Midnight" in *Uptown, Downtown*, a Bank Street Reader) is about a dog that barked at a cat named Midnight. The child read: "The cat's mane is Midnight." In the context of the story, his reversal made no sense. On the other hand, he had previously and without hesitation read the word "name" correctly three times. The teacher had no idea why he misread "mane" for "name," but since the story was about a cat and a dog, she talked with all the children in the reading group about cats and dogs and how they behave toward each other, and invited them to tell what their experiences with these animals had been. At that, the boy said that his family's dog often killed cats and had once even devoured a cat, and he ended by saying that he was afraid the dog might bite him.

His substitution of "mane" for "name" seemed to reflect the wish that the cat should be some other animal, such as a lion, which would scare the dog. The child understood that a big feline animal with a mane could conquer the dog he was afraid of, could even destroy it, whereas a small feline pet called Midnight could not. Despite the similarity of n and m, the reversal hypothesis does not explain why the boy specifically chose to reverse the letters in "name" here but in no other context; that only becomes intelligible on the basis of his later remarks, indicating a specific response to something the story's content evoked in him. And it was an intelligent error, as it replaced one feline animal that could be defeated by the feared aggressor with another that could easily overcome the dog. The reason the boy misread here is probably because at this point in the story the animal is identified with a name. Subconsciously his mind may have run: "The cat's name should be lion, then it would be safe and the dog would be put in its place." He was well aware that the actual name in the sentence was not lion, so his wish that the cat was a lion made him read "mane" for "name."

There are as many different psychological reasons for what are viewed as perceptual errors as there are readers who make these mistakes, each induced to do so by something going on in his mind at the moment of reading that interferes with his conscious intention to read as printed. Another example can suggest the kind of psychological phenomenon which may account for such errors, suggesting that these have nothing to do with an inability to perceive letters.

Some kindergarten children were reading a story about a monkey who tries to sell a shell (*Sell the Shell*, a SWRL reader). This booklet, like others in the series, is a phonics-based reader, the major purpose of which is to teach discrimination between similar-sounding words—here between "sell" and "shell," that is, between "s" and "sh" words, which kindergarten children find difficult to differentiate. One girl read fairly easily and entirely correctly:

> Did Mit see the shell?
> I need the shell.
> See this shell.

and:

> See this sand. I will sell it.

but stumbled on reading:

> I will sell the shell.

In this sentence she first substituted "shell" for "sell" as she read, "I will shell . . ." and then stopped, recognizing that this wasn't right; she either knew that the word she had just read was not "shell," or she recognized that what she had read made no sense. So she reread the sentence, but now substituted for "shell" (a word she had read correctly in several preceding sentences) the word "sheet," reading: "I will sell the sheet." Since she had previously identified and read both "sell" and "shell" correctly, her substitution could not be the consequence of an inability to do so here. She had probably taken in the sentence and for some reason decided that selling the shell was not acceptable, at least not in the form the sentence demanded, which required her to say that it was she who would sell the shell. On the other hand, as her final reading showed, she did not deem it objectionable that she sell a sheet.[1]

Our speculation as to her reason for substituting "sheet" for "shell" would have had to end with the assumption that selling a shell was objectionable to her, and we would have been unable to guess why—of the various possibilities open to her in substituting a word beginning with "sh," she had selected "sheet"—had we not known that the girl had been introduced to the word "sheet" in another reader of this series, a book about a rat that covers a clean sheet with mud. With this information available, one may guess that her misreading expressed her feeling that she would not sell such a desirable object as a shell, but that she was willing and able to sell—i.e., get rid of—something like a dirty sheet.

Since her misreading had shown what she was ready to dispose of, we reacted by saying: "What you read would be a good way to get rid of the sheet." In immediate reaction, the girl read correctly: "I will sell the shell."

This speculative explanation of the misreading was supported by a discussion that had taken place earlier in the reading lesson. Several children, including the girl, objected to the monkey's intention of selling the shell. One child asked: "How come he doesn't want to keep the shell?" All the children were puzzled that the monkey, believing the shell to be valuable, wanted to sell it; they all preferred a pretty shell to any remuneration it could possibly bring. So while they comprehended what the story said, they didn't agree with it. And the children having just settled on the idea that they would not

[1] It was not that the girl failed to discriminate between "s" and "sh" sounds in the sentence "I will sell the shell." Had she been unable to discriminate between these two sounds, she might not have chosen to substitute for "shell" another word beginning also with an "sh" sound, such as "sheet." Her substitution reflects a correct discrimination between the two sounds. She substituted one word beginning with an "sh" sound for another also beginning with it because she wished to give the text a meaning different from that printed.

sell a pretty shell, the girl felt unable to say: "I will sell the shell."

The issues involved in selling a plaything are of vital interest to children of the age for whom these texts are written. But neither text nor teaching situation makes provisions for coping with this issue that the story raises. Instead, text and teachers focus solely on perceptual discrimination, convinced that it is more important than understanding the messages of the text—an attitude strongly reinforced by the guidelines laid down in phonics-based lesson plans.

The story (if it can be called that) and the girl's misreading raise the important problem of how stories for beginners ought to be phrased. It helps the child in his learning to read if he can project himself into a story's character, and he will do so anyway if the character appeals to him. So a good argument can be made for letting the characters speak about themselves in the first person. But as discussed previously, if a person has to say, "I will do this," as he reads a sentence aloud, he is being manipulated to assert something about himself. This is fine, provided that what he reads truly expresses what he would think, feel, or do. But correct reading becomes very difficult for the young child—who has a hard time anyway distancing himself from what he reads or says aloud to another person—if the text requires him to say something about himself that is unacceptable to him.

Thus, while it is psychologically sound to try to write texts for beginners so that they can closely identify with the main characters, doing so requires careful consideration as to whether what these main characters say or do is of such a nature that the child will wish to identify with them and their actions. In fact, these texts often create an inner conflict between the wish to identify and a child's inability to do so, given their vacuous content. If there is a good chance that the child cannot make his own the feelings, attitudes, or actions of a character, then it is much better not to write the story in the first person, so that the child is not forced to say that he would behave in a certain way that is actually odious to him.

To teach reading most effectively, a wide variety of methods should and could be used. But they should be used in order of importance, with reading for meaning taking precedence over all technical considerations, although these, too, have a significant place in reading instruction. Word recognition and word discrimination have to be taught, but they are best taught within a framework of meanings, and with the acknowledgment that the meanings the child spontaneously projects into what he is reading are at least as important for developing his literacy as those the text is trying to convey.

A first-grade girl, whose teacher felt strongly that phonics was the correct approach to teaching reading, was reading the story "Fishing with Mints" (*Sullivan Storybook No. 3B, The Land in the West* [New York: McGraw-Hill, 1966]). It tells about a boy, Ed, who tries to get a bag of mints away from a girl, Peg, by instructing her to put the mints on a fishing hook, which he then grabs from behind a bush. The vocabulary is controlled in the sense that most words have short vowel sounds that appear many times in the different words. In trying to read the story, the girl had difficulty with the children's names. The teacher assumed that this reflected a problem in comprehension and therefore talked about the fact that both are nicknames, standing for Peggy and Edward. To make the use of nicknames more acceptable, the teacher asked the child how she felt about her own. The girl said she didn't mind her parents using it, but preferred to be called by her full name in school. Thereafter she read "Peg" correctly every time it occurred.

However, she continued to misread "Ed." The teacher encouraged her to sound out the word, since an attempt to monitor comprehension had already been tried and in fact had led to the correct reading of "Peg." This teacher, like most others, taught reading by combining phonics with comprehension exercises, believing these to be the two best approaches, and especially effective when used together. So she became puzzled when the child still continued to misread despite the combined use of the two techniques.

The girl, in response to the phonics approach, began to read the boy's name as "Eed," which gave the impression that she thought the *e* was long. When told that it was a short *e*, she then read "It" for "Ed." So the teacher told her that the *e* in the word was the same sound as in "Peg," which she had previously read correctly. The child continued to substitute "It" for "Ed."

The teacher, who had become interested in, and in some measure familiar with, our view that trying to understand what a child expresses through a misreading may facilitate correct reading, decided that further drill on phonics would not work and that another approach was needed. Somewhat exasperated, she stated that even though the boy was fooling the girl, this still did not make him an "it." In response to this remark, which showed some recognition that calling the boy "It" had something to do with disliking him, or what he was doing, the child could come out with her feelings. She hit Ed's picture in the book vigorously and said that Ed was a naughty, naughty boy for fooling Peg, demonstrating that she could easily say "Ed," although she had been unwilling to read his name. Subsequently, she corrected her previous misreadings and read "Ed" without difficulty every time it appeared.

The story evidently had activated the girl's negative feelings about boys because it depicted a boy fooling a girl. She began to enjoy the story only when Peg discovers the trick, at which point she began to read easily, laughing because "Peg is smarter than Ed." She eagerly discussed the content of the text when it had to do with Peg catching Ed in his trickery.

Typically, phonics instruction—insistence that the child sound out the letters—takes the place of efforts to grasp meaning. Emphasizing phonics turns reading into a game with rules to follow in order to please the teacher, but robs it of meaning.

A third-grade boy had been exposed to the phonics approach and no other for the entire three or four years of his schooling. When he came across a word he didn't know, he quite seriously played the game of sounding out, with the result that he didn't comprehend the thought behind what he was reading, nor did he care to do so. He seemed totally bound up with the mechanics of letter sounds. As we read with him, intervening in some positive way when misreadings occurred, a glimmer of interest in the text began to appear. But what he did then was to make fun of phonics by taking it to ridiculous lengths. After we acknowledged that we knew what he was doing, he grinned knowingly and admitted that what he had just read, laboriously looking for the little words in big words, or paying attention to each and every syllable, "doesn't make sense." It didn't make sense because he was not reading for overall understanding.

Typically, he broke a word up into little words as he had been taught to do and read them that way, without the slightest attempt to say the word normally and without any hint that he knew what he was reading. He was reading the story of "The Donkey and His Band."[2] When the donkey meets the dog, the boy read "asleep" as though it were two words— the article "a" and the noun "sleep"—so that the sentence, "[T]he donkey came upon an old dog a sleep at the side of the road," made no sense. He substituted "low" for "loud" in the sentence: "The donkey called to the dog in a loud voice, 'Dog! Dog! Why do you sleep at the side of the road?'" In response to our remark that if the donkey called in a low voice, it wouldn't wake a sleeping dog, the boy immediately went back

[2] A simplified version of the Brothers Grimm's tale "The Bremen Town Musicians," in *It Happened One Day*. New York: Harper & Row, 1962.

to the word and stared at it quizzically, then correctly reread it. He suddenly began to read much better and with expression, demonstrating that he could comprehend the text if he wanted to and when it was communicated to him that its material held meaning. But he soon reverted to looking for the little word in the big word, and lost all interest in the story's content.

The word "join" gave him trouble. Recognizing the "in," he read "join" as "jo in." As always, he let it go at that, apparently satisfied with what was a non-word because he felt he had done what was expected of him. Since we had no idea what his difficulty with reading "join" was, for the moment we did nothing. The word appears in the sentence, "Join in my band. . . ." which is repeated as the various animals in the story are invited to do so.

After having read "jo in" twice in succession, the boy then read "join in" for "join." He thus demonstrated that "join" was a word he knew as part of his spoken vocabulary and that he knew its meaning. He had again concentrated his attention on the little word in the big word—the result of his years of phonics instruction—but this time had added "in." When told that "join in in . . ." makes even better sense, the boy scrutinized the text and read "join in" correctly for the first time.

By now, he had a clear idea of our intention. He then made a substitution that seemed to make fun of phonics instruction. In the sentence, "You sing well in the early morning," he read "airly" for "early." When simply asked, "Airly?," he grinned broadly and without even looking at the text, said matter-of-factly, "Early." We remarked that it took quite some ingenuity to substitute one vowel combination—*a, i*—for another, particularly since "airly" is not a word. From then on, he never made an error without spontaneously correcting himself.

Near the end of the story, in the sentence: " 'Yes, let us be gone before we are killed,' said another robber," the child read "other robbers" for "another robber," again noticing the smaller word "other" in "another." He stopped, puzzled, waited for a moment, then went back to the text and said: "Oh, it says 'another robber.'" He finished the story, about eleven lines, without a single error. When done, he said with pleasure: "I read a lot!"

Having stressed the value of treating misreadings positively, we ought to mention that for many reasons teachers seem to have difficulty in accepting the procedures we suggest. For example, teachers often had the experience that when they paid positive attention to errors, the general tendency to misread did not decrease—although particular substitutions were usually corrected, as predicted. This is because acceptance of misreadings emboldens the child to deal more creatively and assertively with meaning. Over the long run, we found that misreadings did decrease. Teachers might well—and actually did—question the point of treating mistakes as meaningful if the tendency to read correctly is not enhanced. They worried that if positive interest in misreadings encourages them, the tendency to make substitutions might become habitual and much more difficult to give up. But while substitutions did indeed become momentarily more frequent, correct reading was nonetheless the final result. Teachers had a hard time believing that an interim phase of making errors more freely would give way first to spontaneous correction, and then to reading as printed, but now for meaning and with interest—not as an empty exercise in decoding.

Every solution to a problem creates new problems. The best solutions are those that advance us to a point ahead of where we began. If the child by the end of the reading lesson becomes able both to express personal feelings and to read correctly, we feel that the long-run gain is well worth a temporary setback.

CHAPTER 10

An Example from the Literature

It may be objected that the examples on which this discussion has been based so far were selected because they fit so well into preconceived psychoanalytic notions on the meanings of errors, and therefore permit explanation along psychoanalytic lines. To meet such objections, we will consider a case of misreading described in detail by an educator who eschews psychoanalytic interpretations. Herbert Kohl, in searching for better methods of teaching reading to children with learning difficulties, chose it as his foremost typical example to demonstrate his own approach to the problem.[1] Kohl's report highlights the nearly universal concentration on current presumed general causes of reading difficulties, completely disregarding any possible personal reasons a child might have for making errors, and this on the part of an educator already committed to the idea that if a child makes errors in reading, the educator's most important task is to increase the child's confidence in his intellectual abilities.

In his book *Reading, How To*, Kohl speaks at some length about Lillian, a sixth grader suffering from a severe reading disability, who misread "mild" for "wild":

---

[1] Herbert Kohl, *Reading, How To*. New York: E. P. Dutton & Co., 1973.

I asked Lillian to read Maurice Sendak's *Where the Wild Things Are*,[2] one of my favorite diagnostic tools. The language is simple; the story is sophisticated; the pictures are interesting and a bit *scary*. . . . [The] story and the pictures . . . can lead to an interesting talk about *wildness* and the symbols Sendak uses to embody it.

Lillian read the first few pages with no trouble.[3] On about the fifth page she made a *simple* mistake, read *"mild"* for *"wild,"* *a word she previously had no trouble with. Immediately* after making the mistake, *she panicked* and read every other word on the page incorrectly. I noticed *she looked away from the page*, wrinkled her brow, and began to make sound associations that had nothing to do with the story. For example, she read "more" as "four" and then said "door," "boor," "coor" and finally trailed off into some inaudible sounds.

I asked her to stop for a while and rest. She began again and was fine until she made another mistake. Then *the same flight from the page occurred.*

The method Kohl employed to help her read was that "every time she made a mistake we stopped and talked about how she could check herself." Eventually "her tendency to panic disappeared," and she became able to read well. According to Kohl, Lillian had no problem with phonics; and "she knew how to read in a technical sense. Only she could not sustain herself for more than a few sentences. *She had no stamina* and didn't know how to help herself when she made

---

[2] New York: Harper & Row, 1963. (The italics in the following quotes are ours, not Kohl's.)
[3] There are only a few lines per page.

a mistake. . . . It turned out that *Lillian had a problem focusing her eyes* on the printed word."

The action that eventually helped her to read fairly well is described: "She found that slowly counting to five helped *calm her down* after a flight of sound associations."

Despite Kohl's belief that children are naturally bright and know what they are doing even when they have difficulties in reading, when it comes to their misreadings or blocking he makes no practical application of this theoretical conviction. Suddenly, children don't know how to help themselves and block because they have no stamina, or can't focus their eyes. But no evidence is presented to support either of these hypotheses.

The behavioral sign—looking away from what is printed on the page—is taken for its own cause, a piece of circular reasoning barely camouflaged by describing the symptom as "a flight from the page," caused by "a problem [in] focusing her eyes on the printed word." Extremely thin though this kind of camouflage is, it has been successful with numerous writers on the teaching of reading and with practically everyone who specializes in remedial reading. With such an explanation, any search for causes becomes unnecessary, so none are discovered and identified.

The assumption is particularly astonishing in this case because Kohl accurately observed that the girl looked away from the page. From our own experience we know that when we look away from something, we do it for one of two reasons: either we don't want to see what we are looking at, or we want to see something else. We do not look away because of an inability to focus, because we have to refocus immediately anyway. Since Kohl gives no indication that Lillian looked at anything else, we can dismiss the idea that her attention was distracted. The only possible conclusion is that she did not want to see what she was looking at. Yet this conclusion is not reached by Kohl because of his *a priori* conviction that a child can have no reasonable motive for not wanting to read or for misreading; thus, such failures must be due to some cerebral defect, such as the inability to focus.

As for Lillian's having no stamina, most of us have enough to achieve what we wish to achieve or endure what we think important to endure, but very little, or none, for whatever we see no reason to endure. The real question is, why did Lillian wish to stop looking at the page; why couldn't she endure looking at it any longer? Yet educators seem to prefer assuming some defect in a child to explain behavior rather than applying the kind of reasoning they would use in all similar situations.[4]

This belief in a supposed inability to focus is the consequence of the unexamined (and hardly ever explicitly stated) assumption that the beginning reader pays attention only to the word itself, and none to its meaning or the associations it arouses and the emotions these may evoke. Educators are so concerned with promoting word recognition and the correct decoding of single words that they seem to believe the same kind of concentration dominates the child's mind when he is learning to read. But judging from their "mistakes," it appears that even young children know better: the word itself is not important, but the meaning it has for them is.

If the material children are asked to read is too disturbing for them, they do not wish to see or consciously recognize the word that is upsetting them, so they may misread it to reduce its impact. If the emotions a word arouses are too strong, the child cannot look at it; he averts his gaze, as we all do if something in the field of our vision is too upsetting. Adults, includ-

---

[4] An inability to focus would indeed be a remarkable defect if restricted to the printed (and occasionally the written) word, and nonexistent when the child happened to be interested in what he was doing and was not scared by it—such as playing with a ball, or watching a TV screen for hours. But despite evidence that children can focus on other things, when their eyes wander from the page they are being asked to read, inability to focus is a preferred explanation.

ing educators, seem unable to recognize this because they are accustomed to separating the signifier—the word—from what it signifies. That the child may be as compelled to look away from the word "wild" as we ourselves might from an actual or even televised act of wildness, does not occur to these educators. But the child looks away, takes flight from a word and what it signifies, because he is not yet able to fully separate the symbol, i.e., the word, from what it signifies, and he becomes completely unable to make this separation when his negative emotions, such as anxiety, are too strongly aroused. His flight demonstrates that he had focused on the word well enough to know that it stands for something he wishes to avoid.

With an explanation such as inability to focus, there is no need to question why a child like Lillian in some specific situation has difficulty in focusing her eyes and is losing her stamina, i.e., can no longer endure contemplating what the printed word forces on her attention, although she had amply demonstrated a real ability to read well at other moments. And no consideration is given the fact that a word which she had been able to read without difficulty in one context has suddenly provoked flight from the page in another.

Kohl, like nearly all teachers in regard to similar misreadings, declares the child's mistake to be a simple one. We might transcribe such a judgment as "she made a simple mistake," or as her "simply having made a mistake." We are much more likely to say about ourselves, "I simply made a mistake," than, "I made a simple mistake." The reasons for this are at least twofold: we do not like to think of ourselves as "simple," certainly not when we have made an error; but also, deep down, we know that mistakes are not all that simple, certainly not those which *we* make. To say that somebody else made a simple mistake denies him our own complexity of intellect and personality, and relieves us of the task of fathoming the mistake's cause and meaning. By calling something a simple mistake, it is prejudged; no further examination of what took place is then necessary.

Kohl, out of his intuition or sensitivity to the feelings of the girl, accurately described Lillian's state of mind when she suddenly misread a word that she had read correctly a few times before. We are told that "she panicked," "looked away from the page," "wrinkled her brow," and in short took "flight" —either "from the page," or into her fantasies, or both. Her state of mind is further indicated by the fact that she was so upset it took special efforts to calm her down after she had felt it necessary to take flight.

When we panic, something must have aroused great anxiety in us; and the same is true when we take flight, as we try to escape the cause of our anxiety. Kohl, like many other teachers, observed that there is not infrequently a connection between a child's making mistakes in reading and anxiety. Unfortunately, he, like many others, reversed the causal connection. It is not making a mistake that causes the child's anxiety; it is the text, or a child's associations to it, which, when they evoke anxiety, lead to the need to defend against this anxiety—and the text that created it—by making mistakes of various kinds. Many of us have had the experience that we are apt to make mistakes when we are very anxious about something, and we are quite prepared to ascribe such errors to our anxiety. This seems an entirely sufficient explanation to us. Why should it be any different for children?

Kohl writes: "Immediately after making the mistake, she panicked. . . ." Implied in the word "immediately" is simultaneity: according to the *Oxford Dictionary*, the word means with "nothing intervening in time, space, order, or succession"; two of *Webster's* definitions are "at once, instantly." If things happen at once, we cannot be certain which is first and which follows. In this sense, the use of "immediately" indicates uncertainty in regard to sequence and causal connection; yet such uncertainty is denied by the assertion that Lillian panicked *after* she made the mistake.

Kohl could have written either "Immediately on making the mistake, she panicked," or "After she made the mistake, she panicked." Perhaps by using both words he asserts too much; perhaps while "immediately" describes what he actually observed, the "after" reflects his preconceived beliefs concerning cause and effect. Once more, preconceived notions in respect to what causes blocking may have skewed observation, with the biased observation then supporting the original prejudice about what is cause and what effect.[5]

Many observations have confirmed that, if a child panics in connection with a misreading, he does so immediately—to such an extent that it is usually impossible to be sure what preceded what. But even when educators do recognize the child's anxiety, they are convinced that it is the consequence and not the cause of the error.

It would be interesting to speculate why educators are so ready to believe that children are made anxious by having made a mistake. If a child does indeed fear unpleasant consequences, it must be because he is afraid of what the teacher may do. But then the anxiety is not about the mistake, but about the teacher's reaction to it; in short, the source of the child's anxiety lies in the teacher, and not in the mistake. This is an unpleasant thought to entertain for the modern teacher, who wishes to see herself as the child's friend.

True, a child's anxiety about making, or having made, a

---

[5] If it should be objected that we are taking too seriously the literal meaning of the words Kohl used, then we reply that if teachers do not think words need to be taken very seriously, how can their children do so? And if children are not taught to take words seriously, why should they expend energy on recognizing them exactly as they are printed? Indeed, the crux of our argument is that in teaching beginners to read, the prevalently used methods do *not* take the meanings of words as seriously as they ought to, if the purpose is to promote literacy.

mistake may be due to his experiences with others besides teachers. He may have been ridiculed or even punished for making mistakes at home by his parents, or by his siblings, or peers at school. If so, the teacher's response to the mistake is even more important; the teacher must convince the child, whenever possible and appropriate, that the error made is an acceptable and intelligent response to what he is reading.

If it could be generally accepted that mistakes such as misreadings are ingenious psychological phenomena, then the child's anxiety about the teacher's reaction to the mistake would disappear, and with it the teacher's mistaken belief that the child's anxiety is due to having made a mistake. It would then be possible to recognize what in fact is causing the error; sometimes it is anxiety, but anxiety caused by the text, or the associations it evokes—such as thoughts about the dog that killed cats and might attack the child, which made him misread "mane" for "name." More often, the causes of errors are important thoughts that intrude and that need to be attended to before the child can continue to read as printed.

Once again some parallels to psychoanalytic treatment may be drawn. At the very beginning of his treatment, a patient may be embarrassed, even anxious, about a slip of the tongue he has made, for in talking, slips of the tongue are the equivalent of misreadings. But later on, after the patient has experienced how interesting and revealing such slips are, and how much they help to promote understanding of what is going on in his mind, they are welcomed as unexpected vistas on important problems.

It is different when complete blocking occurs, as it does in psychoanalytic treatment when the patient becomes unable to talk. This is always the result of something taking place in the mind of the patient, be it consciously or more likely unconsciously, which is so painful or anxiety-creating that he is quite unable to face it. Although he may consciously know that the analyst will be able to help him, unconsciously he is convinced that this will not be possible. Thus, while verbal slips in psychoanalysis most often are the result of the patient's wanting some thought to come to light despite a certain resistance, blocking is always the result of a strong conscious or unconscious desire to *prevent* a thought from coming to light, due either to anxiety or extreme negativism. (The latter is another form of anxiety, as can be understood from the fact that hatred is an extreme form of negativism, but we seldom hate persons or experiences unless they make us very anxious.)

Educators are most reluctant to accept the fact that learning to read is scary for children, although we all know that learning new things can be very scary, despite the advantages and pleasures we may gain at a later time from having learned them. To be able to swim is pleasant and beneficial, it can be life-saving; but most people are quite anxious at first when learning it. One might object that this anxiety has to do with the reality that in the process of learning to swim, one may drown, or at least swallow water, which is unpleasant. But there are many other learning situations in which we are anxious at the beginning—one common fear being that we may not be able to master what we are trying to learn— although there are, objectively speaking, no dangers involved. But since when has the objective knowledge that no ghost dwells in a dark room prevented people, and particularly children, from being afraid of what might be lurking there? There are some children who are so secure that they are not afraid of the dark, but these are a minority, and so are the children who take to reading as ducks take to the water. Maybe we would be better teachers of reading if we started out with the conviction that learning something so difficult and important as reading is scary for most people, until such time as they securely know all that is involved in it and that they will be able to master it.

From what Kohl writes, one cannot tell on which page of the book Lillian misread "mild" for "wild," after having had no

trouble with it on the preceding pages.[6] It is entirely possible
that her panic anxiety was caused by a cumulative effect, but
in perusing the book we infer the likelihood that she changed
"wild" to "mild" in reaction to the pictures, not the words. For
in this little book the pictures dominate the text in all respects.
The first seven picture pages are not apt to create anxiety; if
anything, they are pleasant and encouraging to the child. On
the eighth picture page, a wild animal appears for the first time
and is called that. This is followed by the first double-spread
picture page, on which the child hero of the story is threatened
by four ferocious wild animals which, again for the first time
in the book, appear massed, in overpowering size and shape.
The text accompanying the page emphasizes this: "And when
he came to the place where the wild things are, they roared
their terrible roars and gnashed their terrible teeth and rolled
their terrible eyes and showed their terrible claws."

The first pages, we are told, Lillian read with no trouble.
On them the story's hero is shown as chasing, possibly threatening, his dog and then, at least by implication, threatening
his mother. Then we see him against some pleasant scenery as
trees grow in his room and he travels in his "private boat"
across the ocean. But on the double-page spread mentioned
above, he arrives at the land of the wild things and *he* is the
one who is being threatened.

The word "wild" appears on this page for the third time (or
counting the title, the fourth time) in the book. Lillian's misreading it on this page would be consistent with Kohl's statement that she previously had had no trouble with it; if she
read it correctly only once before, the author could be expected
to report this fact. If our assumption about the place in the
book where Lillian made her error is correct, then she made it

---

[6] Kohl says that "on about the fifth page she . . . read 'mild' for 'wild,' "
but in the book this word appears for the first time on the third
page of the text, and again on the eighth and ninth pages. It does
not appear on the fifth page.

when she experienced for the first time the full visual impact of the anxiety-creating wildness of the creatures. (If she made it on a later page, this would not greatly change our analysis, since on all the following pages where she could have made the mistake these same creatures are depicted, and the cumulative effect of having been exposed to these anxiety-creating impressions would only have grown.) She cannot possibly have made her mistake on the last pages of the book, which present the happy denouement of the story, since the word "wild" does not appear on them, and since Kohl's "about the fifth page" implies the earlier rather than later section of the book.

We believe that Lillian responded with anxiety to the fear-creating images of the wild, threatening animals in the pictures, and to the word "wild," which further asserts their dangerousness. She might, of course, also have reacted to the text, which vividly describes their wildness. Wishing to deny her anxiety, or the causes of it, as do many children in similar situations, she might have tried to pretend that there was no reason to be afraid of these creatures because, despite their looks, they were "mild" animals.

Since Lillian exchanged only one letter for another (m for w), her misreading is viewed by Kohl as a simple mistake caused by a problem in focusing her eye on the printed word. But it remains unexplained why she could not focus correctly this time when she had done so several times before. Worse, it is not recognized that this inconsistency requires an explanation.

In his account, Kohl mentions first that Lillian "looked away from the page" and "wrinkled her brow" (might we assume in disgust, puzzlement, or fear?), and only later that she has a problem with "focusing her eyes on the written word." If her misreading took place on the page on which we assume it did, then two-thirds of the double-page spread she was looking at was taken up with an impressively drawn and colored picture in which a small, sullen child is being threatened by huge, wild beasts. (The situation is not much different on some of the following pages.) Without a complex measuring apparatus it is practically impossible to be certain exactly where on a page a child is trying to focus. But given the nature of this book, with its pictures dominating the text, it is hard to see how one could feel certain whether it was the pictures or the words on which Lillian failed (or refused) to focus. If she took flight from a page, as we are told she did, isn't it more likely that she was taking flight from the impressively threatening large picture than from the much less impressive words?

There is no way of knowing what went on in Lillian's mind. But her replacement of "wild" with "mild" suggests as a likely explanation that she was trying to deny the wildness of the animals; probably both their anxiety-evoking appearance in the picture *and* what was said about them in the text. If she indeed was trying to pretend to herself that these animals were "mild," then she *had* to look away from the page, since the picture gave the lie to her attempt; the only way she could then maintain this wild-into-mild transformation was by concentrating on the reassuring picture she had created in her mind.

Because Kohl assumes that difficulty in focusing explains this "simple" error, he pays no attention to the fact that emotionally, "mild" is the opposite of "wild." Under normal circumstances—that is, if this were not a situation in which a young child having difficulty in reading was being taught—when a person changes "wild" to "mild," we would *immediately* recognize not only that something is being changed into its opposite but that this exchange is turning something threatening into something benign. It would seem obvious that the change has been made to allow escape from anxiety, or to deny the need for it. But in such discussions of the teaching of reading, all attention is so concentrated on problems of technique (similarity of letters, exchange of one letter for another, inability to focus) that everything we know about normal child behavior, not to mention child psychology, is completely disregarded. If it weren't, we would remember that asserting that something threatening is really benign is a favorite method of young children in dealing with their anxieties, particularly when threatening animals are the cause. The feared lion is called "nice lion," the dog the child is afraid of "nice doggie." When a very bright kindergartener was warned away from stray dogs by being told that although her dog was a "family dog," dogs she encountered on the street might not be family dogs, her solution was to call *every* dog a "family dog."

In choosing "mild," Lillian showed her intelligence by replacing the anxiety-creating concept "wild"' with a word that rhymed with it and retained three of the original word's four letters. Her choice showed respect both for the printed word and for the person who had asked her to read the word correctly, by making the new word as close as possible in tonal quality to that which she replaced through rhyming, through identity of three of the letters and, since opposites are in our minds closely associated with each other, through association.

The panic Kohl observed may very well have been caused or confirmed by the fact that Lillian's replacement of "wild" with "mild" in her effort to deny or escape her anxiety was not accepted as a correct way of dealing with the problem—a response that she may have sensed in Kohl, whether or not he expressed it openly. Even though what she did was not criticized, since Kohl asked her (either right away, or later) to check herself, she must have received the impression that what she had done was unacceptable.

If we accept it when a child calls an anxiety-creating animal nice, more often than not this is the end of it. But if we insist that the animal is in truth ferocious, then either the child insists much more stubbornly that he is right and we are wrong—as happened when in the face of the teacher's insistence that tigers are big, strong animals, the girl persisted in saying that the story was about Tigger—or panic may se

in. By and large, it is the more secure child who will insist on
his way, while an insecure child, like Lillian, is more apt to
panic. But such panic is not, as is often assumed, the simple
consequence of having to accept the dangerousness of the
animal; this would evoke fear, but not panic. Rather, it is
the child's experience that his own defensive efforts—which
alone in the long run can offer him reliable protection—have
turned out to be ineffective that creates panic. The inadequacy
of our methods for mastering anxiety leaves us permanently
vulnerable, whereas an external threat threatens us only
temporarily. Kohl, who is very skillful in his use of words,
chose to describe Lillian's reaction as panic rather than fear,
which adds credence to this admittedly speculative re-creation
of what actually happened.

Children are often reluctant to admit their anxieties to
adults. Here we must remember that Lillian was not a little
child; she was of sixth-grade age. Whereas a small child might
not feel the need to cover up when a picture or a story in a
book makes him very anxious, an older child is much more
reluctant to admit to panic anxiety aroused by a picture or
story. Wishing to cover up her anxiety, Lillian did what many
children do in such a situation: having replaced the scary
word with one that rhymed with it, she pretended that what
she was doing was rhyming, not trying to run away from her
anxiety. Her making up senseless rhymes was akin to whis-
tling in the dark: its purpose was to fool the adult into believing that the cause of her replacing "wild" with "mild" was a
wish to rhyme, not anxiety about what she was reading and
seeing on the page. This mechanism is often employed by
children who do something inadvertently or out of anxiety,
and then claim, "I did it on purpose," giving the appearance
of deliberation to something they could not help doing.[7]

[7] The way Kohl describes the rhyming, it cannot have happened in
connection with the exchange of "mild" for "wild"—and not just because "more" doesn't rhyme with either word. It cannot have happened

So ingrained is the conviction of educators that children's errors in reading have no deeper meaning and are due to lack of technical proficiencies that it did not occur to a man as intelligent as Kohl that Lillian's anxiety, and her wish to escape it, were *appropriate* emotional responses to the material she was reading, and even more obviously appropriate to what she was seeing in the pictures (and the book is so printed that it is not possible to look at the text without seeing the picture accompanying it). Yet Kohl does not make this connection, although he himself says that the book is a bit scary, that the text and pictures deal with wildness and hence must arouse feelings about it, and that the girl panicked.[8]

We are told that when Lillian was ten, "she was involved in a serious car accident. Her head was thrown against the dashboard, and she had suffered severe headaches ever since." This is enough reason to make us believe that her anxiety had to do with the wild things one encounters in life—and throughout this book the only wild things are the animals. Given this background, it seems much more likely that Lillian was afraid of the harm wildness might do to her than that she wished to participate in wildness by proxy, or be wild herself.

Sympathetic and helpful though Kohl was to the girl, hard as he tried to develop her self-confidence and so to convince

---

in the context of reading *Where the Wild Things Are* because the word "more" does not appear in this book. But Lillian might very well have made up meaningless words as rhymes following wild-mild for the reasons mentioned above. Or she might have made them up in reaction to something Kohl said.

[8] In overreaction to antiquated notions about the innocence of children, their enjoyment of wildness and naughtiness is now sometimes so uncritically taken for granted that the anxiety these can evoke is overlooked. Among all groups there are children who have been the victims of violence in their homes or on the streets. This arouses in such children wishes to retaliate, but these desires are weak when compared with their fear that they might again be the victims of aggression. Thus, stories like that of the book Lillian was asked to read, which have for their content a child's wish to be wild or to fantasize about it, can

her—and us, the readers of his book—of her intelligence, still he did not start out with the assumption that it may have been her very perspicacity that led her to exchange one word for its opposite. Kohl says that "every time she made a mistake we stopped and talked about how she could check herself." But they did not talk about why she may have made the mistake. This is because Kohl had already decided that there were no possible reasons for it other than lack of stamina and inability to focus. The procedure he suggested to Lillian—slowly counting to five, to calm herself after a flight of sound associations —suggests some degree of awareness that she had become anxious or over-excited about something, since only in such situations do we need to calm ourselves. But he completely ignored the most important thing in such a situation: discovering what caused the anxiety or excitement, the loss of equanimity, instead of assuming reasons that in normal people would hardly ever cause either excitement or panic anxiety.

Not every child is so quick-witted as to be able to transform ferocity into its opposite by coming up with a word that has the same number of letters as the "dangerous" word, and that even rhymes with the original. Here we must remember that Lillian was of sixth-grade age, much more mature than a normal beginning reader.

The most natural way of dealing with a story that makes one anxious is to deny its validity, to say it is not so. This Lillian did, by calling the animals "mild." Another possibility

---

be very satisfying to certain children and equally anxiety-creating to other children.

This is not to suggest that stories about children being wild or having fantasies about wildness have no place as children's reading material. Aggression is part of life, and fantasies about it form an important aspect of emotional life. But the counterpart of these emotions— anxieties about being wild—must receive equal attention; otherwise the one-sidedness of this kind of modern children's literature would be as great as that of those books in which life is depicted as all sweetness and light.

for dealing with a situation that arouses painful or overwhelming emotions is to try to get out of it. If this situation is that of reading a story, then the way to get out of it is not to read it; in that way the offending situation is destroyed (in a sense). In class, children often do this, not by misreadings but by complete blocking. At home, where they may feel freer to express themselves, they may throw away or tear up such a book. It is their way of getting even with the story and of avoiding reading what is creating too much anxiety or other discomfort. Such kinds of behavior are more primitive and require less intelligence than Lillian's changing into "mild" the wild things of the story.

When they encounter overwhelming dangers, animals attack, flee, play possum, or take other evasive or protective action. Running away and attacking, as well as playing possum, seem more primitive than more sophisticated evasive or protective actions. Blocking may be most readily compared with playing possum and taking flight, but in some subtle manner it is also an attack, since it denies the book the reason for its existence: that it should be read.[9] Lillian, by changing the words, tried to deflect what was causing her anxiety; in this way she was acting evasively and self-protectively. Only when this failed to be effective, because it was met with nonacceptance, did she block. Other children, not able, or not trusting their ability, to take successful evasive action, block immediately when the level of anxiety rises too high.

In the same book in which Kohl describes his experience with Lillian, he also reports another instance of blocking. To test the degree of complexity of reading material children are

[9] If it weren't too costly, and didn't run counter to the ethos of the educational system, it might be more useful psychologically to let a child do away with a book that upsets him. Since we don't usually destroy a book, but simply put it aside when its content annoys us, so children would usually be satisfied with throwing down the offending book rather than tearing it up. If they *do* attempt to destroy a book, this is probably the consequence of their knowing that they will soon

able to master, Kohl used some stories he had developed for this purpose. A child "broke down over the word 'furious.'" Kohl gives no indication of recognizing that what accounted for this blocking was in all probability an emotional reaction to the correctly perceived word and the feelings to which it refers, rather than difficulty in recognizing the word. Indeed, in both of the examples of blocking Kohl describes in his book, the child became unable to read when confronted with a word signifying a threatening emotion: wildness and fury. Kohl's book says a great deal about the kind of content that should be used to teach children reading, yet he pays no attention to the content around which reading became impossible for the children whose reading difficulties he discusses.

Kohl is not unaware, however, of the emotions that accompany a child's inability to read some word. He also describes an experience he himself had as a fifth grader while riding the subway in New York and reading a book that contained some words he could not pronounce or understand: "There were many people in the car reading . . . and I wanted to ask someone to help me with the words but was scared. My fantasy was of being punched, stomped, laughed at, ignored and ridiculed for daring to ask a stranger for such help. I don't think I'm alone. We are accustomed to asking strangers for directions if we're lost, but to ask for help with reading . . . is often looked upon as . . . a threat or challenge." We do not know which words the eleven-year-old Kohl was unable to read and wanted help with, but his fantasy about the strangers' reactions suggests that subconsciously he probably perceived these

---

be asked to read it again; they try to make this impossible by destroying it.

If we permitted or even encouraged children to throw away books that offended them, they would at least be given the assurance that they are allowed to respond actively to the emotions reading arouses in them. Such an active attitude can more easily be transformed into meaningful, active reading than can a passive negativism.

words as provoking violent emotions—which, incidentally, might be why he could not read them to begin with.

This, in fact, explains the phenomenon that bemuses Kohl: that we find it easy to ask strangers for directions but not to explain a word. When asking directions, we feel certain that our request will not be considered offensive. But if we don't know what a word means, and sense that it might be repugnant, then the anxiety that it might evoke aggression in others is not at all strange, particularly in view of the fact that all children have had the experience of uttering a word the meaning of which they don't quite grasp, only to be severely criticized for doing so. Our fear that something untoward may happen to us when we ask for the meaning of a word has a great deal to do with our unconscious fantasies about just what this meaning might be. It is these associations which may not only keep us from asking for help, but which, depending on their nature, may lead to misreadings to cover them up from ourselves and others, or even to blocking.

Since earliest times, and particularly in primitive societies even today, words are believed to have magic properties. Children retain many primitive attitudes and beliefs in their experiencing of the world, attitudes which they shed to varying degrees as they are being educated. In the process of education they slowly learn to separate the word from what it signifies and thereby to divest the word of some of its magic connotations, which gradually become replaced by its abstract meaning. But before this process is complete, children are very sensitive not just to the emotional impact of words but also to their power to affect reality, including the power to do physical harm.

Because the beginning reader still believes in the power of words for good and evil, he blocks or misreads when he encounters a word that arouses over-strong feelings—and hence may seem dangerous. Yet since these words evoke very strong (albeit negative) emotions, this very strength of emotional involvement can, when handled properly, be preserved and the negative charge defused or even changed into a positive one, as Lillian tried to do when she read "mild" for "wild." Such experiences can help make reading become one of the most pleasurable activities life has to offer the child, since few things are as deeply satisfying as when we discover in ourselves the capacity to transform the negative into the positive.

PART THREE

The Problem
with Primers

CHAPTER 11

Misreadings Caused
by Primers

Reading is a difficult cognitive achievement, particularly for the beginner. It requires considerable temporary expenditure, and permanent investment, of the ego's energy. If, because the task seems purposeless or offensive to the child, the cognitive powers of the mind are not invested with mental energy, a wide variety of misreadings may occur. These can be both the result and the expression of a generalized lack of interest in the material the child is supposed to read.

If as adults we become bored or disgusted with a book, we stop reading and may even throw the book away; but the school child is not permitted these alternatives. Compelled by the teacher's demands, or those the child senses coming from his parents, he pretends to attend to his reading while actually he cannot keep his mind on it. He may then try to make the task more interesting by substituting words that reflect his genuine concerns.

Sometimes asking the child to pay better attention in this situation brings results. Fear of the teacher or desire to please her induces the child to invest his ego—his cognitive powers —with some additional mental energy, and he can then read the word correctly. If so, the teacher gathers renewed conviction that the child could not read before because he was not paying attention—which is true enough, but not for the reasons she assumes. Or she thinks the error is due to not sounding out the word adequately, or not comprehending the text. Actually, in such cases the child's error is due to his comprehending all too correctly the vacuity of the text. Yet it never seems to occur to the teacher that an absence of concentration, focusing, sounding out, or comprehending can be the direct result of the meaninglessness of the text.

The substance of what the child is being asked to read requires very little mental energy compared to that demanded in recognizing letters or words. But such work of recognition can occupy our interest for only a short time, and that part of our energy not invested in the actual task becomes "free-floating," which means it seeks other things to attach itself to. These might be thoughts evoked by what the child is reading, by what is going on around him, and also by what is going on in the recesses of his mind—content that remains repressed or unattended to while the child's conscious mind is fully occupied with other things, but that has a tendency to float to the surface when his consciousness is not interestingly engaged.

Some of the ways in which primers and readers talk down to children have been mentioned before, such as their extremely limited vocabulary. There are others: the simplicity of sentences does not encourage investment of mental energy in reading, nor permit the conveyance of anything interesting. The diction used is literally that of "baby" talk, akin to the truncated "telegraphic" speech of toddlers; yet the child should be made to feel that learning to read is progressive, not something that returns him to a manner of thinking and speech he has quite outgrown.

Even more demeaning to a child's budding intellect is the endless repetition of identical words—another throwback to the time when the child was learning to talk and he repeated the same words over and over again, words that became tiresome to the parent. The insensitive or tired parent reacts with indifference to this repetition, which discourages the child and interferes with his intellectual development. The sensitive parent invents interesting games with words, both in order to tolerate the repetitions and to foster the child's speech and intellectual development. But no such play with words is found in the most widely used basic readers. Since a first preprimer (*Janet and Mark,* for example) typically contains only twenty different words, the same words are repeated endlessly. And since so few words are used, there can be no variations in the context in which they appear to invest them with some interest.

Everybody can understand and accept that to learn a new skill, repeated exercise is necessary. What is offensive is the assumption that we should find interest, meaning, and enjoyment in such a training exercise. Young children are exposed all too often to such annoying situations, in which adults think them less intelligent or sensitive than they are; and, like the rest of us, they appreciate it if others are honest with them. Therefore, while children are bored by the many repetitions required for recognizing a word, they do not resent being subjected to them, provided that nothing else is pretended. But when these repetitions are camouflaged as stories, as they are in the basic readers, and are accompanied by pictures depicting situations for the description of which the child knows he would use a wide vocabulary and a rather complex sentence structure, then the pretense that the constant repetition of a few words constitutes a story becomes an insult to the child's intelligence. It gives him the impression that those who want him to learn to read from these books consider him, if not stupid, then of limited capacity and very gullible. How else can he view the fact that they think an endless repetition of words in two-, three-, or four-word phrases can interest him and convince him of the value of reading? He is particularly sensitive to slights involved in being considered less advanced than he is—for these occur too often in his relations with adults for him to take them lightly. He knows he is no longer a baby, and so the baby language of the primers is to him an irrefutable demonstration that his intelligence is being underestimated.

How can the child be interested in reading when mechanical repetition makes these words and phrases even more meaningless than they would be by themselves? Under these conditions, it is very understandable that the child from time to time should try to make what he has to read a bit more varied, interesting, and meaningful through word substitutions. If his effort to apply his mind to what he is reading is rejected and criticized as wrong and he is required to restrict himself to reading the empty sentences of the book as printed, the bright child will conclude that—at least in class—reading is something to which one is not supposed to apply one's intelligence; and the child who is insecure about his abilities will also conclude that he is perceived to be of limited intelligence.

The trouble is that any text the teacher uses is meaningful to her because she is convinced that reading it is good exercise and promotes reading ability; of course she thinks concentration on it is worthwhile. But the child does not see it this way, and from a broader perspective he is more correct in his evaluation than the teacher, because reading can never be meaningful as a mere exercise.

Here, too, the remedy is recognition that in misreading or failing to read, the child's behavior is purposeful: escaping a meaningless and hence odious task. It is not that teachers do not recognize when a child is bored with what he is reading; what is missing is the recognition that a blocking or misreading is due to this boredom. The teachers we observed were quite sensitive to a child's lack of involvement in what he was reading and his consequent inability to concentrate on it. But even the most gifted teachers did not tell the child that his reaction showed good judgment. They felt that doing so would undermine the child's interest in reading in general; they seemed to think that to reject a boring text was tantamount to rejecting all of reading—perhaps all of school learning.

The children, too, did not dare criticize the text, even if they truly felt like it, unless they were first explicitly given permission to do so. They were afraid to criticize a text for fear they would seem to be criticizing the teacher, or school in general. Here, once again, one must take into account the great insecurity of the beginning reader in intellectual matters. If he cannot keep himself interested in an assigned text, he tends to think that there is something wrong with him; it takes considerable self-confidence to conclude that the shortcoming resides in the reading matter.

Telling the child that being turned off by a boring story demonstrates his ability to discriminate and his good aesthetic judgment would considerably strengthen his self-confidence and encourage his interest in reading. This is not mere theory. Whenever we commented to a bored child that the text was indeed boring—which of course we did only when in our opinion it really was—our comment always produced willingness, often eagerness on the child's part to read something more interesting.

Yet teachers seemed reluctant to agree that a specific book the child was reading was boring—perhaps because that would be a negative statement about a book made available in their class. They would simply offer the child something else to read, or ask him what he wanted to read. Unfortunately, these responses did not really work, because they didn't lift the child out of his negativism. That negativism tended to be transferred to the new text, which the child approached with the old lack of interest and the old conviction that nothing worthwhile was to be gained from reading it.

The outcome was strikingly different when we praised the child for the discernment he had shown. Pleased with himself, he would begin to read the new book in a positive frame of mind and would find something of interest in it; if nothing else, he had a desire to make up his mind about the merits of this new book, to display once again his ability to discriminate.

Children also responded positively when told that they didn't have to read if they couldn't find something of interest to them. Given a choice between reading and doing something entirely different, the child usually searched for some book that appeared interesting. Other children, who had been utterly bored and lethargic, eagerly engaged in some entirely different activity. Vital energy was available to the child instantaneously, whenever his activity made an appeal to him. After a while, most of them returned to reading with us, all on their own. Invigorated by doing something that had greatly interested him, his ego reinvested with energy, the child now felt capable of enjoying reading.

The lesson is obvious: it is necessary to offer children reading material that makes a strong positive appeal to their total personality. Unfortunately, most basic readers are designed to be attractive mainly to that part of the child's personality which seeks simple-minded pleasure or satisfaction. These lead the child to seek gratification in the most direct ways, such as through mainly motor activities or very simple fantasy play. If the child is stimulated to think of eating or jumping (as he is by the content of many basic readers), then he wants to eat or jump, not just read about it. Thus content that reminds the child of physical pleasures in the most direct way is unlikely to induce the total personality to invest ego energy in serious reading. Subconsciously, children know all this, and also what is needed in a text to hold their interest.

A third-grade girl, whose teacher felt she had a good sight vocabulary but who never sounded words out, was given some material that forces the reader to make fine distinctions between similar words which start and end with different consonants. The teacher felt that such a controlled vocabulary might teach the child skills that would permit her to decode words not immediately recognizable on first sight. The text was:

I can fan a sad man.
I can fan a tan man.
I can fan a bad man.
Can I fan a mad man?

Nan had a pad.
Nan had a tan pad.
Dad ran.
Dad ran to the pad.
Dad had the tan pad.
Bad Dan.
Mad Nan.

These are words which, because of their similarity and the way they are mixed together, are hard for a sight reader to master —but as tongue twisters, they are even harder to say. To make it possible to be at all interested in these silly word combinations, the girl infused them with personal meaning. In this way she avoided becoming bored or feeling too degraded at having to recite such nonsense.

Possibly the idea of fanning a sad person and thus cheering him up, and of cooling one who felt hot (as somebody who has a tan might feel) were acceptable, so the girl could read the first two sentences without error. Repeating such boringly stupid sentences for a third time was just too much, or maybe saying that she would be fanning a bad person was unacceptable. Or perhaps since what she was reading could not hold her attention, her eyes wandered as she looked at the page and alighted on the one word that had real meaning for her: "Dad." Whatever the reason, in the third line she substituted "Dad" for "bad," reading: "I can fan a Dad man." The teacher, thinking that she was reversing *b* and *d*, asked whether she spelled "dad" with a capital or a small *d*. The child's unhesitating answer was: "With a capital *D*." So her choice of "Dad" could not be explained as an error due to reversal of letters, as her teacher had many times before interpreted the girl's misreadings.

This substitution was most likely the consequence of the girl's inability to keep her attention riveted on such meaningless and repetitious sentences. But it also shows that even a substitution due to boredom is never random. What better way for a third-grade girl to escape boredom and focus her wandering, or to rekindle her extinguished attention, than to think of her Dad?

A more fanciful interpretation might consider that a girl her age is more likely to be interested in fanning a father's emotions than she is in providing him with a slight air breeze, and that this desire might subconsciously have motivated her choice of substitution. Or while consciously aware only of wishing to provide her Dad with some comfort, subconsciously she may well hope that he would respond to such service with great affection. This interpretation must remain conjecture, since—as already stated—we do not think it wise to explore unconscious emotions when the purpose is to teach reading, and hence did not do so. For the same reason we failed to find out whether "bad" might have evoked associations to her father and led to its being replaced by "Dad," because perhaps at this moment she was angry with him and felt that he was bad; or whether, on the contrary, the idea of fanning a man led to the association that Dad was the man whom she wished thus to comfort.

When the girl told her teacher that "Dad" was spelled with a capital D, this ended their conversation; both were quite frustrated by the impasse in which they found themselves, neither seeing a way to resolve it. So we interjected ourselves by saying reassuringly to the girl, "Sure, Dad is a man." Thereupon she immediately corrected the error, spontaneously rereading the sentence as printed, and turned to continue reading with us. She blocked for several minutes on the word "mad," in the next line. Since she had just before misread, "I can fan a Dad man," a sentence which showed that she was thinking about an interaction with a father, we felt it best not to intrude on her mental activities as she blocked. Having recognized subconsciously that the word was "mad," she may have been having difficulty coping with the emotions this word aroused in connection with a father.

By waiting patiently for her to decide how to complete the question of whom she can fan, we tacitly gave her credit for being able, as she had before, to find some solution here too, in her own good time. We remarked that when people feel the word written here, they sometimes think they are bad—in other words, we merely said aloud what children tend to think: that they are bad if they are mad at somebody. Again she immediately corrected herself, rereading the sentence as printed.

She went on to read the rest of the text without any difficulty, discriminating easily in the last two lines between "bad" and "mad." That she could do so readily when the text referred to the nondescript Dan and Nan, as opposed to her difficulty when it referred to her, as in the sentences which began, "I can . . ." "Can I . . . ," suggests that besides boredom with the nonsensical text, her difficulties in decoding the words had to do with being required to say that it was she who fanned bad and mad men. Despite the importance which thoughts about a father have for a girl, it was not associations to him that were the original cause of the misreading; at least this is what she told us later. According to her, the reason was that her attention had wandered away from what she was supposed to read because of its meaninglessness.

After she had read nine more lines of this text without any further errors, we asked if she wanted to continue with it. She definitely did not want to do so, and asked to read instead "a real story with easy and also hard words." In reply to our question, she explained that easy words were those of the phonics text she had just read; hard words were those which were longer and more interesting and were used in telling a good story. That she called the words hard and asked to read them reflected her conviction that reading a good story, while harder, was so much more interesting that it was far preferable to the easy stuff.

She chose to read the story "Some Day" (in *People Read*, a Bank Street Reader). She misread the sentence "Some day I want to have a truck," by substituting "job" for "truck." Having said that some day she wanted a job, this black girl studied the picture in the text of a black girl who dreams of becoming a teacher when she grows up. To express our understanding that she had substituted "job" for "truck," for good reasons, we asked what she wanted to do when grown up, to which she answered: "Read." And then she added, as if this explanation were hardly necessary, that she wanted to be a teacher. So this had been the job she had had in mind for herself—it was not a truck she wanted, but the job of being a teacher. Having said this, she spontaneously corrected her misreading of "job" for "truck."

The teacher had thought the words of a phonics text were harder for this girl than those of a sight text because she seemed unable to sound out words. The girl thought that phonics material was easier, even though she made more mistakes in reading it, than the text she read on sight. Thus, teacher and child misunderstood each other about what was easy and what was hard. The girl tried to express the point that while the words of *People Read* (and other stories) were harder for her to read than the similar "fan," "Nan," "Dan," "mad," "bad," "sad," and so on, she was nonetheless more motivated to do well in reading them because what she read had meaning and interest for her. Her refusal to sound out the simpler words was not due to inability, but to a desire not to do so.

One of the booklets of the SWRL series tells a story about

a snake named Sis. Another animal, a rat, says to Sis: "Sis, see me run." One child read instead: "Sis sees me run." When asked what he would say if he wanted someone else to watch him, he replied: "Look . . . look at me." Since the child could read at least on a beginning level, he knew that the word was "see" and not "look." But the sentence "Sis, see me run" sounded stilted to him; on his own, he would have said instead, "Sis, look at me," or, "Watch me run."

It requires quite some ingenuity to retain the entire sentence as printed, and by adding just one letter, *s*, at the end of one of its words, to change an exclamation or command— "Sis, see me run"—to the narrative statement, "Sis sees me run," and in so doing, make the stilted sentence conform to common speech. One can imagine what it does to a child's feelings about himself, and about reading, if his efforts to make the text more colloquially correct are branded as errors.

One cannot help wondering how animals are selected as the characters of these stories, and how they are named. Most children and adults find snakes and rats repellent. No normal child would spontaneously identify with either animal, or find it sympathetic. Snakes stand for poisonous animals. In the Judeo-Christian tradition for some 3,000 years the snake has been the evil, treacherous animal that caused hereditary sin. And while this religiously based aversion is no longer part of many children's conscious reaction to snakes, the unconscious reason that made the snake's role in the tragedy in Paradise easy to accept for untold generations is still at work in the unconscious mind of the modern agnostic.

Perhaps the intention in naming the snake Sis was to imitate the sound that snakes make. But Sis is what some children call their sisters and what all children know is a nickname for sister. While some child occasionally in an angry moment may think that his sister is a snake, to call a snake by a name which, as he reads it aloud, would suggest his sister is most provocative and repugnant. The snake in the role of a sister is

contrary to very strong, deep, ancient conscious and unconscious responses to this animal, and it runs counter to the
purpose of facilitating reading to force the child to combat unconscious feelings as he has to struggle with the task of
reading. This type of content evokes in the child's preconscious a response that reading does not make sense on a deeper
level; it may even lead to the feeling that reading is offensive.

Nearly the same holds true for the rat. For many conscious
and unconscious reasons, we call a most undesirable character
a rat. It is part of the unfortunate living situation of many
underprivileged children—those who have a much harder time
learning to read because of their home background and life's
circumstances—that rats are their enemies. Rats remind them
that their living conditions are substandard, when compared
with the rest of the population; in the slums of our cities, rats
are among the very few animals that actually attack babies;
and they spoil food which they touch and are carriers of disease. So rats, too, arouse in the child strong negative feelings
which, in the normal course of events, are much more powerful than the desire to learn to read. Having to read about
rats makes reading objectionable. This choice of animal is
even stranger, or more revealing of unconscious attitudes, if
one considers that the SWRL series was created for and is used
in follow-through classes with the specific intention of teaching minority children to read.

Why are the most repulsive animals chosen for children to
read about, when the intention is to make reading easier by
repeating words, trying to elicit interest in humorous stories,
and so on? The most generous explanation is that the authors
of the texts, the educators who approve of them, and the
teachers who use them, view content as completely unim-
portant. Or else that they think young children are so insensitive that "funny" stories, whatever the content, will entice
them to read. All this gives the impression that the secret or
unconscious intention is to impart the message that nothing

ought to distract the child's attention from the decoding of words in isolation.

While reading for meaning occasionally induces misreadings if the meaning the child ascribes to a text is different from what is printed, it nearly always *facilitates* decoding and in the last analysis, is the only reason for undertaking decoding. It is well known and accepted that the purpose of talking is to convey meaning; even the infant's early babbling is a communication of something that seems meaningful to him. Shouldn't the same hold true for the beginning reader?

Little wonder that children have a hard time understanding the content of the SWRL and similar readers. While the stated intention is to elicit the child's interest by presenting stories about the antics of engaging animals, this is rarely accomplished, because the choice of content mystifies children, even when the animal is not one that evokes negative feelings.

Textbook writers, in order to engross the child in reading material, select as the main figures of their stories attractive children of the students' age, who are like them in many other respects also, thereby making it practically impossible for the child not to identify with these figures. But this creates problems if the figure in the story behaves in ways unacceptable to the child, or if the story characters do or say things the child would never say or do.[1] In fact, the child's identification with the main figure he is reading about can be a major source of reading difficulties. Part of the problem is the age at which

[1] In Japan, child psychotherapists use Western-type dolls in their treatment, ones that do not resemble in bodily features the Japanese children who play with them. Similarly, the dolls available in Japanese stores all represent Western white children. The explanation given by the child psychiatrists, psychologists, and educators is that the dolls' not looking like the children themselves greatly facilitated their fantasizing about the dolls, and acting out all kinds of things with them. In this way, the children could identify with the dolls when they wished, but they also knew all along that these were fantasies, because the dolls looked so different from them. Perhaps this is something we might consider in creating the pictures that accompany the stories of

reading is introduced to children. If they were older, they would be much less likely to identify strongly and indiscriminately with what they read about, and would therefore feel less need to reshape the content to make it acceptable as pertaining to themselves.

As we grow older and gain more experience with reading, we learn to identify selectively, with some features of the hero and not with others. But children at the age when they are learning to read still proceed on an all-or-nothing principle, and are least able to separate themselves from the person they are hearing or reading about, particularly when that person is a child about their own age. (If these protagonists are adults, the child is apt to identify them with his parents or other close relatives. Still, it is a little simpler for the child to separate himself from a parental figure, since he knows from his everyday experience that his parents and he often respond differently to things.)

When reading "Kitty and James," in a Sullivan storybook (No. 9a), a girl blocked without first misreading anything. The story is about a puppy, James. The passage in which the blocking occurred reads: "Can you tell why James sits on the floor scratching and barking at the door? I think you can. It isn't hard." With some difficulty the girl was able to read until she came to the word "hard." At that point she declared herself unable to read the word, or to read on.

The teacher, trying to help her, suggested that the word seemed to express how the girl felt about this reading lesson. To that there was no response; if anything, her body and face

---

our textbooks, where all efforts are geared to make the children in the pictures look like the children reading the stories.

Japanese-looking dolls are also available in Japan, of course, and these are very beautiful—elaborately carved and clothed, to represent various historical and literary Japanese characters. But these dolls are not suitable for being played with by children. They are something to be admired from a distance, not to be touched or moved about; they are treated as, and sometimes are, works of art.

seemed to express a hardening of her resistance to reading. So the teacher read the crucial passage to her, but with an important difference: she changed the sentence from a negation to an assertion, reading: "As a matter of fact, it is . . ." With that, the girl without any hesitation decisively read, or one might say, completed the teacher's sentence, by saying "hard."

What seems to have happened here again was that the girl was taking the story very personally, as is typical for her age—something strongly encouraged by the wording of the text as it addresses itself to the reader (i.e., the girl) and asks her a question, namely, whether she can tell what is going on. And without waiting for an answer, in a condescending way the text provides one.

What follows immediately in the text might also have had something to do with the girl's difficulty in reading the word "hard." According to the story, what isn't hard to tell is that James (the puppy) wants to go out to play in the backyard. This, too, the girl may have taken personally. She too may have preferred to go out to play, instead of engaging in the (for her) hard task of reading a story in which she could work up no interest. For her it was indeed hard to do what was asked of her—to read a dull text—and doubly hard to do so when the story itself was reminding her that it is preferable to go out and play.

The statements "It's easy" and "It isn't hard," which abound in primers, either directly or implied, along with the many stories that tell about the pleasures of playing outside, make learning to read all the more difficult. If we want the child to read, which to him is hard work, why use a text that creates conflicts between the desire to play and the need to concentrate on reading? This makes concentration on hard work yet more difficult and undesirable in comparison with play.

If something is stated as being easy or not hard, and I still can't do it, this makes me feel all the more defeated. Indeed, even if I should succeed in doing well something that

I'm told comes easy, no great satisfaction can be derived from it. If, on the contrary, the story—or the teacher's attitude—makes it clear that what is being asked of me is difficult, while this may at first create some hesitation in me to try it, once I attempt it, even if I fail there is no great loss in self-respect. After all, not being able to do something difficult is part of the expectation created by the warning. If, on the other hand, I should succeed in mastering what has been declared difficult, my confidence is greatly increased, and a feeling of well-being is created—and with it enjoyment of reading—because I succeeded even though I had been told that the challenge was a major one.

As this girl knew, learning to read is hard, and it is serious business, as difficult as it is important. Indeed, the stories from which children are taught to read are kept simple because of our recognition that learning to read is such a difficult undertaking. Yet it does not follow from this that the texts have to be simplistic. The task of the educator is to facilitate learning to read, but this is not achieved by making it seem easier than it really is, and certainly not by making it seem dull.

The solution is to use interesting and meaningful texts. Then the learner will strive for word recognition on his own because he wants to get at the meaning of what he is reading. The behavior of those children whose substitutions were taken seriously shows that after this has happened, they, all on their own, gave recognition to the printed word they had previously failed to read. But if word recognition makes accessible a text that is not worth the trouble, the child will have difficulty in being interested enough in the hard work required for *achieving* word recognition.

CHAPTER 12

Empty Texts—
Bored Children

Initial impressions can easily sway our judgments. This is why publishers take great care to lure the reader through a book's title and external appearance. Title and jacket are selected to sell the book to its potential buyers, and reveal what author and publisher believe is most attractive about a specific book. This is particularly true of books designed for children, because children have much less experience than adults, and in general tend to rely much more on appearances and first impressions, making impulsive decisions. For the beginning reader, titles and cover pictures are all the information available to him about a preprimer or primer. Since he knows, however, that the purpose of these books is to help him to learn to read, he will also form certain notions of what reading itself is all about on the basis of these cover messages.

The titles and cover designs of American basic readers are based on the premise that nothing but the potential to provide fun can make reading attractive to the books' prospective audience. Yet in stressing fun and avoiding any reference to reading, these titles and covers are deceptive in regard to the books' true instructional aims, even though they are more or less accurate concerning the emphasis and content of the stories they contain, since the covers as much as the contents stress the fun morality mentioned previously. According to these books, having fun is life's only purpose.[1]

Although there are some truly funny children's stories, and many that are enjoyable, reading these requires greater skill than the beginning reader possesses, so that these stories are not found in primers. Instead of being honest about this, however, primers try to impress on the child that their goal is to entertain him, and that the main value of being able to read is to enjoy an amusing pastime. But this is *not* the reason we teach children to learn to read; we do so because books are man's most important source of information and knowledge, and all later learning requires the ability to read.

What is more, for most children, learning to read is not an entertainment but hard work, a difficult task requiring serious application. Thus, if the titles and the pictures on the covers of basic readers were to represent honestly what the books are for, they would in some fashion convey first and foremost the intention to teach reading, and the reason for teaching it: reading's unique importance in the process of education.

Publishers often alter the cover pictures of primers without changing the titles or contents of their series, and there are states that in adopting a series sometimes request or arrange for their own cover pictures. Thus it is difficult to select specific covers to illustrate our argument. Still, despite small variations, nearly all covers convey the same message as those described below.

The Betts Basic Readers (American Book Co., New York, 1963) begin with *On Our Way*, which shows on its cover a

[1] It has been mentioned that children are strongly influenced by first impressions. To this we might add that the period when children are taught to read is a most impressionable age. If on first encountering reading, and during the years he is taught it, the child is given to understand that reading is only for fun, the deep impact this may make can subconsciously stay with him, despite everything he may be taught later, or come to realize. Little wonder that many children continue to remain influenced by such a viewpoint and in later life read only comics or trite material.

picture of one boy running after a dog, another boy roller-skating, and a third on a bike. These children are indeed on their way somewhere, but it is not to school or learning; nor, as its title indicates, are the children in *Time to Play*, the next preprimer, whose cover depicts one child pouring Kool-Aid for another. The third preprimer, *All in a Day*, carries similar pictures on its cover. (Since this book promises to tell what happens through a child's day, it should be mentioned that his entire day is taken up with playing; there is no place in it for school, learning, leisure-time reading, or being read to.) The primer *Up the Street and Down* carries on its cover pictures of a girl playing with a cat, a boy with his dog, a girl carrying a rabbit, and a boy holding a dressed-up duck.

The first preprimer of another series (Houghton Mifflin & Co., Boston, 1966) is entitled *Tip* and has on its cover a little dog that is either amazed or frightened by a frog. The second preprimer, *Tip and Mitten*, is appropriately adorned with images of a dog and a cat. The last preprimer, *The Big Show*, has on its cover a picture of a circus.

The covers of practically all the widely used primers try to convey the message that play and being entertained are what count in life. According to these books, serious application has no place in the lives of children or adults, nor do books and reading play any role in life. Yet equally characteristic of these primers, which are promising to provide fun and entertainment, is that they contain texts that annoy or bore the child. It is unfair to pick out any one series as an example, because the others do not differ in any significant respects; but to illustrate the points to be made, the Harper & Row Basic Reading Program may serve as an example, since it is used as the basic instrument for teaching reading in large parts of the United States, including California, where much of this study was carried out.

Janet and Mark is the first preprimer of this series, which, without essential changes, replaced the equally widely used

Dick and Jane series. The picture on the cover (California State Series, Sacramento, 1969) shows two girls, one jumping, the other in a pose suggesting she is about to play. But none of the stories are about two girls—they are only about Janet and Mark. Thus even if the title is appropriate, the picture is misleading. Are those who prepare these covers convinced that children are so mindless that they don't become aware of such discrepancies between pictures and text? Actually, the teachers' instructions ask them to discuss the pictures in the books with the children at length!

One of the two girls on the cover picture is dark-skinned, obviously to make the book more attractive to minority children —particularly since Janet is a redhead and Mark is blond. The dark-skinned girl on the cover probably also suggests the publishers', authors', and schools' commitment to desegregation. But while some dark-skinned children do indeed appear in some of the pictures accompanying the text, so far as integration is concerned it has a place *only* in the pictures and not in the text. If integration is an important message, it is once more impressed on the child that paying attention to the messages of these pictures is much more important than learning to read these words.

The book opens to a full-page picture of Janet, followed by one of Mark, with their names printed under their pictures. Janet is shown picking ripe tomatoes off a plant, Mark raking grass. These activities have no relation to learning, school, reading, or to any of the stories in the book. Have they been selected to inform the child that the children about whom he is going to read are not living in a city, as most American children do, but in a suburban or semi-rural environment? Or is Mark shown raking grass to indicate that learning to read is not the only unattractive task adults demand of children? But if so, why do none of the children in the stories themselves engage in any serious or adult-imposed task?

After teaching the child to read the two names, the book

requires him to read the two words "and" and "come." The
first "story" the child is made to read in this preprimer adds to
these three more words: "here," "I," and "jump." It reads:
"Janet and Mark. Come, Mark, come. Come here, Mark. Come
here. Come here, Mark, come and jump. Come and jump,
jump, jump. Here I come, Janet. Here I come. Jump, jump,
jump."

Children typically hate to be told what to do, and they particularly hate the order "Come here!" to which they are so
frequently subjected by their parents. *Janet and Mark* contains
in all 177 lines of text, most of them composed of only 3 or
4 words. The demand to "come here" is repeated twenty-four
times; in addition, the simpler command, "come," or statements that someone is obeying this command, appear forty-
three times. More than one fourth of all the book's lines are
either commands to come, or statements that the command is
being obeyed. The order to "jump" is given nineteen times.

Children also intensely dislike being told to "see" something that is right in front of their eyes, as if they are unable
to observe it on their own. In these 177 lines, Janet and Mark
are asked 39 times to "see" something at which, according to
the pictures, they are obviously looking, or which is right in
front of their eyes; or they are asked to state that they "see"
something at which they are looking.

The second preprimer of this series, *Outdoors and In*, is
about Janet and Mark and their parents. On the cover it has
two boys walking—again one dark-skinned, the other Mark—
but no parents. Maybe the two boys are here to compensate for
the misleading picture of the two girls on the preceding book;
if so, the contradiction between covers and text is compounded
by repeating it in different form.

In this book, too, dark-skinned children appear in some
of the pictures, now accompanied by parents, but these all remain nameless and are not mentioned in any of the stories.
It is as if in these preprimers minority children have an ex-

istence only in the background, as a foil for what goes on in the lives of the white protagonists. Thus the implied promise of the covers that dark-skinned and white children will have equal importance in the books is completely denied by the text: the dark children and what they are doing in the pictures are not mentioned in print.

In this second preprimer the two children again often ask each other, or are asked by their parents, whether they can see such large objects as a train engine that is right in front of them, as if they would otherwise overlook anything not specifically brought to their attention. No wonder a main cause of children's annoyance with their readers is that the texts treat them as if they were idiots.

In the stories of this second preprimer, in which the children's parents appear in dominant roles—as is true for the rest of the series—overall disrespect for the child readers' intelligence and importance as people manifests itself in two main forms: the children are viewed as being so gullible that they will accept obviously false renderings of children's and parents' lives and activities as facsimiles of reality or desirable ways of living; and that they will believe that people like themselves and their parents spend all their time without any serious thoughts or actions. Nowhere in the pictures, which depict all kinds of activities, is anyone reading or working: the only exceptions are a few adults appearing in the pictures (but never mentioned in the text) whose work it is to provide fun for children. These are the engineer of a children's train, a man who sells ice cream, another who provides pony rides, and one who runs speedboats. In the book's last story, the father brings presents to his family. He could easily be shown as bringing a book or magazine to one of them; instead, the story says that he is bringing a bracelet to Jane, a watch to Mark, and a clock to Mother. The pictures show Mark's and Janet's home well furnished and equipped, including a big

TV set; but nowhere is there a book or a place for one—not even a magazine or newspaper is to be seen.

For those unfamiliar with the way these primers present the conversation of parents, this is how the father speaks to his wife at the very end of the second preprimer: "This box is for Mother. Look in the box, Mother. Look for something you like. Look for something you want." To this, the mother replies: "A clock. A clock for me. This is something I like. This is something I want."[2] People who talk like this are supposed to remind the children of their own parents! Is it any surprise that so many children decide there is not much to be gained from learning to read?

To the authors of these books, and to those who teach from them, it seems more important that children learn to decode words like "jump" and "bracelet" than words that refer to learning, such as "read" or "book." It is a hierarchy of values not lost on the children who are being forced to learn to read from these texts.

Young readers, since they must read about Janet and Mark for several years, are implicitly expected to be interested in them—their lives and activities—if not to actually identify with them in some measure. Yet the most elementary facts are not available about these crude role models. For example, Janet and Mark are depicted as being about the same age, and seem to spend all their time together, doing the same things. While in the first preprimer they are not shown as necessarily belonging to the same family (although they seem to live in the same home), the second preprimer permits no doubt that they are siblings, since they have the same parents. As they are the same age, does this mean that they are twins? Is one, or are both, adopted? The child's relation to his siblings is of the greatest importance to him, yet young readers are somehow

---

[2] For the entire story, see page 275.

not expected to wonder how two children with the same parents could be the same age. It would be easy enough to indicate that Janet and Mark are twins, or in some other way to explain their age situation; but since no adult in his right mind could take the stories in these primers seriously, it does not occur to authors, publishers, or educators that children might do so.

Actually, the instructions to teachers suggest repeatedly that they bring material from the stories to the children's attention and encourage them to observe this or consider that. But these suggestions are directed solely to the most superficial phenomena, such as things revealed only in the pictures. One picture shows a big box out of which Mark takes an elaborate space suit that he is proudly wearing on the following page. For these two pictures, the teacher is instructed to ask the children: "What do you think came in the big box?" Since the words "box" and "space suit" do not appear in the text, asking such a question encourages the child to derive all important information from the pictures and makes reading seem superfluous.

Among the next questions the teacher is instructed to ask is: "How does Janet feel about all this?" Again, the text has nothing to say on this point, but the pictures show Janet as delighted as Mark that he has received such an attractive and valuable gift. In fact, Janet, a passive spectator admiring Mark's glory, is depicted throughout as being blissfully happy (like Mark himself). That a sister might be less than pleased when her brother is given such a valuable present and she receives nothing; that she may be jealous or sad at being neglected—these possibilities are not supposed to occur to the children who are being asked to contemplate this story. They are only to think about what is clearly shown in the pictures or explicitly stated in the text; that is, they are not to engage in any thinking or reacting of their own. Thus the material they are made to read remains empty to them, as is all reading matter to which we don't bring something from our own experience, which we don't enrich with something coming from ourselves.

Again, the reason educators restrict children's spontaneous reactions to what they are reading, thus making reading boring for them, is the all-pervasive wish that they should concentrate solely on decoding. This is the result of a single-minded concentration on word recognition at the expense of any attention to meaning, and it reflects the conviction that concern with meaning would distract the children from correct decoding. But actually the opposite is true: the search for meaning or an interest in meaning is the only true motive for learning to read.

City Days, City Ways, the third preprimer of this series, returns to showing two girls on its cover. Among the city ways depicted and discussed in this book, one finds many houses, stores, even an airport, and the city streets are full of cars and buses—but there is not a single school on these city streets. And the city days are filled with all kinds of activities, but reading and learning are not among them. The last preprimer declares by its title, *Just for Fun*, what it is all about: on its cover is a cat wearing a funny hat. The first reader, *Real and Make Believe*, shows children running and playing on its cover and, in line with its title, a man from outer space.

School—but still not learning—makes its first appearance at the end of the second grade in the second reader, *All Through the Year*, which shows on its cover children at play, a dog, a bird, and a boy dressed up as a bird. This book has eight sections, the last entitled "Too Much Is Too Much of Anything." The first story about the things that are too much is about school, and it is entitled "A Feeling in the Air." The feeling is that "everyone was waiting. . . . It was the last day of school. A little while, and it would be all over." The rest of the story tells about children not paying attention but "daydreaming . . . of baseball and swimming and bicycle rides." This is illustrated with a double-spread picture showing children sitting utterly bored in class, dreaming. The picture accompanying the last page of the story shows them streaming out of the school building, suddenly full of life and happiness because school is over for the year.

These primers present definite images to the child, instructing him as to what his attitude in life should be: he should be interested only in playing and having fun, particularly through strenuous motor activities such as running, jumping, and bicycle riding. There is a complete absence of any reference to quiet activities, not to mention books, reading, or being read to. In all of the widely used series, reading in particular is treated as a tabooed subject. The idea seems to be that to indicate what books are really for would have the most undesirable consequences for the children's ability to learn to read. (The instructions to teachers on how to use these readers reflect the same conviction. Surveying these, Chall remarks: "one gets the impression from the manuals that children do not really want to learn to read and will do so only if they are promised an enjoyable story full of surprises and fun. This emphasis does not change from preprimer through 3-2 reader.")[3]

Although there is no reference to books or reading in the texts designed for beginning readers, very occasionally school is mentioned in them. When it is, the child is not left in doubt as to what attitudes he should adopt toward school and learning. For example, one of the stories in the ITA (Initial Training Alphabet) series is called "Jumping," and goes as follows:

If a boy likes to jump, he jumps over, and into, and on. He jumps over a fence and into a puddle and into a bed and into trouble. He jumps into a pool, over some rocks, out of school, into a box. If a boy jumps, he jumps with a shout, and makes girls jump too, because

[3] Chall, *op. cit.*

he yells "Yippee, hy you!" Boys jump! Girls jump! You
jump too!

The child who has to sit still in order to learn to read from
this text is not only consistently reminded of the pleasures of
jumping, but it is suggested to him that he should jump out of
school! This is not a Freudian slip, betraying the author's feelings about the undesirability of being in school. On the contrary, it is a deliberate attitude with which the stories seem to
wish to impress the child, since other stories in this same series
suggest more or less directly that because of school, the child's
whole life is a chain of tedious and senseless activities.

In the morning you get up. You get dressed. You get
breakfast. Even if you get wet you go to school on time.
Then you get out of school and you go home again.
After a day of getting up and getting dressed and getting breakfast, and getting wet, and getting to school,
and getting out of school, and getting hot, and getting
home and getting dinner, you get very tired and get
into bed, so that you can get up the next morning and
start all over again.

The implication seems to be that life is depressing for the child
because he has to go to school, an attitude epitomized in a
story in this series entitled "School Days":

Bill lives in this house. Today is Monday. It is a hot
sunny day. [It seems as if the day is described as hot
and sunny in order to make going to school even less
attractive.] Bill goes to school. Bill rides to school on
the bus. What can Bill do after school? After school Bill
can fish. Bess lives here. Today is Tuesday. It is a
sunny day. Bess goes to this school. What can Bess do
after school? After school Bess can ride. [The picture

shows her riding a horse.] Al lives in this apartment
house. Today is Wednesday. It is a windy day. Al goes to
school. Al rides a bike to school. What can Al do after
school? After school Al can run and play. Pat lives in
this apartment house. Liz lives here too. Today is
Thursday. Pat and Liz go to school here. What can Pat
and Liz do after school? After school today Pat and
Liz can play house. This is Ted's house. Today is Fri-
day. It is cold and windy. It is snowing today. Ted goes
to school. Ted rides on the school bus. After school
today Ted can ride a sled. What can you do after school
today?

There is not a word about anything positive that may happen
during the school day—good things happen only after school
is out! This story suggests that all one can reasonably do during time in class is think about what one can do after school.

In the rare instances when school is mentioned in other
readers, things are not much different. For example, the first
preprimer in the most recent revision of a widely used series
is entitled *Lions* and has on its cover a big lion with a little dog
looking up at it (Houghton Mifflin Co., Boston, 1974). Its
first story, "Jim's Going Fishing," begins with the following
conversation between two little boys:

Here comes the school bus! Come on, Jim!
I am not going to school.
You have to go.
I'm going fishing. And I can't fish in school.

For seven more pages the argument continues that going to
school is no fun, and that fishing is preferable by far. On the
last page of the story, Jim is finally shown as satisfied with
being in class since he can "fish" there. How this is possible to
accomplish cannot be learned from the text but only from the

illustration accompanying it, which shows children picking up paper fish with magnets on their lines.

The next story, "I Can't Smile," has parallel content, only now it is a little girl who refuses to go to school because her photograph is to be taken and she doesn't want to smile because her second front teeth have not yet come in. The third story of this preprimer tells about "Surprise Day at School." The surprise is that a girl brings a frog to school in a box. The frog is released and creates exciting havoc in class. The fourth and fifth stories that conclude this little book and give it its title are about a stone lion in front of a library, which two boys pretend to chase.

Thus, of the three stories dealing with school, the first two project conflict about going because the events that take place there are not viewed as enjoyable. These conflicts are then seemingly resolved by showing that what happens in class (playing at fishing, having one's picture taken) can be fun. The children are not conflicted about going to school in the third story, because each is bringing a surprise to class and on this surprise day no learning is expected of them. There is no indication in any of these three stories that in school something of a serious nature can take place, such as learning, not to mention the possibility that reading can be as enjoyable as fishing, or that what one can gain from becoming literate may be of as lasting value as having one's picture taken.

Psychoanalytic studies of the so-called double bind[4] have shown that nothing is more confusing and disturbing to the child, and has more far-reaching detrimental consequences for his later attitudes, than when significant adults expose him simultaneously to contradictory messages concerning important issues. This is particularly true when a covert, tacit message is contradicted by opposite overt messages: the child, not knowing which of the messages to believe, comes to distrust

[4] G. Bateson, J. Ruesch, et al., "Toward a Theory of Schizophrenia," *Behavioral Science*, 1 (1956).

others, and ends up distrusting his own ability to know what's what. The preprimers and primers described—and most others are very much like them—contain such contradictory messages. The tacit, covert message is that the educational system which requires the child to go to school, and presents him with a book so that he may learn to read from it, considers school and learning most necessary and important. The overt message—conveyed by the cover pictures, the pictures accompanying the text, and particularly the stories—tells the child that he should think (i.e., read aloud and silently) only about play. The implication is that school and learning are so unattractive that the only way to induce a child to go to school is by providing him with enjoyable nonacademic events in the classroom.

This confusing double-bind message is further emphasized by the behavior of adults in these stories and pictures, who also seem to be interested only in having fun or in arranging for their children to have fun, and who are completely uninterested in reading. Or the same message is stated more directly by adults as, for example, in the story about fishing: there, the adults seem to agree with Jim that it would be highly preferable to go fishing—Jim is told by the driver of the school bus and by a policeman that the only reason he has to go to school is that it's a school day. None of the adults seems to think, or consider it worth mentioning, that something of importance can be gained through learning—something of deeper meaning and more lasting significance than can be derived from going fishing; and that this is, if not the only, certainly the most important reason for going to school.

From a psychoanalytic perspective, another serious shortcoming of most widely used primers and first readers is that their content addresses itself solely to the pleasure-seeking ego—the earliest, most basic, but also most primitive motivating force in man. But as the child reaches school age, by around five, he should have learned to exchange (at least partially) living by the pleasure principle for proceeding on the basis of the reality principle, particularly when the enterprise is of some importance. These primers, by presenting content reinforcing a "fun morality," throw the child back to the developmental phase he is trying with difficulty to outgrow. Yet to assume that at the age of six the child is still proceeding on the basis of the pleasure principle alone is an insult not only to his intelligence but to him as a person. This is why children reject such reading matter as empty. It talks down to them; it does not take them and their aspirations seriously.

There would be nothing wrong with presenting the image of a child obeying the pleasure principle (wanting to go fishing) if in the course of the story such pleasure-seeking was found wanting compared with activities that not only satisfy id desires but also conform to ego and superego values. But to exchange one id satisfaction (fishing in the park) for another id satisfaction (fishing in class, having one's picture taken, creating havoc by bringing a frog to school) leaves ego and superego unsatisfied and undeveloped. With such one-sided emphasis on id satisfactions, learning to read is once more deprived of all serious purpose, whereas it is seriousness of purpose that alone can first create, and then sustain, a lifelong interest in and devotion to learning.

This preprimer was discussed here in some detail because despite these shortcomings it is far superior to most others in one important respect. It not only makes the typical strong appeal to the child's id, as do all the others, but it also clearly states the child's central conflict between seeking immediate pleasure satisfaction and the obligation to go to school. None of the other primers even recognize this conflict, although such strong conflicts are what create problems in our lives, motivate us to actions, and require understanding and knowledge to solve them constructively, to our lasting advantage. And as far as school and learning are concerned, the conflict between pleasure and obligation is the child's central conflict.

Another recently developed series of readers, the preparation of which involved much thought and effort, the Bank Street Readers (Macmillan, New York, 1965), at least mentions reading and school in the preprimers; although most of the stories in this series are factual and do not provide new or interesting information. By failing to evoke an emotional response in the child, such content appeals neither to id, ego, nor superego. The facts presented are already well known to the child:

One house,
Two houses,
Three houses,
Many houses.
Many, many houses.

One street,
Two streets,
Three streets,
Many streets.
Many houses.
One city.

Consequently, this nonstory in the first preprimer, *In the City*, evokes neither the interest that comes from thinking about gaining pleasure satisfaction, nor that which a pseudo-conflict arouses.

The primer of this series, *Around the City*, begins by suggesting that pleasure is derived from aimless motor discharge:

All around the city,
All around the town,
Boys and girls run up the street,
Boys and girls run down.

Boys come out into the sun.
Boys come out to play and run.

Girls come out to run and play,
Around the city, all the day.

All around the city,
All around the town,
Boys and girls run up the street,
Boys and girls run down.

One would be hard-pressed to describe a more pointless way
to spend the day; compared to this, going fishing seems a
purposeful enterprise. The assertion that children run up and
down the street "all the day" leaves neither time nor place for
any serious endeavor, certainly not for school or learning, not
to mention reading. A so-called story in *Uptown, Downtown*,
the first reader of this series, epitomizes the depressive emptiness and aimlessness of the lives of children—and so of life
in general—which these basic texts project. Matters are made
worse by the story's title, "What Do You Think?", which evokes
the expectation that it will reveal something about children's
thoughts. Instead, the story suggests that there is *nothing* to
think about, nor anything in life that might make it worthwhile
for the child to seek new experiences and open himself to
them.

What do you think?

The little girl came out of her new house, and what
do you think she saw?
Just a corner.

She went around the corner, and what do you think she
saw?
Just another corner.

She went around that corner, and what do you think she
saw?
Still another corner.

So she went around it, and what do you think she saw?

And what do you think she did?

With that the story ends. It is illustrated by pictures showing a girl roller-skating around the four nearly identical streets and corners of a city block.

When young children are given half a chance, their lives are full of what are to them exciting experiences. But the basic texts from which they are to learn to read suggest that there is nothing to life but shallow "fun," and that, left to their own devices, they act aimlessly. This view of himself, of course, discourages the child, yet this is the subject matter from which he must learn to read.

Even when, in a rare story, the importance of reading is stated, the way it is done interferes with the intended message. The Bank Street Readers contain a story, "People Read," the purpose of which is to impress on the child that reading is important. This is the text: "All over the city people read. People read in stores. People read in houses. Boys and girls read in school. All over the city people read. They read on streets and in stores. They read in houses. And they read in school. All over the city people read." But since we are not told what they read, or why, or what is interesting about reading, or why it is enjoyable, it makes reading sound rather boring and (once again) purposeless. Any advantages one may gain from reading are placed in doubt by the impressive double-spread picture introducing the story. The truly eye-catching central feature that dominates this picture is a huge STOP sign, and other signs in the same picture indicate other prohibitions, such as NO PARKING, NO STANDING, or ONE WAY. The suggestion inherent in this picture—that being able to read allows one to read prohibitions—is not likely to make reading attractive to small children. The only sign in the picture appealing to a child is the one saying PLAY STREET; it and the street sign ELM STREET suggest that possibly being able to read may be useful. But these are both dwarfed by the STOP sign. And while the child is repeatedly told by the text that everybody reads, the pictures suggest that the only point to reading is to read traffic, street, and store signs. But the store signs chosen are such as MEATS, or BARBER, and the purpose of these stores is already quite clear from their window displays, or in the case of the barbershop, from the barbershop pole. The signs are unnecessary, and thus these pictures, too, negate the need to be able to read.

Of the many and various problems facing the child entering school, one is finally mentioned in the first reader, *Uptown, Downtown*, of the Bank Street series. Entitled "Too Little," the story tells how little brothers and sisters taunt their older siblings who have to go to school: "I can play all day, but you can't. Ha! Ha!" The older children's reply is: "You can't go where we can go. You are too little." The story ends: "Down the street went Teddy and Linda and Carlo. Where did they go? They all went to school!"

Here two ways of life—one devoted entirely to play, the other centered on learning in school—are clearly differentiated. But while the merits of being able to play to his heart's content are obvious to the child, no explanation is given of the advantages of going to school. According to this story, the only benefit children gain from going to school is that they can lord it over their younger siblings. Neither in this nor in any of the other stories is anything said about the skills one can learn in school, such as reading, and the important knowledge one can gain thereby; nowhere is it even suggested that reading may be enjoyable as well as useful. The real reason for going to school—to acquire an education so as to become able to master life's difficulties—is implicitly denied by being completely neglected in these stories. On the contrary, the stories suggest only one solution to all of life's problems: one must strive to have fun. (Some children, it should be noted, have a considerably higher opinion of school and learning than the texts from which they are taught reading credit them with. This is illustrated by the way in which one boy recast this story when narrating it to his teacher. According to his version, the story told that: "The older brother said to the little kids, 'I can go to school all day, but you can't! Ha, ha, ha.' ")

The conflict between the wish to remain little, tied closely to mother and home, and the opposite desire to become independent, accounts for many serious school problems—more reason why what one learns in class should help to solve this conflict. And jealousies among siblings, particularly around the issue that the little one is indulged whereas the elder is often expected to meet difficult tasks, are crucial problems in the child's life. These are problems in respect to which the child should receive guidance through what he is taught in school, that is, if school were living up to its inherent promise that it will help the child cope with life's problems.

The most widely used primers and readers were examined by us to see whether they took cognizance of these matters in any form, and if so, whether they suggested constructive ways of dealing with them. A study of the Scotts Foresman, Ginn, Houghton Mifflin, and Harper & Row series from first pre-primer up to and including third-grade readers shows that none of them contain, for example, any stories about the arrival of a new baby in the home, or an older child's reaction to this change in his family, although this common occurrence arouses in the child complex and ambivalent feelings with which he is in need of help. Since many stories describe family situations, a new baby would seem a natural topic, as it is one of the most normal and positive occurrences in a family, typically called a "happy event"—as opposed to deaths, separations, or divorces, which are destructive of family life, common events that are equally absent in the stories.

.   .   .

Since the stories from which children are taught reading have no intrinsic merit, it is not surprising to find that literate persons did not become literate from learning to read them. When doctoral students in education and in the social sciences were asked to recall texts from which they had learned to read, with hardly an exception their memories reflected nothing but disgust at what they had been forced to endure. All paralleled closely the following recollections, which are so typical that they can stand for the rest.

One of the students wrote: "*Fun with Dick and Jane* and *On Cherry Street* were the books from which I learned to read. I have forgotten about everything in them but a few illustrations which I still recall. All I remember is that I felt the stories were terrible, and that I loathed reading as a child because of it."

Another recalled: "I was a good student and went through the motions of pretending to be interested in what I was reading. Actually I was terribly bored. I still remember vividly how I hated the bland reading material I was given. This is the only thing I remember clearly, but nothing else."

A third had this to say: "My memories of class reading time are all about such things as the seating arrangement of my reading group. My most emotionally charged memories are about how edgy I was that I had to spend time reading stories which were meaningless and without a plot.

"It didn't make sense that books I could comprehend when read to me had to be ridiculously simplified for me to understand when reading by myself. To me these stories were a message from adults, 'By yourself you are no good; on your own you can understand only what adults make stupidly simple for you.' I hated these adults who thought so little of me."

After they have read some story, children are frequently asked questions by their teachers about it, most frequently connected with whether they liked it, so we asked children the same question about the stories in their readers. Not quite satisfied with their "No," which was as unanimous as their "Yes" to their teachers, we wondered whether there might not be at least one or another story in these books that might be worth reading. They could not think of a single one.

After the complaint that the stories in their readers were "stupid," the next most frequently voiced objection was that they were not "true to life." The children were all very angry that the primer stories tell about children their own age, and their parents, while making them act in ways neither they nor their parents ever would. One typical example of their reaction to stories they had just finished reading may illustrate this.

One boy's teacher had assigned him, as an exercise in reading, "The Drum and the Hammer."[5] With many word repetitions the story tells about a boy who has been given a hammer, and his sister who has been given a drum (not by their parents, but by a stranger who remains undescribed, and whose reason for giving these presents is unexplained). The boy hammers and the girl drums ever faster and louder, first while their mother is trying to fix dinner and later while their father is trying to take a nap. There is no explanation of why the children act so provocatively toward both parents, and the parents do not wonder about their children's preposterous behavior, nor get angry; they finally just ask them to stop, which the children do. This ends the story.

It is difficult to fathom why textbook writers think this kind of story is good material with which to teach children to read. Maybe they think children enjoy imagining the playing of such tricks on their parents, even driving them out of their minds. But while this may possibly be so, what the author overlooks is that since there is no reason given for the chil-

[5] One of a series of boxed books, published by Lippincott with the title SUPER Books (Stories Unique for Purposeful Extra Reading).

dren's behavior, the child reader is at the least confused, and is often angered, that somebody like himself is depicted as so mindless that he would make life miserable for his parents without having very strong reasons for doing so. Characteristic of these stories for beginning readers is the assumption that the child can hold in his mind only one idea, and a most simple-minded one at that. Here the authors assume that the child would enjoy the fantasy of playing nasty tricks on both his parents, but they fail to realize that the child reading this would not only question why someone would want to do this, but would also be fearful of the consequences of such actions relating to his parents.

The boy's spontaneous reaction was that the story was no good. Since there was no point in asking whether he liked it, he was asked whether he could remember anything of it, because he had had a hard time decoding some of the words and it was unclear how much of the content he had taken in. His reply was an angry "I don't care!" and he was unwilling to say any more, although encouraged to elaborate. He was then asked whether there might be some way the story could be made more interesting for children. His immediate reaction was "By throwing it away!" When asked whether there was really no other way to change the story to make it acceptable, his reply was "No way!" Not willing to give up, and wanting to know some of the reasons for this total rejection, we asked whether the story could not be made more interesting by having the kids get into trouble at the end. He heartily agreed, "Oh yeah!" Invited to suggest what would happen then, i.e., what would make the story more interesting, he said: "Dad would be real mad! They'd be one mad family!" Asked how come they would *all* be mad, he explained that their dad would punish the children and that would make *them* mad, too.

Thus the boy had accurately received the story's single idea, which was indeed hard to miss—that the children wanted to drive their parents to distraction—but this did not make the story interesting or worthwhile to him. Knowing life, he realized that while at first the parents might be made to suffer, in the end the children would be made to suffer also. So, on one level, the reason he wanted to throw the book away was that it told such an incomplete tale; although it described actions that would drive parents mad, it pretended that there would be no dire consequences. Although barely a second grader, the boy already had sufficient literary judgment to know that for a story to be interesting, not only actions but also their consequences must be related.

But there were deeper reasons, too, for his anger at the story and his wish to throw the book away. While reading the first few lines of the story, he had been interested, as indicated by a spontaneous remark he made about the horrendous noise the children were creating. He said (about the father): "He's going to get so peed off!" At that point in his reading, having to some degree identified with the children, he had assumed the story would tell about normal people—like himself—and normal family behavior, such as his own. But when he read on, he came to the conclusion that they all must be "one mad family." So originally he had identified with the children, as the story wanted him to, but afterwards he was forced to conclude that the family situation with which he had identified was that of a mad family. Worse, since the children act so badly without any reason, his alter ego in the story has acted nastily without cause or purpose. If what one gets from reading is the experience of identifying oneself with a child who is nasty without reason and with a family that has to get "mad," then it is far preferable to have nothing to do with such books.

The boy's reactions were typical because—like the other children—he objected most strongly to the absence of appropriate emotions in the figures of the story, that the people in it "aren't anything," are made to act without reason. And since the parents have no reaction to their children's provocations, there is a suggestion that they don't care what the children do, and by implication, don't care about their children.

This boy was turned off reading by a story because the events in it were so senseless. And when talking with other children about why they disliked a story in their reader, usually some such specific feature of the story was mentioned as their reason for rejecting the book, if not for rejecting reading in general. But whatever particular objections children had to the details of a story, when talking about their readers in general, it was striking how uniformly the sweetness and goodness of the children in the stories was mentioned first as what was wrong with them; this always aroused the students' greatest ire. The most frequent explanation of why they completely rejected their basic readers was that they very much resented being thought stupid enough to believe that children were like that.

Children know children best, and for that reason are most sensitive when persons like themselves are presented as being empty-headed. An additional explanation may be children's deep resentment that adults—the author of the readers, their teachers, and by proxy the educational system that forces them to use such books—view children as so one-dimensional, so unable to have deep and complicated feelings or to comprehend the complexity of human relations, the ramifications of actions, and the consequences of events. That this is also the attitude of many of their parents is something of which they are painfully aware. It makes them bitter that when they are learning to read—an important step toward gaining a more sophisticated understanding of themselves and of their place in the world—the material they are made to read implies a view of them that does not take them seriously. Because of their dependent position, they cannot vent their annoyance against the adults who hold such demeaning views of them;

but they can at least direct it against the books that remind them of what adults think of them.

The remedy children advocate to improve their readers is to make the stories either true to life or utterly fantastic. In one case, they would encounter figures in the stories with whom they could identify without insult to their self-respect and in whom they could recognize persons like their parents the way they really are; and they would no longer be tempted to identify with the "plastic" stereotypes of children who have no inner life. In the other case, identification would be with figures who clearly inhabit a world of make-believe fantasy: while reflecting their hopes for themselves—and also their hidden anxieties and vengeful imaginings, as fairy tales do— the figures in such tales do not pretend to be people like them or their parents.

The inadequate vocabulary used in the primers, the endless repetition of the same words, and the many other shortcomings of these texts mainly annoy and bore children. The emptiness of the so-called stories would do no more than that, if most of them didn't speak of family situations and of children interacting with other children. But these are relationships of the greatest importance to the child: they arouse his deepest emotions. And because they do, the shallowness with which they are dealt in the stories makes these all the more offensive; that is why they are at one and the same time so utterly vapid and yet also so effective in arousing adverse emotions. Who can suffer with indifference seeing what is most important to him depicted as utterly bland and meaningless?

There is truth in the idea that we like to read about people and settings similar to those we know, but only if what we read leads us to new, unexpected perspectives, and provides us with new thoughts and a new awareness of motives for our actions and those of others. A story that does all this and in addition is well written will fascinate us. But if instead of giving us new insights into familiar facts, a story merely restates them, then it bores us. And if it describes aspects of our lives in ways that fail to do justice to them, disregards their complexities, makes them seem insignificant, oversimplifies the motives of our actions, and makes our emotions appear shallower than we know they are, then such reading disgusts us.

The children's main complaint about their readers was that the stories are not true to life, that by presenting only pleasant interactions they deny by implication the importance of ambivalent and negative feelings such as anger or jealousy that play such a large role in shaping family life. They wished that the personalities described would be truer to life. But while this would certainly give the stories the depth which the children felt was so sorely lacking in them, one cannot be sure that it would make learning to read easier. It certainly would make it much more *interesting,* and in this way some nonreaders might be induced to invest themselves in reading. On the other hand, stories about fights in a family, or about families in which every member more or less goes his own way, while they would be an antidote against the sickly goodness and sweetness the children objected to, could arouse very strong emotions in the readers which, though in some cases strengthening the cognitive powers necessary to learning to read, in many other cases might seriously interfere with them.

Probably a better solution would be stories truer to the complex and ambivalent aspects of family life, and particularly to the struggles involved in growing up, while at the same time offering suggestions as to how the child can succeed in mastering the vagaries of living. All goodness and sweetness will not do, as the children rightly insisted, but simply adding blackness or storminess will not result in the right mixture either. In a different context, it was suggested why stories in which the child hero meets up with serious difficulties, struggles courageously with them, and finally succeeds are particularly attractive to children.[6] But only experimenting with the use of such stories in the teaching of reading to beginners could permit decisions on their suitability for this purpose. Be this as it may, the question at this moment is: Why are these primers used to teach reading, when children universally object that they find them boring, when they use an unjustifiably limited vocabulary much too repetitiously,[7] and where they obviously fail in their purpose, since all too few of the children taught by means of these texts become literate? And why do teachers continue to use texts that must bore them far more than they do the children?

Once again, the answer to these questions lies in the single-minded conviction of educators that the only important matter is to teach the skills necessary for reading, and that in doing so one can completely disregard the purpose for which these skills are taught, given the assumption that this purpose will automatically gain ascendancy once the skills are mastered. After all, the doctoral students quoted above became literate people despite their loathing for the way they were taught reading.

But is the emphasis on having fun presented by the titles, pictures, and stories in our primers and readers really necessary for children to learn to read today? Are the studious avoidance of any mention of school, of learning and reading, of books and what they are here for—the complete absence in the stories of anything serious, of any of the many difficult

---

[6] See Bruno Bettelheim, *The Uses of Enchantment.* New York: Alfred A. Knopf, 1975.

[7] To give only one example, John Carroll writes: "The language of most primers and 'basal readers' is far short of what most children can handle in lexical and grammatical complexity, and this is a fact that many believe should be reckoned with in making beginning reading material more appropriate to children's purposes and interests"—John B. Carroll, "Psycholinguistics and the Study and Teaching of Reading," in Susanne Pflaum-Connor, ed., *Aspects of Reading Education,* a publication of the National Society for the Study of Education. Berkeley: McCutchan, 1978.

or important problems with which the child has to cope in his life both inside and outside school—are all these necessary to entice the modern child to learn to read, who otherwise would refuse to do so?

Past generations learned to read from primers which, in their texts, severely condemned seeking only fun as immoral and as leading to failure in life. These stressed (and possibly overstressed) the merits of hard work; did not avoid revealing the serious aspects of life; emphasized most strongly the need to apply oneself, to learn what is taught in school, and in particular the great value of being able to read, and to read well. Children taught from these old-fashioned primers learned to read at least as well as the present generations, whose reading scores have gone down as the texts from which they were taught have stressed ever more fun-seeking and as the stories have become ever more vacuous.

Later, in junior and senior high school, our modern reading material changes. One then often finds in the stories an overemphasis on the dark side of life and on all the things that are wrong with our society. Where everything was light and happiness in the primers, now darkness and misery are everywhere. This reflects a negative view of man and his world for which nothing in the youngster's early education has prepared him and which hence comes to some as a great shock.

What are needed are beginning texts that fascinate children, and convince them that reading both is delightful and helps one to gain a better understanding of oneself and others —in short, of the world we live in, and of how to live in it. To achieve this, primary texts should stimulate and enrich the child's imagination, as fairy tales do, and should develop the child's literary sensitivities, as good poems are apt to do. The texts should also present the child with literary images of the world, of nature and of man, as these have been created by great writers. They should be able to render in a few sentences three-dimensional, true-to-life images of people in their struggle with some of life's more serious problems, demonstrating how, through these struggles, people are able to achieve greater clarity about themselves, about their relations to others, about what is required to be able to live a meaningful life.

How to live a good life right now and in the future—this is the greatest concern of all children. They know very well the merits of having fun; they don't need to be taught that in school. But they also know that much more is needed for leading a good life than having fun. To learn about this—of what it consists, what it entails, how it may be achieved—is what school from its very beginning should be all about.

CHAPTER 13

The Case for
Meaningful Primers

By now several generations of American primary-grade children have been cheated out of discovering that reading is the
most stimulating, rewarding, and meaningful experience
school has to offer them. But for schools to afford the beginning reader this experience, the texts from which he is taught
must be stimulating, rewarding, and most of all meaningful.

In theory, there is no lack of recognition that reading ought
to be taught for meaning, but unfortunately it remains mere
theory—an empty declaration of intentions—since educational
practice runs directly counter to this theory and will continue
to do so as long as reading texts are completely worthless. Not
only are the stories from which the child is asked to learn to
read devoid of any merit; with their empty sentences and their
annoyingly boring repetitions of the same few words, they dull
the child's mind instead of stimulating it.

It has been shown that year after year, these texts have
become emptier and emptier, use fewer and fewer words, and
so grow more and more repetitious, more and more boring.
The point is that the texts concentrate solely on teaching the
skills of decoding, irrespective of whether this is done through
sight recognition of whole words or through phonics. Since the
texts have no meaning, the child is expected to learn skills
without their being meaningfully applied, and this makes
such learning uninteresting to the child's ever active and

curious mind. Because they are taught in this way, children are not interested in learning to read, and this has led and still leads to the erroneous opinion that children do not want to learn to read, and that they therefore must be constantly drilled in reading skills. This conviction accounts for texts that emphasize drill, and such texts do indeed confirm children in not wanting to learn to read, because nobody in his right mind would want to learn to read in order to be able to read such stupid stories. With that, the conviction that children do not want to learn to read becomes a self-fulfilling prophecy. The continued use of texts based on the conviction that children do not like to learn to read and which, therefore, concentrate on repetitious drill under the pretext that they tell "fun" stories, "proves" over and over again that children in fact do not like to learn to read. But this is so only if they are taught reading from texts that destroy any spontaneous wish to learn it. In fact, however, there is no need to teach reading from texts that make reading utterly unattractive, and no excuse for doing so.

The universal use in the United States of basic texts that are alike in their repetitious emptiness, and of stories that tell only about the most shallow "fun" activities, makes one wonder whether it is indeed possible to teach reading to modern children by means of texts that are neither condescending to them, nor dull, nor excruciatingly repetitious, nor restricted to the use of a few simple words. Maybe children raised in an industrial, or what has been called a post-industrial, society would prove really unable or unwilling to learn to read if the demand that they should do so were clearly conveyed to them, if they were honestly given to understand that learning to read, not amusement, is the purpose of their primers, and if the stories from which they were taught reading dealt with the more serious aspects of their own and their parents' lives.

So the crucial question is whether reading can be successfully taught to the modern child from texts that have literary merit and hence introduce children to literacy from the start. Unfortunately, this question cannot be answered by comparing the effectiveness of different American basic series, since they vary only in the degree to which they fail to arouse the child's interest in reading (as the fact that so many of our children do not achieve literacy makes glaringly apparent). But a comparison of our primers with those used in other advanced countries may shed light on this question. Children in these other highly industrialized countries do learn to read, and in quite a few of them at least as well as if not better than in this country. Let us examine the titles, cover pictures, and some of the stories in primers used in certain other countries today.

The first Austrian preprimer (*Fibel*, or "alphabet book") *Joyous Learning*, in use today, has been reprinted twenty-two times without changes.[1] The title states the thesis: learning (to read) is enjoyable, but the important task is to learn. In accordance with the title and the book's purpose of teaching the most rudimentary school skills, its cover shows three primary-grade children: two are sitting at their desks, attending to the simplest learning tasks with obvious enjoyment (one is crayoning, the other taking pencils and paper out of his satchel), while the third is just entering the classroom.

Inside, the book begins with a series of single- and double-page pictures without words. The first shows adults engaged in work and a group of children playing on the sidewalk of a busy street. Thus, as suggested in the title, both work and play are important aspects of life. The second and third pages are taken up by a double-spread picture of a family. The father is leaving for work, fondly saying goodbye to his oldest daughter. The mother is getting a little girl ready to go to school,

[1] *Frohes Lernen,* A reader for the beginner. First Part. Vienna: Austrian Federal Publishing House for Instruction, Science, and Art, 1963.

while a somewhat older boy is hurriedly finishing his break-fast. A preschool child is playing on the floor.

The next picture (again a double spread) shows both the adults and the children following their serious pursuits. The children, singly or in groups, are going to school—the school building is the most prominent feature of the picture—while adults are busily at work; only one old man sits on a bench, reading. By implication, it is suggested here that going to school is as important as the work of adults. The following picture—again covering two pages—shows the start of the school day. Some children are already at work at their desks; two are arguing with each other; some others are enjoying a chat. Three children are entering the classroom, among them the girl who in the second picture was being got ready for school by her mother. One child is showing a toy to the teacher, who is standing in front of the blackboard, on which simple exercises have been drawn—a preliminary to learning to print letters.

The next double-spread picture returns us to the family room seen previously. But now the father and the older children are absent. The mother is cooking; the little preschool girl is building with blocks. Many toys surround her—some are on the floor, others stand on a chest. As if to emphasize that all here is play, the dog and the cat are also playing with each other.

The next two pages contain the first printed word, accompanied by eight separate small pictures. In the first of them, we see the girl we know from the preceding pictures draw a simple house and the sun on the blackboard. Next she erases what she has drawn, as we see from the following picture, to print on the blackboard the letter *M*. As we learn from what is printed beside the pictures, this is the first letter of her name, "Mimi."

The name "Mimi" is printed repeatedly the way a child learning to print would do it. The selection of this name is quite ingenious, not only because it consists of two identical syllables, each of only two letters, but because—as is shown on the next page—by an exchange of *i* for *a* the name "Mimi" becomes "Mama." In addition, as the book points out, "Mimi" contains the German word *im*, meaning "inside," while "Mama" contains *am*, meaning "on." These words are then used to form simple sentences.

All through the book's eighty pages, at the bottom of each page or in its margin, simple drawings of well-known animals or objects appear, the names of which contain one of the letters learned on the page, which are printed with these drawings. For example, on this page, among others, is a drawing of a fish with an *i* under it.

Returning to the small pictures on this page: after Mimi is shown printing *M* on the blackboard, she is seen distributing booklets to other children. Then she is sitting at her desk, counting blocks. This is followed by a picture showing her putting her school things into her satchel, ready to leave class. In the last two little pictures of this double page one sees her climbing in the gymnasium, and finally jumping rope in the yard of her home.

This is the last double-spread picture. All following pages —with one exception mentioned below—carry some simple words and sentences. The next single page shows the little girl's mother in small pictures doing chores such as vacuuming, cooking, setting the table, and raking in the garden. The following page shows her first playing with Mimi, later sitting in the garden knitting while Mimi plays ball there.

This sequence of pictures has been described in some detail because here, as in certain American primers, the conflict between work (going to school and learning there) and play is a central topic. It is put at the very beginning of the first Austrian preprimer because the school recognizes that this is not only the first but the central area of conflict for the new school child, who desires both to remain a child at play and to grow up. Here the conflict is neither denied nor belittled; nor are pseudo-solutions offered in place of a true resolution of the conflict. Instead, the child's inner conflict, and with it the child, are taken seriously. The solution offered is the only realistic one: to the school child, both play and serious learning are equally available, each at its appropriate time and place, each with its specific and different rewards.

This is further demonstrated in the following pages on which one or two words are accompanied by little pictures, usually four to a page. In these pictures we see Mimi washing dishes, going shopping for food, and being embraced by her mother, who gives her a kiss, we must assume in appreciation for having done these chores. She is also shown writing, reading, knitting, and playing with the cat. After these two pages in which Mimi is shown mostly working, the next two show her only at play—on a big sandpile with her older brother and sister, by herself, and in a group of children who are flying kites.

So that the rewards of learning to read may accrue to the child in a deeply and personally meaningful fashion, he must internalize his new achievements: learning must become something not just done in class but built into his personality, staying with him all the time. This is illustrated in a nearly full-page picture with only a few lines of text, and it comes just after the child has learned to read some simple sentences. The picture shows Mimi sleeping in her bed, clutching a jumping jack in her hand. In her dream various animals appear to her, each one with the appropriate capital letter, such as *A* under an ape, *D* on top of a donkey, and so on. As all of us use dreams to work through important problems that have occupied us during our waking day, so Mimi is seen here dreaming about learning to read.

This picture speaks directly, appealingly, and convincingly to the reading child about the need for integrating into one's unconscious what one has learned with one's conscious mind, and it does so in ways that permit him to grasp intuitively what is beyond his conscious comprehension. There is hardly a primary-grade child who does not dream about school. This picture indicates that the authors of the textbook—and the teacher who teaches the child from it—know that learning to read is so important to the child that he dreams about it. The expression of such an understanding of his unconscious processes can become a powerful bond tying the child to learning— in this case to reading. And it makes this preprimer an attractive one to learn from, although the child does not consciously know why this is so.

The book follows the events of the school year. Its parts are called "Fall is nice"; "It gets cold"; "It's Winter and we look forward to Christmas"; and finally, "A new year has begun." The preprimer ends here, because by the end of February Austrian first graders are supposed to be finished with this book and moving on to their first reader. The page on which Mimi is shown dreaming should be reached by the child just before All Souls' Day, an important holiday in Austria on which it is customary to visit the graves of dead relatives and decorate them.

Dreaming is the most obvious experience in which our unconscious asserts itself, but it is at work in us in many other ways as well. Some of them are much too complex to permit expression in the as-yet limited vocabulary of the beginning reader; more important, some experiences are too difficult to be put into the appropriate words by the young child. There are things that remain best unsaid. This, too, is recognized in this little book, which nevertheless, in its simple fashion, deals with some of the child's most complex experiences.

The page on which Mimi is dreaming is followed once more—for the last time in this reader—by a picture page without words. It represents All Souls' Day, and the three school-age children and their parents are shown decorating a grave. The unconscious bond that ties us to our ancestors finds silent but nevertheless moving expression here; and so does the idea of death. The serious expression on everybody's face, the way the oldest girl is lighting a candle on the grave while Mimi carries a wreath, and the way her older brother is ready to water the flowers and the grass on the grave—all this suggests that children can, in their own fashion, cope with death, although they are as yet unable to put it all into words. By presenting this picture to the child, he is implicitly given credit not only for understanding the idea of death, but also for realizing that through mourning and appropriate rituals he can keep the memory of his ancestors alive in him, and thus need not lose touch with them completely.

American primers, by contrast, are based on the conviction that for the child to learn, everything has to be spelled out fully and repeatedly, leaving nothing to his imagination— which therefore fails to be enriched by what he reads. This method of teaching deprives the child of one of the most important rewards of reading: being stimulated to penetrate in his understanding beyond the mere recognition of what he already knows, which is there on the page. This stimulation is what makes reading attractive.

In the Austrian preprimer, stories about both active and quiet play alternate with those about serious activities in the pages preceding and following the one showing the child dreaming and the visit to the grave. Birth takes its place alongside death, as there is a picture and story about a birthday party.

As in American primers, one little story tells about the father bringing presents to his children. In the Austrian primer, each child receives a present appropriate to his age. The oldest girl is given some notebooks to write in, the boy a book to read, Mimi crayons, and the little one receives a pull-toy. In various other stories children are also differentiated by age, making it clear that there are definite advantages to growing up (advantages that do not exist in American primers). For example, the play activities of the older children are more advanced than those of the younger ones—not all children play on the same level, as is typically the case in American primers. And children like not only to see children of their own age in their primers but also older ones, including teenagers. The need for this is recognized in the Austrian primer, where, for example, on a given page older children play at cards while younger ones in the same room engage in more childish games.

After several pages telling of the pleasures of St. Nicholas Day—where the little one is shown as being afraid of St. Nicholas, hiding in Mother's skirt, while the older children take it in their stride—the mishaps of family life find equal recognition. A simple story of everyday life, "Mother isn't here," tells of the ability of a child of grade-school age to cope with some of the more difficult aspects of family living:

Susi comes home.
Mother isn't in the kitchen.
It is cold in the kitchen.
Poor Mother is sick.
She can't cook.
So Susi does everything.
She searches for a wrap for Mother.
Then she fetches rolls and a cake.
She boils the milk and prepares a cup.
Now it is no longer so cold in the kitchen.

On the next page Father has come home:

Just look in the kitchen.
Our father cooks.
Susi, quick the dumplings!
Mimi, fetch an egg.
Toni, cut a slice of cake for Mother.
Here is the cup of milk.

Susi sets the table.
Father brings the dumplings.
Toni the bowl with the salad.
Now everybody eats.

This little story shows that school, as represented by this book, gives full due to the child's ability to develop initiative in an emergency and to cope with it adequately. In this way the story buttresses the child's self-esteem and makes him feel good about himself. What better reason to learn to read than that it makes you feel you are a worthwhile person! The story expresses the idea that responsible work and satisfaction go together, as the child derives enjoyment from being able to cope with things well, and from being important to others. This story, too, impresses on the child how he grows with age, as the oldest child shows the greatest initiative, doing most of the work, with the boy and Mimi helping with simpler things, each one to the best of his abilities. As the book's stories take the child seriously, they help him to take himself and learning seriously.

These stories also show that the child need not give up more primitive satisfactions (receiving presents from St. Nicholas) just because she is capable of higher achievements (taking care of her sick mother). Even subtle psychological phenomena find expression as the story relates how cold the kitchen feels with Mother unexpectedly not there, but how warm and cozy it becomes when the child gets busy as she realizes she is able to care for both Mother and herself. Again, this is not spelled out—as it would be in our readers if they contained such subtleties, which they do not—but the child is implicitly given credit for understanding why the kitchen at first felt so cold and later so cozy.

This rather complex story is read by the Austrian first grader early in December—that is, three months after he has learned to read his first words. He can do it, because from the beginning what he has been asked to read was stimulating, and learning to read was made worth the effort required to make fast progress. American authors are aware that for learning to read to seem important and worth the effort, the child must be given interesting things to read. But since they believe that only "fun" things are interesting to children, stories about these "fun" things are all that they offer the child as reward for learning to read. With this in mind, let us examine the kind of significant story the American child is offered after having completed his *first two* books. After reading the 48 pages of *Janet and Mark* and the 71 pages of *Outdoors and In* —that is, after nearly 120 pages of reading—the American child's reward is to be offered the story "Something in My Pocket":

> Come to the window.
> Come to the window, Mother.
> Here comes Daddy.
> Look, Mark.
> Come on, Mark, come on.
>
> Look in my pocket.
> Look in my pocket, Janet.
> One pocket is for you.
> One pocket is for Mark.
> This pocket is for you.
> Look for something you like.
>
> Here, Mark.
> Look down in this pocket.
> This pocket is for you.
> Look for something good.
> Look for something you want.
> I have something for you.

A bracelet.
Look, Mark.
A bracelet. A bracelet.
Daddy, Daddy.
I like my bracelet.
Look, Mother, look.

A watch.
Daddy, Daddy,
A watch, a watch.
This is something I like.
This watch can go.
This watch can go.

Come here, Janet and Mark.
See this box.
This box is for Mother.
Look in the box, Mother.
Look for something you like.
Look for something you want.

A clock.
A clock for me.
This is something I like.
This is something I want.
My clock can go here.
I like my clock, Daddy.

Look, Daddy.
See this pie.
This pie is not for me.
This pie is not for Janet.
This pie is not for Mother.
Mother can make good pie.
This pie is for you.
For you, Daddy.

Early in the Austrian *Fibel*, Mimi's dream was shown mostly by means of the picture, the three lines of text accompanying it expressing Mimi's wonder as to whether her dream was reality. A few months later, after having read only seventy-one pages (that is, a little more than half the pages the American child has had to master to be rewarded by "Something in My Pocket"), the Austrian child is once more presented with the theme of dreaming, now in the form of a nightmare. Children, of course, frequently have nightmares, which are among their most scary experiences, and thus play an important role in the child's life; they are experiences with which children need help—all the more reason to read about them.

The Austrian story is "Toni Dreams." (Toni is Mimi's brother, who is about one or two years older than she.)

Toni runs through the garden,
    across the path,
    out on the meadow.
Toni runs and runs.
Everywhere there is ice.
Icicles hang on the houses,
    on the trees,
    on the shrubs.
A thick white ice cover
    has covered the big pond.
How the ice sparkles!
Many children skate on the ice.
Toni, too, skates out—far, far!
He skates faster than all others.
There—the ice crackles—it cracks!
    Help! Help!
Toni sinks—deeper, always deeper.
    Father! Mother!

At that Toni wakes.
Mother is there.
She stands by his bed.

This story is read in February, when ice covers all the lakes in Austria and when practically all children skate, so skating is a timely topic in life and in dreams. The dream expresses the child's temptation to skate faster and further out than all the other children, and his anxiety about the dangers involved. But it also tells the reader that trust in one's parents is the best remedy for anxiety, and gives assurance that the child's cry for help will immediately bring Mother to the rescue; that parents will protect their child against real as well as imaginary dangers. It suggests what the child should do when having a nightmare: call for help to his parents. But it also permits the child to assess what he has gained from having learned to read—how little he could read about the first dream, which he had to understand from the picture, and how much he can understand about the second dream through reading. Incidentally, this story is not illustrated by a picture. There is no need for one, because the words the child can read say it all.

The comparison of this story with "Something in My Pocket" shows how insipidly children and their parents are rendered in American basic texts and how vacuous the stories themselves are, in contrast to those from which children may learn to read in other countries. It is impossible to compare the treatment of dreams and nightmares in the first Austrian preprimer with that in American preprimers, primers, or readers, because dreams are not mentioned in any of the latter. But both Austrian and American basic books contain animal stories, so here some comparison is possible.

In the Harper & Row series, the first true animal story, "The Jeep Ride," appears in the fourth and last preprimer, *Just for Fun*. In it, a little goat drives a jeep and invites several other animals to ride with it. They ride to a store where the goat gets itself a feather; a kitten gets itself some red mittens; a turkey, earrings; and so on, without rhyme or reason. If a child enjoys this story, it is because the animals act so stupidly; at best it is cheap entertainment, talking down to the child.

In the next story in this preprimer, "Up to the Moon," a frog rides all by itself in a rocket to the moon, so that a little owl now sees an image of a frog next to the Man in the Moon. The story ends:

"Look up, Mother, look up,"
said little Owl.
"Do you see the man in the moon?
I see the man in the moon.
But I see Little Frog, too.
Can you see Little Frog?
I can.
Yes, I can."

Incidentally, no little owl was mentioned previously in the story, but the child reading it is not supposed to wonder how a little owl that knew nothing about the frog's ride to the moon can see it there.

The first primer, *Secrets*, of the Houghton Mifflin series mentioned before contains an animal story about a mule that tries to be all kinds of other animals; for instance, the mule puts on a sweater to disguise himself as a zebra. Similarly, the first animal story in the Bank Street Readers—also in the first primer, *Uptown, Downtown*—is about a donkey that wishes to be a lapdog and jumps onto a man's lap. The moral of these stories is that one should not try to be anything but oneself. True enough, but the animals are depicted as acting and thinking like people, and silly people at that. The only purpose to these animals' existence, so far as these stories are concerned, is either to teach children a lesson, or to amuse them through pure silliness.

In the Austrian series, the first animal stories appear in the first-grade reader, *We Are Already Able to Read,*[2] in a section entitled "Blossoms in All Gardens." This section includes three little poems about animals that might naturally be found in a garden. In the first, five chickens fight over a worm; as soon as it is gone, they get along with each other again. The second poem, called "The little birds and the cat," tells how birds in an apple tree warn each other of the approaching cat. The birds fly off, and the cat slinks away, probably thinking to itself, as the text says, "I'll catch you next time," while the sparrow laughs, "We'll be careful, good riddance, cat." In these simple little poems, the main concerns of real animals in a garden—for food and for safety—are charmingly rendered. The last of these poems is "So speaks the dog." (The translation, trying to remain true to the words of the original, fails to do justice to the text's subtle, attractive, and childlike poetic quality.)

Bow wow, bow wow! Go away from this house!
Master and Lady are not at home.
I have to be the watchman here,
and I'll bite you in the leg
if you keep standing here any longer
and don't take off for your own house right away!

Listen, listen, dear mistress:
Someone came to our house, bow wow!

[2] *Wir können schon lesen. Ein Lesebuch für kleine Leute* (*We Are Already Able to Read. A Reader for Little People*). To be used in the first grade. Published by the Vienna *Fibel* Commission, Austrian Federal Publishing House, 1963. This book has on its cover the picture of a girl and a boy, carrying their school satchels, looking very pleased with themselves and the world (we assume because, as the title printed under their picture states, they are able to read). Most pieces in this primer for the second half of the first grade are not accompanied by any

But I chased him away,
told him clearly right away:
Off with you, you villain!
No stealing while I'm here!
Bow wow.

This is how a young child thinks an animal may view and meet its tasks. This dog has dignity and purpose; animals in American primers do not. But children feel considerable closeness to animals and tend to identify with them; therefore they want adults to think of animals as acting responsibly and intelligently. Such identification is encouraged in American primers when in their stories children and animals both do things that are fun. But when the stories depict animals as foolish, the child fears that the adults who write such stories and teach him reading from them may think the child as foolish as the animal.

Unfortunately, the seriousness with which the child himself and his life are treated in the Austrian primers cannot be compared in any specific way with its absence in the American series. Instead, a few more examples may round out the suggestion that it is quite feasible to deal in basic texts with some of the serious problems the child encounters in life, and in this way help him with them by giving him the feeling that what he is being asked to read not only recognizes the validity of what he is struggling with but offers solutions, thus providing the child with a most convincing demonstration of the value of reading.

We have mentioned that up to and including third grade,

---

illustration, and whatever illustrations there are do not suggest what the text is about.

The second-grade reader in this series is appropriately entitled *Wir lesen gern (We Like to Read)*. For these second graders, learning to read is no longer a problem; they have mastered it by the end of first grade. In their second-grade reader they are taught to understand longer and more complex texts—content they may very well enjoy reading.

no stories in American series refer to the arrival of a new baby, or an older child's reaction to one, although this is a crucial event in the lives of most children. By contrast, a section of the Austrian first-grade primer just described is entitled "Little Brother and Little Sister." It begins with the poem "Little Brother":

> A little child has arrived.
> I hear his little voice crying.
> Mother took him to her heart.
> Now it's our little brother.
> How we are going to play and laugh
> and be gay with the little one!
> I'll give all my toys
> to the dear little brother.
> But the mother says: "Be quiet
> and don't make noise or roughhouse!
> He needs to sleep
> after his long voyage."

The first four lines tell not only about the arrival of the new-comer, but also that he has taken the place at Mother's heart (and breast, by implication). The next four lines tell about the children's expectations that they'll have a good time with their little brother. In the last four lines, Mother brings the children back to reality by telling them that they have to be quiet, because the baby is tired and needs to sleep after his arrival in this world. In a few lines, with simple words and in a pleasant way, the poem expresses the mother's concentrated interest in the newborn; the children's unrealistic expectations about the play companionship the baby will provide; and the necessity to make adjustments to the new situation, which will interfere to some degree with what they are allowed to do.

This poem is followed by a little story telling about all the mishaps in the life of an infant: how he cries, is afraid of a black cat, falls down, is hungry; but also how each time an older child helps him out. The story ends with the baby being happy again, and the older siblings being pleased about it.

Then comes a story about a boy proudly showing off his new roller skates. This leads to others wishing to use them, and a scuffle ensues. After they have fought it out, the children are again able to enjoy each other's company. This is a story about sibling rivalry among age mates.

Next comes a little poem that takes up the problem of sibling rivalry toward the infant brother:

Are you cross, my little brother?
Look, I'll act differently!
I won't tease you any more,
nor pinch you, or pull your hair,
if it hurts you so much!
Let's be friends again, little brother!

Here the aggression the older child feels toward the baby who replaced him near Mother's heart is accepted as normal, in a matter-of-fact way. It suggests to the child that he need not feel guilty about having such feelings, not even about occasionally acting them out by pulling the baby's hair. But the poem also communicates the idea that the desire to hurt the infant competitor is no stronger than the wish to befriend him, and that it is easy for positive feelings to gain ascendancy after negative emotions have been acted upon.

Parents, too, are shown realistically in the Austrian primer, which not only helps the child learn to understand them better but also to get along with them better. The last story of this section is "Mami, Please!":

"Mami, please, a piece of bread!" says the child.
"Yes," says the mother and cuts a piece for the child.
"Mami, please, read me a story!" says the child.

"Later," says the mother.
"Why later?" asks the child.
"Listen!" says the mother. "Don't you hear anything?"

At that the child is very quiet and listens.
"Mami, please wash us!" call the dishes.
"Mami, please polish us!" call the shoes.
"Mami, please mend us!" call the stockings.
"Mami, please sweep me!" calls the room.
"Mami, please fetch the milk!" calls the milk jug.
"Mami, please iron me!" calls the laundry in the basket.

Oh, what an awful noise!
The child covers his ears.
At that the mother says:
"That's how it goes all day."
Now the child says:
"Jug, come, we'll help Mother. The two of us will go and
    fetch milk."

A hungry child cannot be expected to postpone his desire for
food, so that need is satisfied immediately. But to be read to
will have to wait. The mother does not mention all the work
she has to do, but simply asks the child to observe, which he
does. Since he is neither told what needs to be attended to,
nor asked to help, he decides to do so on his own and chooses
in which way he will aid his mother.

Joyous Learning occupies Austrian first graders through
the initial twenty-three weeks of the school year, which begins
around September 1. From it they move on at the beginning of
March to their first reader, *We Are Already Able to Read*,
which is organized in weekly units. The first of these, "Evening and Night," begins with a story of fourteen lines called
"It Got to Be Evening," which tells of two children who have
been sledding but have to stop because it gets to be dark. Then
they look up at the sky and admire the beauty of the stars. A

story follows about how sleepy the youngest child has grown and how the mother undresses her and puts her to bed. Then comes: "The Children Want to Stay Up," a problem all too familiar to first graders and their parents. The mother tells the children that they have to go to bed, but they beg to stay up longer. The mother offers a compromise: they may remain up a short while longer, but *then* they'll have to go to bed. The message is that a child cannot always have his way, but that when he can't, to accept a reasonable compromise is a good solution. Four well-known and beloved bedtime verses follow, each of four lines. One assumes that with these verses the mother sings the children to sleep.

With the children now in bed, the time has come for "When the Children Sleep":

"Listen, Father," says the mother,
"Susi needs new shoes!
The old ones have gotten too small."
The father says:
"Oh my, shoes are expensive!"

"Oh, Father," says the mother,
"our Toni needs some new pants.
I can't mend the old ones any longer."
The father says:
"Oh my, they cost a lot of money!"

"And, Father," says the mother,
"Mimi needs a new bed,
and you are out of warm shirts!"
The father says:
"Mother, we'll have to economize a lot!" [meaning, to be
    able to buy all these things]

There are few things a child is more curious about than what his parents are up to while he is asleep; what they talk about when he cannot hear them. This story not only recognizes the child's desire to know about his parents' private conversations, but by implication suggests that through being able to read, he may actually find out what these conversations are.

The story also shows how reading can be wish-fulfilling, for it satisfies the child's desire that he and his well-being should stand at the center of his parents' private talks and planning. At the same time, the story is true to reality: taking care of the needs of children is expensive, and satisfying the needs of all the members of a family demands good planning and economizing. But the story makes these restraints on the ego and superego eminently acceptable to the child, because it satisfies his wishes that everything be done for him out of love and concern for his well-being. The fact that not only his necessities, but also the other children's, are taken into account, removes any guilt the child may feel about having selfish desires. And the final remark—about the needs of the father—shows the parents' concern for each other and assures the child that the parents care for each other and are working together to ensure the well-being of everyone.

Two stories follow that demonstrate that the child's childish ways of doing things are accepted. The first, "Time to Get Up," is about the children's reluctance to get up in the morning because it is still dark and cold. So their mother good-humoredly comes a couple of times to get them out of bed. The second story tells how the children proceed on the basis of their impulses, rather than with their parents' high standards of cleanliness:

A Cat's Lick

Susi dips her finger into the water.
But not too deep, just the fingertip.
With the wet finger
she takes a stroll over her face:

across the front
across the left cheek
across the chin
across the right cheek.
Then she calls:
"Mami, I'm all through washing myself!"
After three days
she has a face
like a chimney sweep.

The story's title is a well-known German expression, which both children and parents use in referring humorously to a perfunctory cleaning up (the way we say, "A lick and a promise"). This title, combined with an untranslatable four-line expression in dialect following it, which makes fun of the pleasure involved in washing out a little child's soiled shirt, makes certain that the remark about Susi ending up looking like a chimney sweep is not meant critically, but expresses sympathy with a child's enjoyment in being good and dirty.

There are also some stories about disagreements between parents and children because they see things differently. Among the stories in the unit *Early Spring* is:

Short Socks—Wool Stockings

In the morning Erika says:
"Mami, it's real warm.
May we wear our socks?"
But the mother doesn't permit it.
She says: "No, no, children!
It's still much too cold for socks.
You would catch a fine cold!"
The children make a face, showing their annoyance,
but they have to put on the wool stockings.

The unit in which this story appears is preceded by one on *Being Sick*, in which one story tells about Susi being absent from school because she has the measles, and another about her brother suffering from a toothache. Both stories end with the children being restored to good health by the ministrations of a physician in the first case and those of a school dental clinic in the second. These stories make the mother's concern about catching a cold and her insistence on warm clothing more understandable. But the story also shows the children openly displaying their displeasure with their mother's decision while still having to obey it.

These few sentences—as well as many other stories—convey to Austrian first graders what education is all about: "An incitement to the conquest of the pleasure principle and to its replacement by the reality principle. . . . Actually the substitution of the reality principle for the pleasure principle denotes no dethronement of the pleasure principle but only a safeguarding of it."[3] The same idea has also been put into different terms: "Impulse is primary and intelligence is secondary and in some sense derivative. There should be no blinking of this fact. But recognition of it as a fact exalts intelligence. For thought is not the slave of impulse to do its bidding. . . . Intelligence converts desire into plans."[4]

In this and other stories, Austrian children learn to replace acting on impulse or on the basis of the pleasure principle because in the long run it is to their advantage to do so—in this case because wool stockings help prevent illness. But they are not expected to find it easy to give up acting on impulse; it is only natural that they make faces when made to conform to the demands of reality. It is the task of the parent to present to them the need to live by the reality principle, but also to help make this acceptable to them by giving full recog-

[3] S. Freud, "Formulations on the Two Principles of Mental Functioning," *op. cit.*, Vol. XII, 1958.
[4] John Dewey, *Experience and Education.* New York: Macmillan, 1938.

nition to the fact that living by it creates displeasure at the moment.

These examples from Austrian primers have not been presented to suggest that they are perfect instruments for teaching reading to beginners, which they are not; nor to suggest that all children taught reading from these texts grow up to be literate persons, which they do not.[5]

Also, each of these primers has its own questionable features. For example, it may be thought that the Austrian primers stress good behavior and good manners too much. But although some of the stories in the first-grade book just discussed are on the moralistic side, or are over-insistent on teaching manners, they still manage to make children and parents sound far more real than they do in our primers:

Susi says to her mother: "Give me some bread!"
The mother does not answer.
"I want some bread!" says Susi.
But the mother again does not answer.
Instead she tells a story:

Once there was a magic garden.
It was perfectly beautiful!
That's why everybody wanted to enter it,
But the door was securely closed.

[5] This is not the place to go into the question of why, despite far superior primers, by no means all or even the majority of children taught with them become truly literate later on in life. Since most of the examples are taken from Austrian primers, it might be mentioned that the main reason only a segment of the Austrian population becomes literate is that the secondary educational system is divided into a minority who are university-bound and a majority who are not. The two strands of education separate after the fourth grade, with only a selected minority entering the Gymnasium or similar higher schools, while the majority continue in a system that does not stress education for literacy. Still, because of the way all children are taught reading, nonreaders and children suffering from severe reading retardation are much rarer in Austrian grade schools than in ours.

First the people wanted to climb over the wall.
But it didn't work. The wall was too high.
Then they wanted to break the door down.
But their hatchet broke.
And when they tried to burn the door down
The fire went out.
Then came a child
and said only the little word Please.
At that the door opened itself wide
and the child ran into the garden.

Susi got red in her face and said:
"Please, Mami, give me some bread!"

The moral of the story is obvious enough, yet the child is not told directly what to do, as is typically the case in our primers where he is constantly told what to see or do, to run, jump, or play. The implication is that the purpose of becoming literate is to be able to draw one's own conclusions from what one reads.

Whether the child is shown as giving in to impulses in not really washing herself but only pretending to have done so, or as becoming aware of his obligation to help an overworked mother with some of the chores, or enjoying acting responsibly in taking care of a sick mother; whether the child disagrees with his parent about bedtime or what clothing to wear; whether he teases or even hurts the baby, or befriends him— in all the various situations the Austrian stories depict, the child is shown as three-dimensional, beset by ambivalences, wanting to enjoy himself but serious when the situation demands it, and competent when his or her help is needed—in short, as a real person. And so are the parents, worrying about how to make ends meet, trying to make their children aware of their obligations, but also understanding that they are still children, and that telling them a story and letting them draw their own conclusions from it is more effective than giving them orders.

The Austrian primers are by no means the only ones that manage to teach reading while respecting the intelligence and dignity of the child. In Switzerland, the world's oldest democracy, primers are traditionally entitled simply *Reader (Lesebuch)* or *New Reader (Neues Lesebuch)*, using the shortest possible statement to convey their purpose. This does not seem to deter Swiss children from learning to read from them. The most recent Swiss series of basic texts—published by the governmental educational publishing house in Bern, the capital—consists of three preprimers and a primer. The preprimers are looseleaf booklets, each page (with a single exception) carrying an illustration appropriate to the few lines of text on the page, the lines containing only a few words each. The covers of the booklets carry no pictures, only their titles. With the absence of programmatic pictures on the covers, the child is encouraged to form through his reading his own opinion as to what each booklet is all about.

The first preprimer is called *We Are All Here*, meaning here to read together. Its first page has only two words: "I am." Since this page is the only one in all three preprimers that bears no illustration, it emphasizes and symbolizes the unique importance of this assertion of selfhood.

The Swiss child's reading thus begins with the strongest statement of self-assertion imaginable. Since no one illustration could be truly representative of every child seeing it, there is no illustration on this page. Such a beginning lets the child know that through learning to read he will not only be able to assert himself better, he will also not be expected to adjust to, or otherwise have to cope with, alien ego images. On the contrary, being able to read will, if anything, permit him to be more definitely himself. The child's individuality having thus been emphasized, the second page, illustrated by a group of children, carries the words, "We are all here," the booklet's title. After sixteen more pages with a few words on each of them for the child to learn, the remaining twenty-eight pages either contain parts of well-known songs or a few lines from various fairy tales with which all Swiss children are familiar. In this way the first book leads to the next, *Once Upon a Time*, which consists of five of the best-known Grimm's fairy tales in quite simplified versions that, nonetheless, in all essentials are true to the originals. The first of the tales is "Hansel and Gretel," followed by "Brother and Sister," and so on.

The third Swiss preprimer, *Edi*, tells about a child who definitely is other than the child reading about him. The first page of this booklet shows Edi with his school satchel on his back, standing between his father and mother. The father is a mail-carrier; the mother holds in her hand a shopping bag filled with food. The text says simply: "Edi, Mama, Papa." The next page shows the house in which they live; the third, Edi eating a meal. On the fourth page Edi is sick in bed, being examined by a physician. On the following pages he is leaving in a train to stay with relatives so that he will recuperate out in the country, where he is lovingly welcomed by them. Soon the words and pictures tell about the animals to be met with on the farm and in the country. At the end of this preprimer, Edi, his health fully restored, returns home to the delight of his mother. But his absence did not only have the purpose of helping him get well; he was also staying with relatives because Mother was having another child. So on his return, Edi finds a baby sister. Thus Edi's story deals with some of the most serious and important events in a child's life: sickness and the birth of a sibling.

The primer of this series is entitled *It's Your Turn*—that is, "It's your turn" to read; the subtitle, "Reader for the first year of school," makes this clear. The book's title finds its explanation on the first page, which carries only two lines of text in addition to a large illustration of a city with houses, cars, factories, and a church on one side of a river, and a country village on the other. The two lines of text are those of a well-known Swiss children's counting rhyme that ends with "It's your turn!" This introduces the book's first part (of eleven), and it consists of other counting rhymes and little songs typically sung by children as accompaniment to their games. All these rhymes and songs are already very well known to the children, so it is most likely that their early attempts at reading will be error-free, since they know how the words they are decoding ought to read.

The children's confidence in their ability to learn to read thus supported, the following sections of the book describe the course of the year, as the book's subtitle has implied. The first of these sections is entitled "Fall," the next "Evening." Then comes "The First Snow and St. Nicholas." (St. Nicholas' Day, December 6, is a very popular children's holiday, celebrated in all German-speaking parts of Europe, as well as in several other European countries.) Next come "Christmas" and "Winter." By then it is time to branch out, and so there are sections called "Animals," "Riddles," "Occupations, Professions," "Morning Sun." The last section in the book is "Spring, Easter." So the children read about the seasons as they occur.

The book is pleasantly illustrated with colorful pictures, which in some way relate to the text they accompany. But these pictures stimulate the child's interest in reading the text because it is impossible to guess from the pictures what the text is specifically about. For example, a poem by the famous poet Christian Morgenstern, "Winternight," is illustrated by a picture showing a town at night all covered with snow, which is still falling; the picture conveys the spirit of the poem without permitting any conclusion regarding its text. This reader contains a number of poems and short stories, many by very well known German authors, both living and dead. The range extends from Hans Magnus Enzenberger, a very famous contemporary (and controversial) German poet, back through to poets of the Romantic and classical period to Martin Luther and beyond—to ancient folktales, counting rhymes, and riddles.[6]

This first Swiss reader, like its American counterparts, tries to introduce children to reading through what is considered attractive and fairly easy reading matter. The chief difference is that none of the pieces in the Swiss reader talks down to the child; there is no deviation from ordinary language or ordinary usage. The counting rhymes are those that children have been reciting to each other for hundreds of years. No words are changed on the grounds that they might be difficult—and they prove not to be, because the child who uses them in everyday conversation is already familiar with them.

All the stories and poems are enjoyable; many are delightful. In one way or another, they all appeal to children of primary-grade age. In many of them a child is speaking—in the section "Animals," for example, the child speaks about his kitten and what it does; in the one on Easter, the child addresses the Easter Bunny; and so on. In none of the poems or stories are children engaging in active play. If anything, the pieces are on the contemplative side, but always with a very light touch. But what is most impressive about this book compared to its American counterparts is the literary quality of many of its selections. The Swiss first-grade reader manages to introduce the child to literacy even as it is teaching him the rudiments of reading.[7]

[6] The primers and reader discussed here are: *Wir Sind Alle Da* (*We Are All Here*); *Es War Einmal* (*Once upon a Time*); *Edi;* and *Du Bist Dran* (*It's Your Turn*). Bern: Staatlicher Lehrmittelverlag, 1968.
[7] These primers used in the German-speaking parts of Switzerland have a special relevance for some of our problems. It might be argued that our primers have to employ such an exaggeratedly simplified language because many minority children speak a different language at home, such as the so-called black English. But *all* children growing up

Even if it were feasible to survey the basic readers of all countries, which is hardly possible, this would not be the place to do so, nor is it necessary. But perhaps a quick look at the primers from which children in some Communist countries learn to read may be of interest. For despite the fact that in such countries children are indoctrinated from the moment they enter school, their primers take the child much more seriously than ours do.

Generations of Polish children both before and since Poland became a Communist country have learned to read from what is essentially the same book: *Elementarz*, meaning "Elementary Reading."[8] Beneath the title of this preprimer, the cover shows six children—three girls and three boys—sitting together in two groups on a bench under a tree, reading books with obvious pleasure. Even the dog lying attentively at their

---

in the German parts of Switzerland speak a language at home entirely different from the standard High German which they are taught in school, and which is also the language used in the primers just discussed. At home and playing with each other, they speak a dialect called Swiss German (*Schwizer Dütsch*), which contains many words that are unique to it, and in which even words identical to those used in High German are pronounced so differently that this dialect is incomprehensible to all Germans who have not been reared in Switzerland or lived there for many years. Thus when Swiss children enter school, they have to learn to read and speak a language very different from that which they have been speaking until then. During the first few months of school the teacher speaks to the children in their dialect, but they learn immediately to read only the High German in which their primers are printed. The fact that Swiss children speak a different language at home and among themselves does not interfere with their ability to learn to read from texts printed in an unfamiliar language— unfamiliar even though it has many words in common with the dialect the children do speak, although these are pronounced quite differently. But the same is true for so-called black English. That the Swiss children learn to read High German from their primers without difficulty stems to a great extent, we believe, from the fact that what they are given to read is of interest to them.

[8] Although mostly unchanged from other editions, the one referred to here is M. Falski, *Elementarz*. Warsaw: 1961.

feet seems to be watching and listening with interest to what they are reading.

The book's initial eight pages have colorful pictures without any text. On the first of them one sees a bookstand under an awning in a park. Some sixteen children of about first-grade age are either reaching for books two ladies are distributing to them, or are showing their books to each other, or are already reading in them with concentration. Some adults passing by watch this scene with interest. The next page shows a little girl saying goodbye to her mother, who is handing her a package as she opens the door for her—one assumes the package contains a snack to be eaten in school. Since the child is carrying on her back the kind of satchel that European children wear when they go to school, the child seems headed there. A coffee pot, cup, and so forth on a nicely set table suggest that the girl and her mother have just had breakfast; on a side table there are four books.

On the next page, the same girl is shown walking on the sidewalk of a busy street, obviously on her way to school. On the following page, another girl is seen leaving a farmhouse for school. On the next page, she and six other children, all carrying school satchels, are walking down a road toward a village where, one assumes, their school is located, while in the background farmers are working in the fields.

On the sixth of these picture pages, the children who appeared on the preceding pages, and many others, are entering a schoolyard, in which some boys are playing ball. Other children who have reached the school's entrance are being welcomed by a teacher. The seventh picture shows a teacher helping a group of children to take off their overcoats and shoes. The last of these pictures without words depicts the children in class, their books open on their desks, the teacher standing in front of them with an open book in her hands. Two children stand at the blackboard—a girl who is reciting to the teacher and a boy who is drawing on the board.

When we look at these pictures and compare them to those introducing American children to their primers, the contrast is truly impressive. The Polish preprimer projects an atmosphere of serious devotion to reading and learning, and everything else school stands for, while the American primers convey a life concentrated on insignificant fun and play.

In Russian primers, the pictures without words show children who seem less relaxed than their Polish counterparts, more serious and self-contained, and more regulated; but they appear equally content with their lives, interested in going to school, and concentrating on their reading. The first two preprimers from which Russian children are taught to read are called *Alphabet* and *Companion to Alphabet*. On their covers these books show children walking to school with flowers in their hands, the customary way in which Russian children celebrate the big event of the first day of school.[9]

The first Russian primer has a large picture on its cover of a girl and a boy standing behind their desk, on which is lying a book with the same cover. Opening the book, the inside shows a full-page picture of children walking toward a school building, holding flowers in one hand and their school satchels in the other; again, it is obviously the first day of school. The next page is still a picture page, showing children sitting at their desks, either working or listening to their teacher, who stands in front of them at the blackboard, indicating the first exercise preliminary to learning to write and read. The next pages have illustrations appropriate to the letters the child is learning to read on that page. The first word the children are taught is "Mama," accompanied by the picture of a mother with her two children sitting beside her. She is shown reading to them, one child holding the book open for her. The second

---

[9] *Alphabet*. Moscow: Ministry of Education, Enlightenment Publications, 1965. *Companion to Alphabet*. Moscow: Ministry of Education, Enlightenment Publications, 1972.

word taught in this primer is "Papa," illustrated by a picture of a man at work in a workshop.

The second book in this series carries on its cover a large picture of the same children, now a little older, reading a book that is clearly their first reader, as one can see its cover, which again repeats the cover picture. The two children are standing in front of a window looking out over Moscow, and in the distance one can see Moscow University. The only large picture in this book, which comes at the very beginning, shows children working seriously on their assignments at their desks. Now the teacher is no longer standing in front of them but at their side, watching what the children are working on, bending over to help one of them.

The third book in this series has on its cover a much smaller picture, of a wheatfield. Its message is grasped as one opens the book to the only full-page picture, in which two girls and one boy are seen in the foreground standing in a park. The girls are reading an open book, on the cover of which one can see the same wheatfield depicted on the primer's cover; that is, the girls in the picture are reading the very book they are in. The boy, who is watching them with interest, is holding a closed book in his hand. Behind these children, in the picture's middle ground, two girls sit on a bench reading a book held open on their laps. Most significantly, behind them and the trees of the park one now sees very clearly and in some detail Moscow University, dominating the entire picture. Thus the progress from beginning to read to an ever closer approach to the university is clearly suggested by the sequence in the central pictures of these books.

A different Russian first reader, designed for use in rural areas, has on its cover three boys and two girls walking from a farm area to their school, wearing school uniforms and carrying school satchels.[10]

[10] The Russian books mentioned carry the imprint of State Publishing House, Moscow, and are dated between 1958 and 1978. These

From the very first, these Russian primers indoctrinate the child in Communist ideology. Lenin figures prominently even in the books for first grade. Parents are shown as hard-working. Children and adults alike are devoting their lives to the well-being of the nation. The stories encourage children to like school, study hard, and be good comrades. Other stories are designed to build character.

But there are also pieces, in poetry and in prose, of considerable literary merit, whose purpose is to instill in young children a love for reading. Most of these are written by the most famous pre-Communist Russian authors—even the first-grade reader, for example, contains stories by Tolstoy. And in the second- and third-grade readers, most of the great Russian writers are represented. All this is possible because by the end of first grade, the vocabulary used in these readers contains about 2,000 words, and by the end of second grade, this figure has doubled.[11]

Russian children are educated for life in a Communist society, and they have been raised under conditions very different from those characterizing the upbringing of American children. The stories in the Russian primers appeal most strongly to the child's conscience, to his feelings of obligation to obey his teachers and to serve his country. In this way the contents of his readers do not merely appeal to the child's superego, but attempt to increase its domination over the child's id, and force him to form his ego and his values in line with the demands that the collective and the state will make on him. If for no other reason, there is little of value we can learn about how to teach reading to our own children

---

readers have been reprinted in essentially the same form for many years, and, with the exception of the prereaders mentioned before, called *Alphabet* and *Companion to Alphabet*, are all entitled *Native Language*.

[11] For a discussion of Russian primers, see Arthur S. Race, Jr., *What Ivan Knows That Johnny Doesn't*. New York: Random House, 1961.

from such one-sided attempts to develop only certain aspects of the child's personality, suppressing others and concentrating on deliberate political and social indoctrination.

So let us conclude our short survey of European primers with an example from France. One French book, definitely designed for the beginning reader, that is widely used at present is entitled *Reading and the Child*.[12] There is no pussyfooting as to what this book is all about. In addition to the title, in which the word READING stands out in bold, red lettering as the most important, the cover shows two children of primer age, a girl and a boy, sitting at a table and reading a book with obvious pleasure. On the floor, beneath the table and nearby, a colorful array of very attractive toys is visible—two balls, several blocks, a teddy bear, and other items—all of which, at this moment, are clearly being neglected owing to the stronger appeal of reading.

The French primer begins with the story of "The little elephant." It has three short chapters, each consisting of only a dozen lines of large print, entitled: "An only child," "His mother," and "The awakening." "An only child" presents the experiences of a newborn elephant. It asks first what its nose (trunk) is there for. The mother's answer is: "That's very complicated." This is the kind of frustrating reply children typically receive from their parents in answer to some of their most pressing questions, so it endows the story with an immediate feeling of verisimilitude.

Next, the infant elephant asks what it will eat. "Grass and fruit, during day and night, right now only milk. . . . And, if you please, don't put your nose into your fingers." This injunction—to behave and not play with its own body—is also well known to all children. Reading this gives the child the feeling

---

12 R. Millot, *L'Enfant et la lecture* (the inside title page has the subtitle, "A first reading book"). Paris: Librairie classique Eugène Belin, 1965, 1975. As a first reading book, it is preceded by a preprimer from which the child learns to spell and read simple words.

that the book reflects an understanding of some of his most difficult experiences, and establishes right at the beginning of the child's reading experience an empathy between the child's inner life and the content of books.

The story continues: "The elephant child sat down and did not say anything more during its first day, but it looked around, hoping to see another little elephant like it, which would be its friend." In one short sentence the disappointment in its mother is described, how this brings about a withdrawal into oneself, and the wish to have somebody one's own age for a companion to understand the child's need to question, and accept and share in its childish behavior. Once more the feeling is reinforced that what the child is reading truly gives words to how he feels when having difficulties with his parents.

The second chapter tells that the elephant mother was so big, the child could not see all of her at once. When it rained, the child was well protected under the mother's large body. It still wished for some companions, but none came, so it rested its head against its mother's foot and discovered that her body was much warmer and softer than anything else, and it fell asleep.

Again, in only a few short lines some early and crucial experiences of the infant are sketched: his experience of the huge size of the parent, and the protection and security this offers; how, disappointed by the coldness of the larger environment and his social isolation, the child returns to seeking comfort from his mother and discovers that this is where he can reliably find it. Thus satisfied in his deepest longings, he can safely fall asleep.

In the last chapter of this little story, the mother awakens her baby by pulling its tail. That annoys it, and deliberately it does not move. When the mother pulls the baby's trunk with her own, it struggles and groans. But the baby loves it when the mother takes it so softly by foot and neck, and calls it her dear little elephant baby. This makes it feel so happy that it wants to laugh and run. It says to itself: "Today I'll find a friend for sure." Then the mother takes her baby to the land where the other elephants live. Having been able to establish a loving relationship with its mother, the elephant child is now ready to meet the wider world.

In thirty-eight lines and in simple words this story manages to tell of the most important events in a child's life: his birth, the discovery of his body, and his attempts to explore it and that of his mother. It tells also how the child seeks satisfaction from his own body, and how, despite his need for stimulation of his body by his mother, he also struggles against this need to assert his bodily independence, but happily accepts it when he feels he is loved. The story tells of the child's need to know from where his food is going to come; of his need to feel protected by his parent, and how only the feeling that he is loved by his mother gives him the courage to move out on his own. It further describes how the child needs to be with children his own age, and how the good parent provides for this desire by guiding his child on his way out into the world. And it relates the child's frustration when his questions are not answered or his behavior is criticized, and how then, discouraged, he withdraws from the parent into himself. Thus the child in the story has both happy and not so happy experiences, as indeed life consists of having both. All this is told in the simplest and most direct manner, thinly disguised as the story of a baby elephant (an appealing animal, by the way, as opposed to the snake and rat of the American reader described previously).

This story is followed in the primer by various short folktales and stories, most of them adapted from those of well-known authors. The book ends with some lovely poems by famous poets—the last one by the great French poet Verlaine about horses on a merry-go-round. An earlier story is about a wooden merry-go-round horse, about how boring it is to always have to go round and round, and how angry this makes it. In its sleep, the wooden horse dreams of becoming a real horse, and the story tells about the adventures it has in this dream, but at the end, the dream is over and the horse finds it is still only a wooden horse. Thus in the very first book from which the child learns to read, not only such important topics as an infant's birth and the discovery of its body and that of its mother are dealt with, but also the wish-fulfilling nature of dreams, which attempt to compensate in imagination for the shortcomings we experience in our real lives.

It would be easy to ask the rhetorical question: Where are the common American readers that expect the first-grade child— or more correctly, give him a chance—to read poems by the English equivalents of a Verlaine, a Martin Luther, a Christian Morgenstern? It would also be easy to score off the American primers at greater length by comparing them with European ones. But there would be little point to this since it would only further demonstrate what has already been illustrated: that these foreign primers treat the beginning reader with respect for his intelligence, for his interest in the more serious aspects of life, and with the recognition that from the earliest age on he will respond positively to writings of true literary merit. The fact is that children taught from readers such as those just described learn to read much faster and better than American children. By the end of first grade, the reading vocabulary of the European child is many times larger than that of American children, and with their vocabulary these foreign children are able to enjoy reading much sooner and much more fully than our children do—if indeed ours enjoy it at all, which is questionable for many of them. Reading retardation, the curse of so many of our children, is much less frequent among European children, and when it does occur, it is almost always far less severe.

Among the reasons these foreign primers can present the

first grader with interesting stories of literary merit from practically the very beginning is that there is no hesitation at asking the child to learn to read "difficult" words. But these words prove *not* to be so difficult because they arouse the child's curiosity and challenge his intelligence, a challenge that makes reading that much more interesting. Children love to learn these "big" words which, to them, seem to carry "magic" powers; to master them makes children feel important. Whereas it bores them to learn the easy, little words, which are the only ones our primers present them with, and they feel belittled if this is all they are given to read. This fact has been pointed out not only by those who have thought seriously about good literature for children, but by those who have written it.

E. B. White, the author of one of the very few books for children by a living American that deservedly became a classic almost on publication, says:

Anybody who writes down to children is simply wasting his time. You have to write up, not down. Children are demanding. They are the most attentive, curious, eager, observant, sensitive, quick, and generally congenial readers on earth. They accept, almost without question, anything you present them with, as long as it is presented honestly, fearlessly, and clearly. I handed them, against the advice of experts, a mouse-boy, and they accepted it without a quiver. In *Charlotte's Web* I gave them a literate spider, and they took that. Some writers for children deliberately avoid using words they think a child doesn't know. This emasculates the prose and, I suspect, bores the reader. Children . . . love words that give them a hard time, provided they are in a context that absorbs their attention.[13]

[13] E. B. White, "The Art of the Essay," *Paris Review*, 48 (Fall 1969).

It is not just the use of interesting and challenging language, free of simplifications and of talking down to the child, that makes learning to read from the European primers so much more attractive. The language used in them is only one of the many ways in which the dignity of learning and of respect for the child and his intelligence are conveyed by these primers, from their cover pictures and titles throughout their contents. Everything in these books suggests to the child that he can be justifiably proud of having become able to read. These primers demonstrate to children that the printed word can express clearly ideas and feelings of which the children had been only vaguely cognizant before. And the children in the stories are treated with dignity and are accorded the respect they deserve. All this makes it easy to want to learn to read, to enjoy reading, and to feel from the beginning that one will gain greatly from becoming literate. It helps in making literacy a meaningful aspect of children's lives—as does the inclusion in their primers of poems and stories of literary merit.

In order for children to learn to read, there is no need to depict them in primers as empty-headed fun-seekers; nor to require them to read stories that show neither them nor their parents any respect; nor to drill them in word recognition by endlessly repeating the same few words over and over again. It is quite possible to introduce children early in their reading experience to the idea that reading is for meaning, that it is the source of valuable information and of aesthetic pleasure.

It is high time that children and teachers were freed of the yoke and the blinders that are the direct result of teaching reading as if its ultimate purpose is the acquisition of decoding skills, and as if the only way to become able to recognize a word is to be exposed to it innumerable times. The truth is that words are learned easily and fast if we are interested in what they mean to us. If we want our children to grow up to be literate, reading must be exciting from the very beginning, and never become a chore the way raking grass is for a first grader—the symbolic activity with which reading is introduced on the first page of *Janet and Mark*, revealing exactly what the constructors of these primers think learning to read may be best compared to.

The first literature probably consisted of myths, which tried to explain the nature of the world and of man; it was a literature through which man tried to understand himself. Out of myths grew poetry, and later science, the sources of the "two cultures" that are still two avenues for understanding ourselves and the world. If we wish to open the world of literacy to our children, what they are asked to read should from the very beginning help them to understand themselves and their world. Their primers ought to contain only selections that have both meaning and literary merit. From such readers —particularly when we respect how they want to read them— children will be able to learn to read all by themselves, will enjoy it, and will begin their lifelong progress toward ever greater literacy.